T0399601

FAIRY-TALE REVIVALS IN THE LONG NINETEENTH CENTURY

FAIRY-TALE REVIVALS IN THE LONG NINETEENTH CENTURY

Edited by
Abigail Heiniger

Volume II
Fairy-Tale Revival Dramas: Writing Wonder in
Transatlantic Ethnic Literary Revivals, 1850–1950

Routledge
Taylor & Francis Group

LONDON AND NEW YORK

First published 2024
by Routledge
4 Park Square, Milton Park, Abingdon, Oxon OX14 4RN

and by Routledge
605 Third Avenue, New York, NY 10158

Routledge is an imprint of the Taylor & Francis Group, an informa business

British Library Cataloguing-in-Publication Data
A catalogue record for this book is available from the British Library

ISBN: 978-0-367-47267-2 (set)
eISBN: 978-1-003-03451-3 (set)
ISBN: 978-0-367-47277-1 (Volume II)
eISBN: 978-1-003-03464-3 (Volume II)

DOI: 10.4324/9781003034643

Typeset in Times New Roman
by Apex CoVantage, LLC

CONTENTS

CONTENTS

ACKNOWLEDGEMENTS

Creating this compilation of fairy tales in the middle of a global pandemic was only possible through the ingenious support of librarians and archivists who found new ways to make invaluable documents available. I am indebted to librarians and archivists at the British Library, the National Library of Ireland, the National Library of Jamaica, the National Library of Wales, the Smathers Libraries at the University of Florida, the New York Public Library, the National Archives in Ireland, the National Gallery in Ireland and Lincoln Memorial University who hunted down attributions and patiently helped me find texts and images I did not even know I needed. Thank you for all the ways you brought the world of literature to us when we could not come to you.

This research was liberally supported with grants from the Appalachian College Association and Lincoln Memorial University. Thank you for not only investing in this project but also enabling me to navigate a new world of international travel in the midst of lockdowns and quarantines, with special thanks to Carolyn Gulley and Marshall Flowers for all their guidance.

I cannot name all the colleagues whose generously shared their knowledge and time. Without their encouragement this project would have failed before it began. Special thanks to David Anderson, Cristina Bacchilega, Rebecca Brackmann, James Deutsch, Anne Duggan, Marian Gray, Lewis Hatcher, Jennifer Schacker, Veronica Schanoes, Peter Stevenson, Anca Vlasopolos, Chaka Ward-Hatcher and Christy Williams who organized conferences, introduced me to new narratives, read drafts and made this project a shared adventure. I will be forever grateful for the doors you opened and the ways you made this field of fairy-tale studies a beautiful place to be – I am honoured to work with such amazing people.

The family members who spent vacations with me travelling through hurricanes and reading stories kept this adventure fun. Thank you for doing life with me.

Finally, I want to offer a heartfelt thanks to Fabian Coverley and the Louise Bennett-Coverley Estate (LBCE) which has given me permission to print unpublished texts here for the first time. It is such an honour to be a part of sharing the Rt Hon Dr Bennett-Coverley's revolutionary work in fairy tales.

GENERAL INTRODUCTION

Fairy-Tale Revivals in the Long Nineteenth Century: Writing Wonder in Transatlantic Ethnic Literary Revivals, 1850–1950

Abigail Heiniger, PhD

Henry Clarke's illustrations depict the hidden costs colonial populations pay in the imperial promise of happy endings. In *The Fairy Tales of Charles Perrault*,[1] Irish artist Henry Patrick 'Harry' Clarke (1889–1931) exposes the exploitation inherent in fairy-tale promises of empire.[2] The first full-colour illustration, 'The Fairy', anchors the imperial exploitation in the wonder and magic of the fairies themselves. The image depicts the good youngest daughter of the story facing the transformed fairy who is about to grant her a gift. Dressed in the clothes of different centuries, the women are united by the pale skin they share. The fairy is followed by a small goat-footed faun with pale brown skin who is never mentioned in the text (see Figure 0.1). Apparently, even fairies must exploit colonial labour to work their magic.

Throughout Clarke's illustrations in *The Fairy Tales of Charles Perrault*, the white protagonists are repeatedly enabled to rise with the silent support of diminutive and rather ambiguous servants of colour, who are never mentioned in the text.[3] One image occurs twice: both 'The Fairy' and 'Sleeping Beauty' end with the same black-and-white line-drawing that underscores the colonial exploitation inherent in the white heroine's happy ending (see Figure 0.2).

In this line-drawing, a Caucasian bride and groom walking off together followed by a servant of colour wearing a turban. He is carrying a parasol in one hand and a baton with two birds-of-paradise[4] imported from the southwest Pacific in the other. The repetition of the image in the collection implies that the exploitation of both colonial labour and colonial resources are as necessary to the fairy tale's happy conclusion as the marriage of the couple. Clarke's illustration imposes this message of colonial exploitation on Perrault's imported fairy tales: fairy-tale happiness is promised to colonizers while colonized workers are excluded from the happy endings dependent upon their labour.

"' AM I COME HITHER TO SERVE YOU WITH WATER, PRAY ?'"

30

Figure 0.1 Clarke, 'The Fairy', *The Fairy Tales of Charles Perrault*, p. 30.

The Fairy Tales of Charles Perrault was Clarke's final collection of illustrations before his early death. It was published in 1922, just months after the Irish War for Independence (1918–1921) finally ended nearly 800 years of British

Figure 0.2 Clarke, *The Fairy Tales of Charles Perrault*, pp. 32, 64.

colonial rule in Ireland. Although Clarke was not known for being overtly political, his work in stained glass made him a leading figure in the Irish Arts and
Crafts Movement (1890s–1920s), a branch of the Celtic Revival in Ireland that
dealt with artistic media such as metalwork, mosaics, stained glass, furniture and
textiles. Like the Irish Literary Revival, the Arts and Crafts Movement was profoundly shaped by Ireland's shift from colonial rule to independence in 1921;
even the aesthetics of the Revival Movement were seeped in political meaning.[5]
Although Clarke's critique of empire is clear in the *Ireland's Memorial Records*,
which he was illustrating at the same time he worked on this collection,[6] there is
no indication that Clarke is also critiquing the imperial abuses he illustrates in *The
Fairy Tales of Charles Perrault*. Whatever his intention, Clarke projects Britain's
colonial empire onto the fairy tale. By positioning the white heroines as the heirs
of fairy-tale promises, he necessarily exposes the racism and abuse inherent in
colonialism. *Fairy-Tale Revivals in the Long Nineteenth Century: Writing Wonder
in Transatlantic Ethnic Literary Revivals, 1850–1950* features fairy tales from the
literary revivals in the US, UK and the Caribbean, created by storytellers who
write back to the expectations and exploitations that Clarke depicts, recentring
the narrative on heroes and heroines that empire allowed to be painted only in the
margins.

FAIRY-TALE REVIVALS INTRODUCTION

Fairy-Tale Revivals in the Long Nineteenth Century: Writing Wonder in Transatlantic Ethnic Literary Revivals, 1850–1950 is primarily a collection of politicized fairy tales[7] created by ethnically or culturally marginalized storytellers in the Anglophone world.[8] The contexts for these fairy tales are the loosely interconnected cultural renaissances and revivals that rippled through the United States and the British Empire in the nineteenth and early twentieth centuries: the Celtic Renaissances (which included Irish, Welsh, Scottish and Manx literary revivals), the Harlem Renaissance in the United States and the Caribbean Renaissance in the British Caribbean.[9] All of these literary renaissances were preceded by academic or scholarly revivals that featured the collection of distinctive ethnic folklore. This folklore, in turn, became a part of the cultural inspiration for a new generation of writers and storytellers who generated new wonder tales charged with the politics of cultural revivals.

Fairy-Tale Revivals brings together a wide range of wonder tales by storytellers writing back to imperialist fairy-tale promises between 1850 and 1950. Many of these fairy tales by historically marginalized authors are out of print or otherwise inaccessible, and some manuscripts included here have never been printed before.

'SEE WHAT IS A FAIRY TALE'

Just as literary revivals revised and recreated genres, blending old traditions with new art, the cultural revivals' fairy tales remain as fluid as quicksilver.[10] The term 'fairy tale' here incorporates wonder tales, both magical and non-magical. It also encompasses responses to fairy tales, such as fairy-tale satires and anti-tales. The majority of these tales include recognizable fairy-tale tropes which allow the texts to be identified as fairy tales by their intended historical audiences. However, there are a few texts included here because they have traditionally been identified as fairy tales within the community where they were created, regardless of the tropes within the narrative. As with other broadly inclusive definitions of the fairy tales, privileging content over literary genre may create a lopsided view of the fairy tale. However, this expansive interpretation of the fairy tale as a genre reflects deliberate interventions into this narrative tradition by communities that have been historically excluded from fairy-tale studies. Uncovering and interrogating this history and the mediations made by revival and renaissance authors is essential to maintaining a critical approach to fairy-tale studies and expanding our understanding of the diverse uses of the fairy tale in Anglophone literature.

A nebulous concept of the fairy tale explicitly circulated around different Anglophone ethnic literary revivals between 1850 and 1950. For example, in 1895, Scottish fantasist George MacDonald[11] defined the fairy tale as an experience of reading a wide range of texts more than a literary genre: 'Were I asked, what is a fairytale? I should reply, *Read Undine: that is a fairytale; then read this and that as well, and you will see what is a fairy tale'* (1895, emphasis in original).[12] Similarly, Katharine Capshaw Smith describes the fairy tale as an ideology rather than a specific literary form in *The Brownies' Book Magazine* (1920–1921) edited by Harlem Renaissance giants W. E. B. Du Bois and Jessie Fauset:

> Revising fairy tales became a crucial response to Du Bois's emphasis on revitalizing black home life. . . .
> . . . Not simply applying a black face to a white genre, fairy tales in *The Brownies' Book* offer children black values in fairy tale form.[13]

As a part of these values, fairy tales in *The Brownies' Book* often retain the wonder of the fairy tale without any apparent magic or supernatural intervention.[14] Bacchilega situates modern activist responses to 'Disneyfied fairy tale[s]'[15] as stories with the potential to unlock possibilities, asking: 'how does [this] story change people's sense of what is possible?'[16] This potentiality pulses in the hopeful heart of literary revivals, seeking what might be.

A BRIEF HISTORY OF THE FAIRY TALE IN THE AGE OF ANGLOPHONE LITERARY RENAISSANCES

Anglophone literary revivals and renaissances generally occurred in waves that began with a combination of amateur and scholarly cultural studies of literature and language. In the many iterations of the Celtic Revival across the United Kingdom, early revival studies resurrected pre-Conquest medieval texts and pre-Conquest Celtic language, while current Celtic narratives and language were compiled and preserved through the collection of local folklore from oral storytellers. The pure and authentic folktale recorded from an oral storyteller is a fabrication of the nineteenth-century nationalist folklore projects. Folklorists frequently embellished tales or took them verbatim from other printed sources.[17] Despite heated debates about the folklorists' replication of the authentic voice of the storyteller, folklore became a touchstone for societies like the Gaelic League (*Conradh na Gaeilge*), which were established to cultivate Celtic language and literature. Anglophone Celtic Revival artists like the Welsh writers Goronwy Owen (1723–1769) and Amy Dillwyn (1845–1935), the Scottish writers Sir Walter Scott (1771–1832) and James Hogg (1770–1835), the Irish writers W. B. Yeats (1865–1939) and Sinéad Ni Flanagan de Valera (1878–1975) and the Manx writer Sophia 'Cushag' Morrison (1859–1917) all created new stories that responded to their regional folklore.

A celebration of linguistics and folklore also converge in the work of Caribbean Renaissance artists like the Rt Hon Dr Louise Bennett-Coverley[18] (1919–2006), who went by 'Miss Lou' for most of her artistic career. Her use of Jamaican vernacular in the original literary fairy tales, songs and dramas she developed out of the folklore she grew up with was acknowledged as revolutionary during her lifetime:

> [Her vernacular] language . . . in fact defied the Eurocentric dictates of colonial life. And without firing a shot, without being violent, without resorting to polemics, Louise Bennett has been herself a symbol of a kind of cultural revolution in Jamaica and the Caribbean.
>
> (Prof. Rex Nettleford, recorded by the
National Library of Jamaica 2017: 45:05–46:00)

Bennett-Coverley incorporated folktales in a wide range of written and performed works, including literary fairy tales. She interrupts and transforms traditional European fairy tales, such as 'Bluebeard' and 'Rumpelstiltskin', with the Jamaican figure of Anancy.[19]

In 1892, Anna Julia Cooper, an African American feminist and a pioneering member of the Washington Negro Folk Lore Society [sic], offered a 'prescient'[20] argument about the need to gather new stories to inspire new art:

> Emancipation from the model is what is needed. Servile copying foredooms mediocrity: it cuts the nerve of soul expression. The American Negro cannot produce an original utterance until he realizes the sanctity of his homely inheritance. . . . And this to my mind is the vital importance for him of the study of his own folklore. . . . These [folktales] must catch and hold and work up into the pictures he paints.
>
> (July 1894)[21]

As Gates indicates in the 'Foreword' to *The Annotated African American Folktales* (New York: Norton, 2018), Cooper's insight into the future power and potential of African American folklore came to fruition in the Harlem Renaissance as new folk narratives paved the way for new literature and new art.

As Cooper predicts, the regional and ethnic folklore inspiring the work of literary revivals and renaissances not only created new art, but art that had the power to break free from hegemonic narratives and imperial messages. The regional and ethnic catalyst of revival and renaissance art was frequently paired with an infusion of regional politics. From the Rebecca Riots in Wales and Home Rule in Ireland on one side of the Atlantic to the NAACP Marches in New York and Independence in Jamaica on the other, revival and renaissance art was often charged with politics that had the potential to negotiate or resist imperialism, even when it was not overtly political. The distinctive nature of renaissance and revival fairy tales could do politically charged work without polemics or even without intentions.

The folklore that permeated these literary revivals and renaissances was part of a transnational trend to gather folk narratives. Throughout the late eighteenth and the nineteenth century in Europe, folklore emerged as an integral part of 'multinational movement[s] to retrieve and preserve regional and national distinctiveness'.[22] The work of Jacob and Wilhelm Grimm, and their popular fairy-tale collection *Kinder-und-Hausmärchen*, quickly became emblematic of the 'uses and abuses'[23] of this nationalistic European trend.[24]

Neither the United States nor Great Britain created a single nationalistic folklore tradition as the Grimms did in the newly created nation of Germany. In Great Britain, folklore became a product of a diverse empire; it was collected at the Celtic edges of the United Kingdom or by British people who 'governed colonies, planted missions, and travelled the globe, diligently [amassing] folk traditions and customs'.[25] Popular collections of Irish, Welsh, Scottish, Manx and Caribbean folklore were avidly consumed by the growing reading public in Great Britain. Similarly, the diverse populations in the United States produced regional and ethnic folklore rather than a hegemonic folklore tradition.[26] However, this regional and ethnic folklore could still be used to promote broader nationalistic messages.

Folklore could easily be appropriated to reinforce ethnocentric imperialist ideology;[27] it is no accident that the Folklore Society in London and American Folklore Society in Cambridge, Massachusetts were established within the hegemonic cultural centres of the Anglophone world. Both British and American consumption of folklore could take a 'colonial approach'[28] to the compilation of folklore collections, reinforcing assumptions and prejudices about the differences between the literate audience and the constructed illiterate storytellers. The conflicting uses of ethnic folklore and fairy tales to both reinforce and challenge colonial oppression often occurred simultaneously in colonial contexts.[29] In *The Annotated African American Folktales*, Gates identifies this tension as one that has 'always already' been negotiated by ethnic folklore, especially as that folklore becomes incorporated into literary revivals and renaissances with nationalistic and regional politics.[30] Even social activists with the same goals disagree about the uses and abuses of folklore.[31]

IMPERIAL FAIRY-TALE PROMISES

Although England and the US did not produce a hegemonic nationalistic folklore, imported European fairy tales and appropriated regional folktales were infused with the politics of empire. Harry Clarke's illustrations are a perfect example, projecting the racialized exploitation of the British empire onto Perrault's imported fairy tales. The amorphous concept of an imperialist fairy-tale promise has been widely explored and analyzed.[32] In 'America's Cinderella' (1977), Jane Yolen describes it as a belief that is shared 'subvocally along with the pledge of allegiance in each [American] classroom' (p. 21). Children unconsciously absorb the belief that the female rise tale is an American right; all good girls (and boys) get what they need to rise in American society and, therefore, those who do not achieve socioeconomic success do not deserve it in the first place. Schacker positions imperialistic approaches to fairy tales and folklore as one of perspective rather than explicit promise in *National Dreams* (pp. 1–4). The consumption of the diverse folk traditions imported from across the British Empire had the potential to 'other' colonized people as exoticized or illiterate.[33]

Fairy-Tale Revivals

Most of the short stories in *Fairy-Tale Revivals in the Long Nineteenth Century: Writing Wonder and Transatlantic Ethnic Literary Revivals, 1850–1950* come from newspapers or literary magazines dedicated to the literary traditions of specific communities, like *The Red Dragon: National Journal of Wales* (1882–1887) or *Ireland's Own*, the longest running literary magazine in Ireland. Unlike large folklore collections produced by folklore societies, most of these popular journals were edited and produced by members of the communities they served, like *The Brownies' Book Magazine* (1920–1921) produced during the start of the Harlem Renaissance by editors Fauset and DuBois.[34] These literary journals also tend to feature literary fairy tales by a single author rather than folktales recorded from oral storytellers.

All of folklore recorded here negotiates the storyteller's meaning and purpose.[35] The concept of 'folk' as authentic creators of culture was constructed as a part of nineteenth-century nationalist movements, and there was a perpetual war for political ownership of their authority.[36] This collection does not attempt to resurrect that battle. The stories included here are situated in their specific historical context and juxtaposed with similarly politicized tales from different traditions. As many scholars have pointed out, even these contexts are presumptions; both amateurs and professionals engaged in what Bo Almqvist calls 'criminal'[37] folklore, passing off copies of printed tales as 'authentic'[38] or creating a fictive folk context for narratives. In fact, there is a plagiarized story in Volume 1: 'Rouchy' (1930) is 'Maureen Rua' (1939) with the name of the heroine changed. Both stories were published in *Ireland's Own* nearly a decade apart. And they are both identical versions of Patrick Kennedy's earlier 'Hairy Rouchy' published in *Fireside Stories* (1870). The repetition of this tale is as culturally significant as the collection of unique tales in many ways. It demonstrates the interchange ability of the narrative for its Irish audience, but it also demonstrates the manipulation of the concept of 'authentic' folk narratives.

Fairy-Tale Revivals is an Anglophone collection. It does not reflect the myriad multilingual influences on folklore and fairy tales in the US and the UK. The only stories in translation here are the Welsh Romani and Traveller tales because those tales were told in a bilingual context. The translated tales were circulated throughout Wales and incorporated into the ongoing cultural renaissance. Although the collection, appropriation and dissemination of these tales is as problematic as any folklore collection from this era, it also gestures towards the complex cultural intersections within literary revival movements.

Many of the fairy tales written specifically for children in this collection eschew the use of dialect entirely. Tales from literary magazines like *The Brownies' Book* (1920–1921), an offshoot of *The Crisis* published in New York, and the 'family friendly' *Ireland's Own* include fairy tales for children written in standard American and British English with sanitized narratives. Even Sinéad de Valera, founding member of *Inghinidhe na hÉireann* (Daughters of Ireland) and a long-time member of the Gaelic League, writes her fairy tales for children in standard British or Irish English, although she occasionally includes a Gaelic term, which she explains and defines for her readers. These tales are sharply contrasted with the use of dialect in both folklore collections and the works of renaissance artists like Manx writer Sophia Morrison, known as 'Cushag', or Caribbean author and artist Bennett-Coverley, as well as more stereotyped dialect in other amateur and scholarly folklore collections.[39] Language and the storyteller's voice are always already an essential to the wonder of the fairy tale. The tales here have been reproduced as they were originally recorded without revising or editing the language, including language that may be offensive or triggering.

CINDERELLA AND EVERYONE ELSE

Cinderella became a metaphor for empire across a wide range of genres. For example, the satiric pamphlet *Cinderella Erin*'s (1874) uses the ATU 510 narrative to address the traumatic history of Ireland and advocate for greater independence from colonial oppression (see *Fairy-Tale Revivals*, Volume 1). In the 1850s, fugitive slave Hannah Crafts incorporated an anti-Cinderella tale into *A Bondwoman's Narrative* (ca. 1854) to expose the exploitation of slave labour inherent in the American rise narrative. Julia Kavanagh, Charles Chesnutt and Jessie Fauset all expose colonial exploitation with pernicious Irish and African American Cinderella narratives. And Afro-Jewish Jamaican author Herbert de Lisser concludes his career as the most influential British Caribbean author of the late nineteenth and early twentieth century with a tragic novel, *Psyche* (1944), that merges Cinderella with Beauty and the Beast.

Although Cinderella was not the most popular fairy tale told and retold by authors in the colonial Anglophone world, it was a touchstone in protest literature in the British Empire and its former colonies. The concept of Cinderella Ireland inspired Caribbean responses to colonial rule; islands in the British Caribbean borrowed the term 'Cinderella of Empire', occasionally referencing the Irish fight for independence directly in discussions of colonial abuse or neglect in the Caribbean.[40] By contrast, Cinderella became incorporated into the American rise tale in the US.[41] Harlem Renaissance writers critiqued this rise formula with new Cinderella narratives that expose the silent exploitation that enables the white heroine's rise. The diversity and variety of fairy tales and folklore crafted by colonized storytellers is beautifully reflected in a wide range of collections.[42] As this collection evolved, Cinderella eclipsed other popular tales in its representation because it was frequently used to expose either the abuse of the Cinderella colony or challenge the belief that the imperialist fairy-tale formula will either fulfil happiness or 'unlock social and public possibilities'.[43] This formula depends on the presence of a supernatural helper who can overcome the impossible social and material barriers to the abused heroine's rise. And like the ten Home Rule League fairies in *Cinderella Erin*, the helper is never quite powerful enough. The colonized Cinderella never actually gets to the ball with Prince Home Rule until she internalizes the fairies' power and makes her own happy ending, as she does in stories like 'Hairy Rouchy',[44] 'A Girl's Will' or *Psyche*.

Cinderella narratives both support and undermine imperial metanarratives in this collection. In *Fairy-Tale Revivals*, the definition of 'Cinderella' begins with folkloric distinctions in the Aarne-Thompson-Üther (ATU) Index: a supernatural helper, a recognition test and a fitness trope. Although some of the most popular folklore collections were created by scholars such as Joseph Jacobs and T. Crofton Croker, the collection of folk narratives also became a communal activity in places like Ireland.[45] The literary revival movements popularized a widespread interest in gathering local stories. In turn, a community's engagement in gathering folklore appears to have spread popular acceptance of folklorists' categorizations of tales and motifs. However, 'Cinderella' is also a label that takes on meaning completely apart from ATU 510 motifs. Narratives like 'Enchanted Island', 'A Girl's Will', 'Hairy Rouchy', 'Ashapelt' and 'Adventures of Maureen Rua' are all identified as Cinderella narratives despite an apparent lack of folkloric Cinderella motifs.[46] These stories demonstrate that the meaning of 'Cinderella' as a fairy tale exceeds any boundary or definition for storytellers. Sometimes a Cinderella story is because it is. As Cristina Bacchilega states in the 'Foreword' to *Cinderella Across Cultures: New Directions and Interdisciplinary Perspectives* (2016), 'Cinderella cannot tell one story only' (p. xiii).

In the shadows of the Cinderella narratives included here are also 'Name of the Helper', 'Little Mermaid', 'Bluebeard', 'Beauty and the Beast' and 'Tar Baby' stories and dramas. These tales, rather than Cinderella, represent the bulk of the narratives surrounding ethnic literary revival movements in the UK and the US. The inclusion of these tales here gestures towards the diversity of Celtic, Caribbean and African American tales without representing it.

VOLUME 1: ARTICLES AND SHORT FICTION

The first volume of *Fairy-Tale Revivals in the Long Nineteenth Century: Writing Wonder and Transatlantic Ethnic Literary Revivals, 1850–1950* contains a wide variety of articles and short wonder tales, satires and anti-tales written between 1840 and 1950. It is divided into six parts: Cinderella Articles, Cinderella Narratives, Cinderella Alternatives, Cinderlad Tales, Fairy Lore, Tricksters and Wonder Tales. Within the parts, similar texts are grouped together and then arranged in roughly chronological order. The first part opens with the pamphlet *Cinderella Erin* and the review of the pamphlet published in *The Nation*. This pamphlet, out of print since 1874, is not even available in the wonderful collections in the National Library of Ireland.

VOLUME 2: DRAMAS

The second volume of *Fairy-Tale Revivals in the Long Nineteenth Century* contains several fairy-tale dramas. Although British fairy-tale pantomimes always had the potential to become political, the politics in these dramas are distinctive because of the ways they negotiate ethnic literary revivals and the pantomime tradition. This volume includes two Bluebeard dramas, two Cinderella dramas, one non-magical fairy-tale play by Langston Hughes, and two fairy-lore dramas.

Bluebeard and Brer Anancy (1944), by Caribbean Renaissance author Bennett-Coverley, is identified as the first Caribbean pantomime. Although reviews of the play do not adequately reflect its revolutionary cultural and political work, it was the beginning of a uniquely Jamaican dramatic tradition. For the first time, this play is available here in print with the permission of the Louise Bennett-Coverley Estate (LBCE) and the support of the National Library of Jamaica. In the 1940s, the revolutionary pantomimes of The Little Theatre Movement (LTM) in Jamaica were central to the Caribbean literary renaissance.

CONCLUSION

The term 'folklore', coined in 1846, was politicized from its inception, 'fuelled by an idea of national identity rooted in the rural working classes, those seemingly closest to the earth'.[47] In the midst of competing claims to the voice and authority of these narratives, a rich and resistant literary tradition developed. On 28 February 1891, George C. Camplejohn's article on the potential for profit of harvesting sea sponges off the coast of the Bahamas with cheap native labour made the front page of the longest running Caribbean newspaper, *The Nassau Guardian*. Camplejohn concludes his discussion of exploiting Caribbean resources and labour with a fairy tale that he appropriated from the men of colour who worked as divers to demonstrate that they were a contented group fit for their dangerous work. The fairy tale, called 'Enchanted Island', is classified as either a Bluebeard tale or a Cinderella tale by Camplejohn in the text of the article. The protagonist, Jack, is double-crossed by his captain and cheated out of the treasure and the lost princess he rescued. The tale ends with Jack outwitting the lying captain, who is put in a tar barrel and set on fire. It concludes with a statement in a stereotypical Caribbean dialect: 'Moral: "Neber trick a poor sponger out of his shares, for the Debil's tar barrels burn mighty hot"' (p. 1). With a single sentence, presumably the moral of the original storyteller, Camplejohn's appropriated story challenges the imperial exploitation of the Caribbean, and the writer seems to miss it completely. Camplejohn's tale is included here as an example of the potential power of fairy tales to make social critiques even when those tales are appropriated and retold to support colonial exploitation.

CONTENT WARNING

Although the texts in this collection make important critical intervention, they contain material that may be triggering or offensive. These texts use extensive tropes from the traditions they critique, including biased language, bigotry and violent situations that may or may not have been considered humorous by the authors. All the material here is original to the source texts. The editorial material in this collection deals critically with the long history of colonial exploitation in the Anglophone fairy-tale tradition. Uncovering and interrogating this history and the mediations made by revival and renaissance authors is essential to maintaining a critical approach to fairy-tale studies and expanding our understanding of the diverse uses of this genre.

NOTES

1 Clarke, H., ill., *The Fairy Tales of Charles Perrault* (London: George G Harpe and Co., 1922).
2 While Clarke's intention is unclear, the distinctive addition of racialized characters sets it apart from all of Clarke's earlier collections, especially *Fairy Tales of Hans Christian Anderson* (London: George G Harpe and Co., 1916). The racialized characters included here are a new addition to Clarke's illustration style and extraneous to the text of the stories.
3 See 'Cinderella' (pp. 87, 92), 'Riquet with the Tuft' (p. 104), and 'Donkey-Skin' (p. 145).
4 Birds-of-paradise all belong to the *Paradisaea* family of birds. These birds, known for their spectacular feathers and mating dances, are frequently identified as 'the most beautiful creatures on earth' ('Birds of Paradise Project', The Cornell Lab). These birds are found in New Guinea and Indonesia in the southwest Pacific. Tens of thousands of birds-of-paradise skins with their feathers were imported to Europe to be used in women's millinery and in flyfishing lures (see Kirsch, S., 'History and the Birds of Paradise', *Expedition Magazine*, 48:1 (2006)).
5 William Dowling, manager of the Clarke Studios sums up his perception of Clarke's politics: 'I do not think that Harry Clarke gave much thought to politics, but due to his close associations with cultural resurgence it is inevitable that he would have absorbed its national atmosphere' (Griffith, A., M. Helmers, and R. Kennedy, eds., *Harry Clarke and Artistic Visions of the New Irish State* (Dublin: Irish Academic Press, 2018), p. 1).
6 *Harry Clarke's War: Illustrations for Ireland's Memorial Records 1914–1018* explores the complex history and subtle critique of Clarke's work in *Ireland's Memorial Records*, which list the names of Irish soldiers in the Great War (see Helmer, M., *Harry Clarke's War: Illustrations for Ireland's Memorial Records, 1914–1918* (Dublin: Irish Academic Press, 2016)).
7 These narratives either have explicit political messages or they are a part of a highly politicized fairy-tale landscape. For example, the political message of Lady Bell's Anglo-Irish *Bluebeard* (1896) is subtle and conflicted. It is a stark contrast to the rich political message in the Rt Hon Dr Louise Bennett-Coverley's *Bluebeard and Brer Anancy* (1949).
8 Jack Zipes's keynote speech at 'Thinking with Stories in Times of Conflict: A Conference in Fairy-Tale Studies' in August 2017 concluded with a rousing call to 'find truth in the [unexplored] margins' of fairy tales and folklore. His call resonates with Bacchilega's earlier invitation to expand the boundaries of the fairy-tale genre in *Fairy Tales*

Transformed? (Detroit, MI: Wayne State P, 2013), pp. 201–2. Recent English-language fairy-tale and folklore collections have both expanded and reoriented fairy-tale studies. Notable collections like *The Annotated African American Folktales* (New York: W.W. Norton and Co., 2018) and *Folk Stories from the Hills of Puerto Rico* (New Brunswick, NJ: Rutgers University Press, 2021) do deep folkloric dives into the work of historically marginalized storytellers from this period in the Anglophone world. This collection complements such focused anthologies.

9 Welsh, Scottish, Irish, Manx, African American and Caribbean literary revival movements all informed and inspired each other. The connections between the Welsh, Scottish, Irish and Manx Celtic Revival movements are relatively obvious, driven by a shared study of the Celtic language. In fact, Irish linguists like de Valera travelled to Wales and the Isle of Man helping to start neighbouring Celtic language societies. Similarly, Jamaican-born Harlem Renaissance writer Claude McKay is one of the many figures who provides a concrete link between African American and Caribbean Renaissance authors. However, Tracy Mishkin demonstrates that the relationship between all of these Anglophone literary revivals in the later nineteenth and early twentieth centuries was once 'well known in intellectual circles, both black and white' (*The Harlem and Irish Renaissances: Language, Identity, and Representation* (Gainesville: U Florida P, 1998), p. xiii.). Not only did literary revival authors face similar issues and develop similar ideas across different movements, artists and their work circulated over regional and national borders, such as the Abbey Theatre tour of the United States in 1911, which was attended by future members of the Harlem Renaissance (Mishkin, *The Harlem and Irish Renaissances*, p. 1).

10 In the 'Series Preface' to *A Cultural History of Fairy Tales in the Long Nineteenth Century* (2021), series editor Anne Duggan gives a broad definition for the fairy tale across different historical periods and geographical locations:

> 'Fairy tale' here serves as a broad umbrella term for what more generally could be referred to as a 'wonder tale,' which encompasses but is not limited to texts that feature fairies, witches, enchanters, djinn, and other beings endowed with supernatural powers; anthropomorphized animals; metamorphosis . . . ; magical objects; and otherworlds and liminal spaces. 'Fairy tale' also refers to texts that may not include any of these qualities but have been received as – that is, read or categorized as or are generally considered to be – a fairy tale.
>
> ((London: Bloomsbury Academic P, 2021), p. ix)

11 MacDonald's work was intertwined with the Celtic Revival in Scotland.

12 Wood, N. J., 'Introduction: Fairy Tales and the Long Nineteenth Century', *A Cultural History of Fairy Tales in the Long Nineteenth Century*, vol. 5 (London: Bloomsbury Academic P, 2021), p. 4.

13 Smith, K. Capshaw, *Children's Literature of the Harlem Renaissance* (Bloomington: Indiana UP, 2004), p. 30.

14 Smith, *Children's Literature of the Harlem Renaissance*, p. 31.

15 *Fairy Tales Transformed?*, p. 195.

16 See Frank, A. W., *Letting Stories Breathe: A Socio-Narratology* (Chicago: U Chicago P, 2010), p. 75 and Bacchilega, *Fairy Tales Transformed?*, p. 195.

17 This collection contains examples of what Bo Almqvist, editor of *Béaloideas: The Journal of the Folklore of Ireland Society*, called 'criminal' folklore copied verbatim from previous print sources (p. 13). Also see Zipes, J., trans., 'Introduction', *The Complete First Edition of The Original Folk and Fairy Tales of the Brothers Grimm* (Princeton, NJ: Princeton UP, 2014), p. xxxii; Sumpter, C., *The Victorian Press and the Fairy Tale* (London: Palgrave Macmillan, 2008); Killick, T. *British Short Fiction*

in the Early Nineteenth Century (Abingdon: Taylor and Francis, 2008); Woods, N. J., 'Introduction', *A Cultural History of Fairy Tales in the Long Nineteenth Century*, vol. 5 (London: Bloomsbury Academic P, 2021), pp. 7–10.

18 The hyphenation of Dr Bennett-Coverley's name here follows the example in the two volumes of the *Journal of West Indian Literature* devoted to critical approaches to her work: volumes 17 and 18 (2009).

19 Bennett-Coverley uses the distinctive incarnation of Anancy that is featured in Anglophone Caribbean folktales, although Anansi is a mythic character 'whose origins can be traced back to the Akan of Ghana in West Africa' (Zobel Marshall, E., '"Nothing but Pleasant Memories of the Discipline of Slavery": The Trickster and the Dynamics of Racial Representation', *Marvels and Tales: Journal of Fairy-Tale Studies*, 32:1 (2018), p. 59).

20 Gates, 'Foreword', *The Annotated African American Folktales* (New York: W.W. Norton and Co., 2018), p. xxv.

21 Gates, 'Forward', pp. xxv–xxvi.

22 Wood, 'Introduction', p. 7. Also see Schacker, J., *National Dreams* (Philadelphia: U Pennsylvania P, 2003), pp. 1–7.

23 Schacker, *National Dreams*, p. 3.

24 The Grimms' body of work exceeded their popular fairy-tale collection, including linguistic studies, but the fairy-tale collection was their most popular. In the context of Anglophone folklore studies, Bo Almqvist, the editor of *Béaloideas: The Journal of the Folklore of Ireland Society*, specifically references the Grimms as an inspiration for collecting folklore in Ireland, alongside Irish folklorists like Thomas Crofton Crocker and Patrick Kennedy (1979: 7).

25 Dorson, R., *The British Folklorists: A History* (Chicago: U Chicago P, 1968), p. 1, and Schacker, *National Dreams*, p. 4. Also see Hobsbawn, E., *Nations and Nationalism since 1780* (Cambridge: Cambridge UP, 1990), p. 104; Simpson, J., and Roud, S., 'Introduction', *A Dictionary of English Folklore* (New York and Oxford: Oxford UP, 2000); Wood, 'Introduction', pp. 4–5.

26 This is also apparent in publications like the *American Folklore Society Journal*, which identifies the ethnic or regional source in the title of all the folklore it published, like Charles Edwards's 'Some Tales from Bahama Folklore' (1891) or William Carso's 'Obijwa Tales' (1917).

27 Wood, 'Introduction', pp. 7–9; Gates, 'Foreword', pp. xxix–xxx; Schacker, *National Dreams*, pp. 1–3.

28 Wood, 'Introduction', p. 8.

29 Schacker, *National Dreams*, pp. 49–58.

30 Gates, 'Foreword', p. xxxii.

31 Gates, 'Foreword', p. xxix–xxx.

32 Schacker, *National Dreams*; 'Unruly Tales: Ideology, Anxiety, and the Regulation of Genre', *The Journal of American Folklore*, 120:478 (2007), pp. 120, 381–400, 478.

33 Schacker, *National Dreams*, pp. 7–10.

34 For Fauset's role as editor of *The Brownies' Book Magazine*, see Smith, *Children's Literature of the Harlem Renaissance*, p. 43.

35 Gates, 'Foreword', pp. xxix–xxx.

36 Wood, 'Introduction', pp. 8–9; Schacker, *National Dreams*, pp. 139–41.

37 Almqvist, 'The Irish Folklore Commission: Achievement and Legacy', *Béaloideas: The Journal of the Folklore of Ireland Society* (1979), p. 13.

38 Wood, 'Introduction', pp. 7–8; Schacker, *National Dreams*, pp. 138–9.

39 See Nwankwo, I. K., 'Introduction (Ap)Praising Louise Bennett: Jamaica, Panama, and Beyond', *Journal of West Indian Literature*, 17:2 (2009), pp. 8–25 and Rodis, K. V., 'Vernacular Literacy and Formal Analysis: Louise Bennett-Coverley's Jamaican English Verse', *Journal of West Indian Literature*, 18:1 (2009), pp. 60–72.

40 See 'Patriotism at a Discount' (11 November 1890) in the *Port of Spain Gazette* (1) and 'The Colonial Office and the Crown Colonies' (11 September 1909) in *The Nassau Guardian* (1).

41 Yolen, 'America's Cinderella', pp. 21–2; Heiniger, 'Passing as the American Cinderella'.

42 Recent collections like *The Annotated African American Folktales* (2018) and *Folklore from the Hills of Puerto Rico* (2020) both include and analyze the rich range of tales in the fairy tale and folklore traditions of traditionally marginalized storytellers.

43 Warner, M., *From the Beast to the Blonde: On Fairy Tales and Their Tellers* (New York: Farrar, Straus and Giroux, 1996), p. xx; Bacchilega, *Fairy Tales Transformed?*, p. 5).

44 Also known as 'Hairy Rucky'.

45 Almqvist, 'The Irish Folklore Commission', pp. 8–14.

46 See Smith, *Children's Literature of the Harlem Renaissance*; Christiansen, 'Cinderella in Ireland', *Béaloideas*, 20:1/2 (1950), pp. 96–107.

47 Wood, 'Introduction', p. 7.

BIBLIOGRAPHY

PRIMARY TEXTS

'Adventures of Maureen Rua', *Ireland's Own: A Journal of Fiction, Literature, and General Information*, 7 October 1939, pp. 12–13.

Alcott, L.M., 'A Modern Cinderella', *The Atlantic Monthly*, 6:36 (1860).

Barrie, J.M., *A Kiss for Cinderella: A Comedy* (London: Hodder and Stoughton Ltd, 1916).

Barton, G.W., 'The Fairy's Bride: A Legend of Llangarren', *The National Magazine of Wales*, 9:1 (January–June 1886), pp. 13–18.

Battey, 'Cover Picture', photograph, *The Brownies' Book Magazine*, 1:1 (January 1920), cover.

Bell, F.E.E.O., 'Bluebeard', *Fairy Tale Plays and How to Act Them* (London: Longmans, Green, and Co., 1896).

Bennett-Coverley, The Rt Hon Dr L., 'Anancy an Alligator', *A Laugh with Louise: Pot-pourri of Jamaican Folklore, Stories, Songs, Verses* (Kingston, Jamaica: City Printery, Ltd., 1961 [unknown]), p. 45.

——— *Bluebeard and Brer Anancy*, MS National Library of Jamaica (NLJ), 1944.

——— 'Unkle Sekrey and Anancy', *A Laugh with Louise: Pot-pourri of Jamaican Folklore, Stories, Songs, Verses* (Kingston, Jamaica: City Printery, Ltd., 1961 [unknown]), pp. 46–7.

Bird, A., 'Impossible Kathleen: A Story', *The Brownie's Book Magazine*, M. Hawkins, ill., 1:10 (October 1920), pp. 297–304.

Burne-Jones, E., 'Depth of the Sea', *Painting* (1886).

C., E., 'Two Jamaicans Write and Produce a Pantomime', *The West Indian Review*, December 1949.

Camplejohn, G.C., 'Enchanted Island', *The Nassau Guardian*, Nassau, New Providence, Bahamas, 28 February 1891, p. 1.

'Celebrating Baby Week at Tuskegee', photograph, *The Brownies' Book Magazine*, 1:1 (January 1920), pp. 16–17.

Cinderella (Waterloo Road, London: March's Farthing Library, 1849).

'Cinderella', *Rhyl Record and Advertiser*, 31 December 1898.

'Cinderella at the Empire', *The Irish Independent*, 28 December 1915.

'Cinderella Dance in Bandon', *Skibbereen Eagle*, Skibbereen, County Cork, Ireland, 17 March 1894.

Cinderella Erin (Dublin, Ireland: W.B. Kelly, 1874).

'Cinderella Erin', *The Nation*, Dublin, Ireland, 17 October 1874.

'Cinderella Fund', *Flintshire Observer Mining Journal and General Advertiser for the Counties of Flint Denbigh*, 12 March 1914.

'Cinderella in Skibbereen', *Skibbereen Eagle*, Skibbereen, County Cork, Ireland, 1 August 1898.

'The Cinderella of the Empire', *The Nation*, Dublin, Ireland, 7 September 1867.

'Cinderella Parties', *The Aberystwyth Observer*, 30 March 1878.

Clarke, H., ill., *The Fairy Tales of Charles Perrault* (London: George G Harpe and Co., 1922).

—— *Fairy Tales of Hans Christian Anderson* (London: George G Harpe and Co., 1916).

'The Colonial Office and the Crown Colonies', *The Nassau Guardian*, Nassau, Bahamas, 11 September 1909.

'Complaint Over Anglican Cinderella', *The Nation*, Dublin, Ireland, 6 January 1872.

Crawshay-Williams, E., *Hywel and Gwyneth: A Modern Fairy Tale*, S.C. Williams, ill. (Cardiff: William Lewis, 1930).

Curtin, J., 'Fair, Brown, and Trembling', *Myths and Folklore of Ireland* (Boston: Little, Brown and Company, 1890), pp. 78–92.

Danaher, K., 'Máirín Rua', *Folktales of the Irish Countryside* (Bloomington: Indiana U, 1967), pp. 102–7.

De Valera, S., 'Ashapelt', (ca. 1930).

—— 'The Miser's Gold', *The Miser's Gold and Other Stories* (Dublin, Ireland: Fallons, 1970 [unknown]), pp. 6–9.

—— 'Pooka', *Fairy Tales of Ireland* (Dublin, Ireland: Fallons, 1967 [unknown]), pp. 13–19.

—— 'The Stolen Treasures', *The Miser's Gold and Other Stories* (Dublin, Ireland: Fallons, 1970 [unknown]), pp. 46–52.

—— 'Well at the End of the World', (ca 1930).

'Fairy Tales', *The Library World* (UK: André Deutsch, 1914).

Fauset, A.H., 'Catskin', excerpted from 'Negro Folk Tales from the South (Alabama, Mississippi, Louisiana)', *The Journal of American Folklore*, 40:157 (1927), pp. 243–5 at https://doi.org/10.2307/534988 (accessed 26 June 2022).

—— 'The Friendly Demon', excerpted from 'Negro Folk Tales from the South (Alabama, Mississippi, Louisiana)', *The Journal of American Folklore*, 40:157 (1927), pp. 248–9 at https://doi.org/10.2307/534988 (accessed 26 June 2022).

—— 'Little Claus', excerpted from 'Negro Folk Tales from the South (Alabama, Mississippi, Louisiana)', *The Journal of American Folklore*, 40:157 (1927), pp. 253–5 at https://doi.org/10.2307/534988 (accessed 26 June 2022).

—— 'The Seventh Son', excerpted from 'Negro Folk Tales from the South (Alabama, Mississippi, Louisiana)', *The Journal of American Folklore*, 40:157 (1927), pp. 255–7 at https://doi.org/10.2307/534988 (accessed 26 June 2022).

—— 'Tar Baby', excerpted from 'Negro Folk Tales from the South (Alabama, Mississippi, Louisiana)', *The Journal of American Folklore*, 40:157 (1927), pp. 228–31 at https://doi.org/10.2307/534988 (accessed 26 June 2022).

'The Folklore of the Negroes of Jamaica', *Folklore*, 15:1 (1904), p. 92.

Geldart, E.M., 'Little Saddleslut', *Folk-Lore of Modern Greece: The Tales of the People* (London: W. Swan Sonnenschein and Company, 1884), pp. 27–30.

'Hairy Rouchy', *Transcript*, JML, pp. 513–25.

'Hengler's Grand Cirque', *The Nation*, Dublin, Ireland, 29 May 1869.

Holt, A., *Fancy Dresses Described; Or, What to Wear at Fancy Balls*, 5th ed. (London: Debenham and Freebody, 1887).

Hughes, L., 'The Gold Piece: A Play That Might Be True', *The Brownies' Book Magazine*, 2:7 (1921), pp. 191–4.

Hyde, D., 'The Bracket Bull', *The Irish Fairy Book*, A.P. Graves, ed., G. Denham, ill. (London: T. Fisher Unwin, 1909), pp. 117–24.

'The Imperial Institute and Colonial Trade', *The Port of Spain Gazette*, Trinidad, 21 April 1891 at www.dloc.com (accessed 10 June 2022).

'Ireland on Stage', *The Nassau Guardian*, Nassau, New Providence, Bahamas, 10 November 1880.

Johnson, J.H., 'Folk-Lore from Antigua, British West Indies', *The Journal of American Folklore*, 34:131 (1921), pp. 40–88 at https://doi.org/10.2307/534935 (accessed 26 June 2022).

Kavanagh, J., *Queen Mab* (Leipzig: Berhard Tauchnitz, 1863).

Kennedy, P., 'Hairy Rouchy', *The Fireside Stories* (Dublin: M'Glashan and Gill; and Patrick Kennedy, 1870), pp. 3–9.

Kilpatrick, A.T., 'Gyp a Fairy Story', *The Brownies' Book Magazine*, 1:1 (January 1920), p. 31.

Madden, E., 'A Girl's Will', *The Brownie's Book Magazine*, H. Wilkinson, ill., 1:2 (February 1920), pp. 54–6.

Moore, T., 'The Young May Moon', *The Oxford Book of English Verse: 1250–1900*, Arthur Quiller-Couch, ed. (Oxford: Claredon Press, 1919) at www.bartleby.com/101/582.html (accessed 1 May 2020).

Morrison, S., 'Cushag', *Eunys, or The Dalby Maid* (Prospect Hill, Douglas, Isle of Mann: G&L Johnson, 1908).

——— 'Joe Moore's Story of Finn MacCooilley and the Buggane', *Manx Fairy Tales* (London: David Nutt, 1911), pp. 42–6.

——— 'The Mermaid of Gob Ny Ooyl', *Manx Fairy Tales* (London: David Nutt, 1911), pp. 71–5.

Morrisson, S., and A.W. Moore, *A Vocabulary of the Anglo-Manx Dialect* (London: Oxford UP, 1924).

Murphy, G., 'Coat of Rushes and the Prince', *Tales from Ireland* (New York: Desmond and Stapleton, 1947), pp. 22–31.

Noël-Paton, M.H., *The Hidden People: A Play Based on the Ballads of Tam Lin and Thomas the Rhymer* (London: George Allen & Unwin Ltd, 1933).

Nutt, D., ed., 'Ashy-Pelty', *Folklore: A Quarterly Review of Myth, Tradition, Institution, and Custom* (London: David Nutt, 1895), pp. 305–8.

——— 'Cul-fin, Cul-din, and Cul-corrach', *Folklore: A Quarterly Review*, Mrs. Whelan, Storyteller, L. Duncan, recorder, vol. 5 (London: David Nutt, 1894), pp. 203–9.

Ocasio, R., *Folk Stories from the Hills of Puerto Rico* (New Brunswick, NJ: Rutgers University Press, 2021).

Parsons, E.C., 'Blue-beard' excerpted from 'Tales from Guilford County, North Carolina', *The Journal of American Folklore*, 30:116 (April–June 1917), p. 180 at www.jstor.org/stable/534337 (accessed 19 November 2022).

——— 'Brave Little Tailor', *The Journal of American Folklore*, 38:148 (April–June 1925), pp. 267–92.

———— 'Cinderella', *Folk-Lore of the Sea Islands, South Carolina* (Cambridge, MA: American Folklore Society, 1923), p. 120 at https://babel.hathitrust.org/cgi/pt?id=uc1.32106000764198&view=1up&seq=8 (accessed 19 November 2022).

———— 'Ramstampeldam', *Folk-Lore of the Sea Islands, South Carolina* (Cambridge, MA: American Folklore Society 1923), pp. 23–4 at https://babel.hathitrust.org/cgi/pt?id=uc1.32106000764198&view=1up&seq=8 (accessed 19 November 2022).

'Patriotism at a Discount', *The Port of Spain Gazette*, Trinidad, 11 November 1890 at www.dloc.com (accessed 10 June 2022).

Poe, P., 'Little Miss Ginger-Snap', *The Brownies' Book Magazine*, 2:11 (November 1921), pp. 312–15.

'The Princess and the Fairy', *Ireland's Own: A Journal of Fiction, Literature, and General Information*, 4 May 1935, pp. 572–3.

Robertson, W.G., 'The Slippers of Cinderella', *The Slippers of Cinderella and Other Plays* (London: William Heinemann, 1919).

'Rouchy', *Ireland's Own: A Journal of Fiction, Literature and General Information*, 56:1455 (18 October 1930), pp. 2–3.

Sampson, J., 'Google-Eyes', *The Journal of the Gypsy Lore Society*, 2:2 (1923), pp. 101–10.

———— 'Laula' (1923), *Welsh Gypsy Folk Tales* (Wales: Gregynog Press, 1933), pp. 4–8.

———— 'The Little Slut', *Journal of the Gypsy Lore Society*, 2:2 (1923), pp. 99–113.

S.H., 'Cinderella', *The Cambrian*, 21 December 1883, p. 7 at https://newspapers.library.wales/view/3337060/3337067/51/cinderella (accessed 1 December 2020).

'Skating Cinderella', *Llandudno Advertiser and List of Visitors*, Llandudno, Conwy County Borough, Wales, 16 May 1908.

Spence, A.A., 'The Wonderful Pipe', *The Brownies' Book Magazine*, Marcellus Hawkins, ill., 1:10 (1920), pp. 294–6.

Stevenson, P., *The Moon-Eyed People* (Cheltenham, UK: The History Press, 2019).

———— *Welsh Folk Tales* (Cheltenham, UK: The History Press, 2017).

Suggs, J.D., 'The Mermaid', *American Negro Folktales*, Richard M. Dorson, ed. (New York: Dover, 1956), pp. 252–3.

Thomas, W.J., 'Peregrine and the Mermaid', *The Welsh Fairy Book*, Willy Pogany, ill. (London: Fisher Unwin, 1907), pp. 138–40.

Tobias, L., 'The Purim Ball', *The Nationalists and Other Goluth Studies* (London: C. W. Daniel, LTD, 1921), pp. 56–64.

Williams, E., *Cinderella*, typescript, Emlyn William Papers, National Library of Wales (NLW), 1924.

'A Working-Girl: A New Cinderella', *Harper's New Monthly Magazine*, 66:395 (1883).

SECONDARY TEXTS

Aarne-Thompson-Üther Folklore Index (ATU) S. Urban, curator at https://sites.ualberta.ca/~urban/Projects/English/Motif_Index.htm (accessed 1 January 2019).

'About *Ireland's Own*' (2022), *Ireland's Own*, website at www.irelandsown.ie/about/ (accessed 1 January 2022).

Aldred, B.G., 'Beauty and the Beast', *The Greenwood Encyclopedia of Folktales and Fairy Tales: A-F* (London: Greenwood Press, 2008), pp. 104–9.

Almqvist, B., 'The Irish Folklore Commission: Achievement and Legacy', *Béaloideas: The Journal of the Folklore of Ireland Society* (1979), pp. 1–47.

Auerbach, N., *Woman and the Demon: The Life of a Victorian Myth* (Cambridge, MA: Harvard UP, 1982).

Bacchilega, C., *Fairy Tales Transformed? Twenty-First-Century Adaptations and the Politics of Wonder* (Detroit, MI: Wayne State P, 2013).

———— 'Foreword', *Cinderella Across Cultures: New Directions and Interdisciplinary Perspectives* (Detroit, MI: Wayne State UP, 2016), pp. xi–xiv.

Barnes, G., 'Revolutionary Jamaica: Interpreting the Politics of the Baptist War', *Age of Revolutions*, 23 January 2017 at https://ageofrevolutions.com/2017/01/23/revolutionary-jamaica-interpreting-the-politics-of-the-baptist-war/ (accessed 13 July 2022).

Barrett, L.E., 'Anancy and Miss Lou', *The Sun and the Drum: African Roots in the Jamaican Folk Tradition* (Kingston, Jamaica: Sangster's Book Stores, 1976).

Bennett, L., 'Evening Time', *Jamaicans.com* (2003) at https://jamaicans.com/eveningt/ (accessed 1 June 2022).

Bennett, L., and D. Scott, 'Bennett on Bennett', *Caribbean Quarterly*, 14:1/2 (1968), pp. 97–101 at www.jstor.org/stable/40653061 (accessed 2 November 2022).

'Birds of Paradise Project', *The Cornell Lab* at www.birdsofparadiseproject.org (accessed 1 January 2022).

Bottigheimer, R., 'Beauty and the Beast', *The Oxford Companion to Fairy Tales* (Oxford: Oxford UP, 2015), pp. 47–9.

———— 'Cinderella: The People's Princess', *Cinderella Across Cultures: New Directions and Interdisciplinary Perspectives* (Detroit, MI: Wayne State UP, 2016), pp. 27–51.

————, ed., *Fairy Tales and Society: Illusion, Allusion, and Paradigm* (Philadelphia, PA: U Pennsylvania P, 1986).

Bowe, N.G., *Harry Clarke: The Life and Works* (Dublin: The History Press Ireland, 1989, 2012).

Bown, N., *Fairies in Nineteenth-Century Art and Literature* (Cambridge: Cambridge UP, 2001).

Boxill, I., 'The Two Faces Of Caribbean Music', *Social and Economic Studies*, 43:2 (1994), pp. 33–56 at www.jstor.org/stable/27865958 (accessed 5 October 2022).

Bracken, D., 'Ua Briain, Toirdelbach [Turlough O'Brien] (1009–1086)', *Oxford Dictionary of National Biography* (Oxford: Oxford UP, 2001) at http://doi.org/10.1093/ref:odnb/20468 (accessed 1 January 2022).

Brathwaite, E.K., *History of the Voice: The Development of Nation Language in Anglophone Caribbean Poetry* (London: New Beacon Books, 1984).

Bunce, J.T., *Fairy Tales, Their Origin and Meaning; with Some Account of Dwellers in Fairyland* (London: Macmillan, 1878).

Burnard, T., 'The Ambiguous Place of Free People in Jamaica', *Jamaica in the Age of Revolution* (Pennsylvania: U Pennsylvania P, 2020), pp. 131–50 at https://doi.org/10.2307/j.ctv11vc955.8 (accessed 13 July 2022).

C., E., 'Two Jamaicans Write and Produce a Pantomime', *The West Indies Review*, December 1949, p. 12.

Camplejohn, G.C., 'Enchanted Island', *The Nassau Guardian*, Nassau, New Providence, Bahamas, 28 February 1891, p. 1.

Carter, S., 'Coupling the Beastly Bride and the Hunter Hunted: What Lies Behind Chaucer's "Wife of Bath's Tale"', *The Chaucer Review*, 37:4 (2003), pp. 329–45 at www.jstor.org/stable/25096219 (accessed 1 May 2018).

'Census Results – Census 2022', *Central Statistics Office Ireland* at www.cso.ie/en/census/ (accessed 1 November 2022).

Chansky, D., 'Little Theater Movement', *The Routledge Encyclopedia of Modernism* (London: Routledge, 2016) at www.rem.routledge.com/articles/little-theater-movement (accessed 1 October 2022).

Christiansen, R.T., 'Cinderella in Ireland', *Béaloideas*, 20:1/2 (1950), pp. 96–107 at https://doi.org/10.2307/20521197 (accessed 1 May 2018).

——— 'A Norwegian Fairytale in Ireland?', *Béaloideas*, 2:3 (1930), pp. 235–45 at https://doi.org/10.2307/20521594 (accessed 1 May 2018).

Clark, R., 'Aspects of the Morrígan in Early Irish Literature', *Irish University Review*, 17:2 (1987), pp. 223–36 at www.jstor.org/stable/25477680 (accessed 1 January 2021).

Collins Dictionary (Glasgow: Harper Collins Publishers, 2022).

Cooper, A.J., 'Paper by Miss Anna Julia Cooper', *Southern Workman*, 22:7 (January 1894), p. 133 at https://babel.hathitrust.org/cgi/pt?id=hvd.hngblm;view=1up;seq=537 (accessed 1 May 2022).

Cooper-Clark, D., *Dreams of Re-Creation in Jamaica: The Holocaust, Internment, Jewish Refugees in Gibraltar Camp, Jamaican Jews and Sephardim* (Victoria, Canada: Friesen Press, 2017).

Cost, B., 'British version of "Saturday Night Live" Currently in the Works', *New York Post*, New York, 10 December 2021 at https://nypost.com/2021/12/10/british-saturday-night-live-in-the-works-at-sky/ (accessed 25 September 2022).

Cox, M.R., 'Cinderella', *Folklore*, 18:2 (1907), pp. 191–208 at www.jstor.org/stable/1254354 (accessed 1 May 2018).

Crawford, S.W. and J.A. Alfaro, 'Esther: Bible', *Shalvi/Hyman Encyclopedia of Jewish Women*, 23 June 2021 at https://jwa.org/encyclopedia/article/esther-bible (accessed 18 October 2022).

Crawshay-Williams, E., *Hywel and Gwyneth: A Modern Fairy Tale*, Sybil C. Williams, ill. (Cardiff: William Lewis, 1930).

Dance, D.C., *Folklore From Contemporary Jamaicans* (Knoxville: U Tennessee P, 1985).

Davis, J., 'Only an Undisciplined [Nation] World Have Done It': Drury Lane Pantomime in the Late Nineteenth Century', *Victorian Pantomime: A Collection of Critical Essays* (London: Palgrave MacMillan, 2010), pp. 100–17.

Denson, L.A., 'The Drought of 1925', *Journal of the Elisha Mitchell Scientific Society*, 42:1/2 (1926), pp. 109–12 at www.jstor.org/stable/24331944 (accessed 20 November 2022).

De Valera, Sile, 'Forward', *The Magic Gifts* (Dublin, Ireland: Wolfhound Press, 2000).

De Valera, Terry, *A Memoir* (Ireland: Currach Press, 2011) at https://web.archive.org/web/20110927044319/www.currach.ie/shop/images/book_samples/1856079112.pdf (accessed 1 June 2020).

Dickens, C., 'On the Decadence of Pantomime', *The Theatre*, 1 January 1896, pp. 21–5.

Dictionary of Jamaican English, F.G. Cassidy and R.B. Le Page, eds., 2nd ed. (Kingston, Jamaica: U of the West Indies P, 2002).

Dictionary of the Scots Language, Scottish Government and University of Glasgow (2022) at https://dsl.ac.uk

Dictionary of Welsh Biography (2022) at https://biography.wales

'Dion Boucicualt Dead', *The New York Times*, 19 September 1890, p. 5 at www.Newspapers.com (accessed 17 September 2022).

Dorson, R., *The British Folklorists: A History* (Chicago: U Chicago P, 1968).

Duggan, A., 'Series Preface', *A Cultural History of Fairy Tales in the Long Nineteenth Century*, Naomi J Wood, ed., vol. 5 (London: Bloomsbury Academic P, 2021), pp. ix–xi.

Dundes, A., 'Fairy Tales from a Folkloristic Perspective', *Fairy Tales and Society: Illusion, Allusion, and Paradigm*, Ruth Bottigheimer, ed. (Philadelphia: U Pennsylvania P, 1986), pp. 259–70.

Eichhorn-Mulligan, A.C., 'The Anatomy of Power and the Miracle of Kingship: The Female Body of Sovereignty in a Medieval Irish Kingship Tale', *Speculum*, 81:4 (2006), pp. 1014–54 at www.jstor.org/stable/20463930 (accessed 1 January 2021).

Elkins, C., *Legacy of Violence: A History of the British Empire* (New York: Knopf, 2022).

'Enabling Gypsies, Roma, and Travellers Plan', *Welsh Government*, 15 June 2018 at https://gov.wales/enabling-gypsies-roma-and-travellers-plan (accessed 1 June 2022).

'Fairy Tales', *The Library World* (UK: André Deutsch, 1914).

Fennetaux, A., 'Fashioning Death/Gendering Sentiment: Mourning Jewelry in Britain in the Eighteenth Century', *Women and the Material Culture of Death*, Maureen Daly Goggin and Beth Fowkes Tobin, eds. (New York: Routledge, 2013).

Frank, A.W., *Letting Stories Breathe: A Socio-Narratology* (Chicago: U Chicago P, 2010).

Gates, H.L., Jr, 'Foreword: The Politics of "Negro Folklore"', *The Annotated African American Folktales*, H. Gates and M. Tatar, eds. (New York: W.W. Norton and Co., 2018), pp. xxiii–lii.

Gates, H.L., Jr, and M. Tatar, eds., *The Annotated African American Folktales* (New York: W.W. Norton and Co., 2018), pp. xxiii–lii.

Geldart, E.M., 'Little Saddleslut', *Folk-Lore of Modern Greece: The Tales of the People* (London: W. Swan Sonnenschein and Company, 1884), pp. 27–30.

General Assembly, 'Negro Womens Children to Serve According to the Condition of the Mother (1662)', *Encyclopedia Virginia* (2021) at https://encyclopediavirginia.org/entries/negro-womens-children-to-serve-according-to-the-condition-of-the-mother-1662 (accessed 15 July 2020).

The Greenwood Encyclopedia of Folktales and Fairy Tales, Haase, Donald, ed. (London: Greenwood Press, 2008).

Grenby, M.O., 'Tame Fairies Make Good Teachers: The Popularity of Early British Fairy Tales', *Lion & Unicorn*, 30:1 (2006), pp. 1–24.

Griffith, A., M. Helmers, and R. Kennedy, eds., *Harry Clarke and Artistic Visions of the New Irish State* (Dublin: Irish Academic Press, 2018).

Griswold, J., *The Meaning of 'Beauty and the Beast': A Handbook* (Peterborough, Ont: Broadview Press, 2004).

Gubar, M., *Artful Dodgers: Reconceiving the Golden Age of Children's Literature* (Oxford: Oxford UP, 2009).

Hall, C., 'White Visions, Black Lives: The Free Villages of Jamaica', *History Workshop*, 36 (1993), pp. 100–32 at www.jstor.org/stable/4289254 (accessed 13 July 2022).

hAodha, M.Ó., 'The Traveller Colonised', *'Insubordinate Irish': Travellers in the Text* (Manchester: Manchester UP, 2011), pp. 9–25 at www.jstor.org/stable/j.ctt155j9t5.6 (accessed 28 October 2022).

Harry, O.G., 'Jamaican Creole', *Journal of the International Phonetic Association*, 36:1 (2006), pp. 125–31.

Hearne, B., *Beauty and the Beast: Visions and Revisions of an Old Tale* (Chicago: U Chicago P, 1989).

Heiniger, A., 'The British Empire's Lost Slipper: Dangerous Irish Cinderellas', *Contemporary Fairy-Tale Magic: Subverting Gender and Genre*, L. Brugué, ed. (Netherlands: Rodopi, 2020).

——— 'Passing as the American Cinderella: Disenchanting Fairy Tales in the Writings of Hannah Crafts, Charles Chesnutt and Jessie Fauset', *Marvels and Tales*, 32:2 (2018), pp. 221–44.

Helleiner, J., 'Origins, Histories, and Anti-Traveller Racism', *Irish Travellers: Racism and the Politics of Culture* (Toronto: U Toronto P, 2000), pp. 29–50 at www.jstor.org/stable/10.3138/9781442676312.5 (accessed 28 October 2022).

Helmer, M., *Harry Clarke's War: Illustrations for Ireland's Memorial Records, 1914–1918* (Dublin: Irish Academic Press, 2016).

Hermansson, C.E., *Bluebeard: A Reader's Guide* (Jackson: UP Mississippi, 2009).

Higman, B.W., 'The Slave Family and Household in the British West Indies, 1800–1834', *The Journal of Interdisciplinary History*, 6:2 (1975), pp. 261–87 at https://doi.org/10.2307/202234 (accessed 13 July 2022).

Hill, E., *The Jamaican Stage, 1655–1900: Profile of a Colonial Theatre* (Amherst: U Massachusetts P, 1992) at https://search-ebscohost-com.lmunet.idm.oclc.org/login.aspx?direct=true&db=nlebk&AN=22394&site=ehost-live&scope=site (accessed 1 June 2022).

——— 'Perspectives in Caribbean Theatre: Ritual, Festival, and Drama', *Caribbean Quarterly*, 46:3/4 (2000), pp. 1–11 at www.jstor.org/stable/40654161 (accessed 1 August 2022).

Hines, S., 'Collecting the Empire: Andrew Lang's Fairy Books (1889–1910)', *Marvels & Tales*, 24:1 (2010), pp. 39–56 at www.jstor.org/stable/41389025 (accessed 1 May 2021).

Hintz, C., and E.L. Tribunella, *Reading Children's Literature: A Critical Introduction* (New York: St. Martin's P, 2013).

'The History of the Nassau Guardian', *The Nassau Guardian*, 3 August 2007 at https://web.archive.org/web/20070807124404/www.thenassauguardian.com/history/guardian-history.php (accessed 16 June 2022).

Hobsbawn, E.J., *Nations and Nationalism since 1780: Programme, Myth, Reality* (Cambridge: Cambridge UP, 1990), p. 104.

Holland, P., 'The Play of Eros: Paradoxes of Gender in English Pantomime', *New Theatre Quarterly*, 13:51 (1997), pp. 195–204.

'The Hon. Louise Bennett-Coverley', *Jamaica Information Services* website (2022) at https://jis.gov.jm/information/famous-jamaicans/louise-bennett-coverley/ (accessed 18 November 2022).

Horne, R.H., 'The Burlesque and the Beautiful', *Contemporary Review*, 18 (1871), pp. 390–406.

'How the Skibbereen Eagle Kept a Watchful Eye on the Czar of Russia', *Medium*, 23 March 2017 at https://medium.com/@allgoodtales/how-the-skibbereen-eagle-kept-a-watchful-eye-on-the-czar-of-russia-5d64d4b75fed (accessed 18 May 2020).

Hursh, C.R., and F.W. Haasis, 'Effects of 1925 Summer Drought on Southern Appalachian Hardwoods', *Ecology*, 12:2 (1931), pp. 380–6 at https://doi.org/10.2307/1931640 (accessed 20 November 2022).

Jackson, A., *Home Rule: An Irish History, 1800–2000* (Oxford: Oxford UP, 2004).

Jewish English Lexicon at https://jel.jewish-languages.org.

'John Canoe', *About Jamaica* (2017) at www.about-jamaica.com/john-canoe/ (accessed 1 October 2022).

Johnson, J.H., 'Folk-Lore from Antigua, British West Indies', *The Journal of American Folklore*, 34:131 (1921), pp. 40–88 at https://doi.org/10.2307/534935 (accessed 26 June 2022).

Joosen, V., *Critical and Creative Perspectives on Fairy Tales: An Intertextual Dialogue Between Fairy-Tale Scholarship and Postmodern Retellings* (Detroit: Wayne State UP, 2011).

Jorgensen, J., 'A Wave of the Magic Wand: Fairy Godmothers in Contemporary American Media', *Marvels & Tales*, 21:2 (2007), pp. 216–27 at muse.jhu.edu/article/241686 (accessed 1 January 2021).

The JPS Dictionary of Jewish Words (2001) at https://jps.org/books/dictionary-of-jewish-words/.

Kader, E. 'Jack in Ireland and Appalachia: The International Tale at Home and Abroad', *The Irish Review*, 44 (2012), pp. 42–59 at www.jstor.org/stable/23350174 (accessed 1 November 2022).

Keating, G., *The History of Ireland* (1857), Edward Comyn and Patrick S. Dinneen, trans., Ex-classics Project at www.exclassics.com/ceitinn/foras.pdf (accessed 1 June 2022).

Killarney Chamber of Tourism & Commerce, 'The Magillicuddy's Reeks Walks', *Kilkarney: The Town in the Park* (2022) at https://killarney.ie/listing/the-macgillycuddy-reeks-walks/ (accessed 1 June 2022).

Killick, T., *British Short Fiction in the Early Nineteenth Century: The Rise of the Tale* (Abingdon: Taylor and Francis, 2008).

Kirsch, S., 'History and the Birds of Paradise', *Expedition Magazine*, 48:1 (2006) at www.penn.museum/sites/expedition/history-and-the-birds-of-paradise/ (accessed 9 October 2022).

'A Kiss for Cinderella', *The Bournemouth Graphic*, 1 September 1916, p. 4.

'A Kiss for Cinderella', *Evening Express*, 6 October 1916, p. 2.

Krappe, A.H., 'The Sovereignty of Erin', *The American Journal of Philology*, 63:4 (1942), pp. 444–54 at https://doi.org/10.2307/291559 (accessed 1 January 2021).

Kruse, J., *Who's Who in Faeryland* (Somerset, UK: Green Magic Independent Publishers, 2022).

'The Late Margaret Ryan, Skibbereen', *The Skibbereen and District Historical Society* (2020) at https://skibbereenhistorical.ie/the-late-margaret-ryan-skibbereen/ (accessed 18 May 2020).

Lees, F.R., *The Selected Works of F.R. Lees* (London: National Temperance Publishing Depot, 1885), p. 125.

'The Little Theatre Movement – The Early History', *LTM Pantomime: Over 70 Years of Jamaican Theatre* (Kingston, Jamaica, 2004) at www.ltmpantomime.com/pages/panto-hist.html (accessed 1 August 2021).

Liverpool, H.U., 'Origins of Rituals and Customs in the Trinidad Carnival: African or European?', *TDR (1988–)*, 42:3 (1998), pp. 24–37 at www.jstor.org/stable/1146677 (accessed 5 October 2022).

——— 'Researching Steelband and Calypso Music in the British Caribbean and the U. S. Virgin Islands', *Black Music Research Journal*, 14:2 (1994), pp. 179–201 at https://doi.org/10.2307/779483 (accessed 5 October 2022).

Locock, M., 'Emlyn William Papers', *National Library of Wales*, March 2003 at https://archives.library.wales/index.php/emlyn-williams-papers-2 (accessed 1 May 2022).

MacDonagh, O., *States of Mind: A Study of Anglo-Irish Conflict 1780–1980* (London: Allen and Unwin, 1983).

'Marketing and Business Profile: Breadfruit (*Artocarpus Altilis*)', *RADA: People, Land and Opportunity* (2019) website, Rural Agricultural Development Authority at www. rada.gov.jm/content/marketing-business-profile-bread-fruit-artocarpus-altilis (accessed 1 July 2022).

Matthews, J., 'Back Where They Belong: Gypsies, Kidnapping and Assimilation in Victorian Children's Literature', *Romani Studies*, 20:2 (2010), pp. 137–59 at www.muse.jhu. edu/article/403958 (accessed 1 June 2022).

'Maude Adams at Academy', *The Baltimore Sun*, Baltimore, Maryland, 17 December 1916, p. 30.

McCaffrey, L.J., 'Home Rule and the General Election of 1874 in Ireland', *Irish Historical Studies*, 9:34 (1999), pp. 190–212 at www.jstor.org/stable/30005687 (accessed 25 July 2022).

McFeely, D., *Dion Bouciacault: Irish Identity on Stage* (Cambridge: Cambridge UP, 2021).

Merriam-Webster Online (Springfield, MA: Merriam Webster Inc., 2022) at www.merriam-webster.com (accessed 1 January 2019).

Merton, A., *The Athenæum*, 862:3 (August 1846).

'Michigan Heritage Award', *Michigan Traditional Arts Program* (2003) Michigan State University at http://traditionalarts.msu.edu/programs/michigan-heritage-awards/mha-awardee/?kid=A2-369-48 (accessed 23 September 2022).

Mishkin, T., *The Harlem and Irish Renaissances: Language, Identity, and Representation* (Gainesville: U Florida P, 1998).

Mokyr, J., 'Great Famine', *Encyclopedia Britannica*, 1 April 2022 at www.britannica.com/event/Great-Famine-Irish-history (accessed 17 September 2022).

Monaghan, P., *Encyclopedia of Goddesses and Heroines* (Novato, CA: New World Library, 2014).

Morris, M., 'Louise Bennett in Print', *Caribbean Quarterly*, 28:1–2 (1982), pp. 44–56.

―――― 'Miss Lou: Any Which Part Mi Live – A Jamaica Mi Deh!', *A Tapestry of Jamaica: The Best of Skywritings, Air Jamaica's Inflight Magazine* (1972–2002), Linda Gambrill, ed. (Oxford: Macmillan Caribbean, 2003).

―――― 'On Reading Louise Bennett, Seriously', *Jamaica Journal*, 1:1 (1967), pp. 69–74.

Murphy, X., and S. McLean, '80 Common Jamaican Patois Sentences That Will Help You Learn the Language', *Jamaicans.com* (2003) at https://jamaicans.com/talk/ (accessed 1 October 2022).

Musser, J., ed., 'Introduction', *"Girl, Colored" and Other Stories: A Complete Short Fiction Anthology of African American Women Writers in The Crisis Magazine, 1910–2010* (Jefferson, NC: McFarland & Co., Inc., 2011), pp. 1–23.

National Library of Jamaica, 'Miss Lou and the Early Jamaican Theatre', *YouTube*, 7 September 2017 at www.youtube.com/watch?v=M6mZUxGP8XA&t=1931s (accessed 1 June 2022).

Nelson, L., *The Normans in South Wales, 1070–117* (Austin and London: U Texas P, 1966) at http://vlib.iue.it/carrie/texts/carrie_books/nelson/ (accessed 1 January 2021).

Nord, D.E., *Gypsies and the British Imagination, 1807–1930* (New York: Columbia UP, 2006) at https://doi.org/10.7312/nord13704 (accessed 28 October 2022).

Nwankwo, I.K., 'Introduction (Ap)Praising Louise Bennett: Jamaica, Panama, and Beyond', *Journal of West Indian Literature*, 17:2 (2009), pp. 8–25 at www.jstor.org/stable/23019943 (accessed 1 May 2022).

Ó Crualaoich, G., 'Non-Sovereignty Queen Aspects of the Otherworld Female in Irish Hag Legends: The Case of Cailleach Bhéarra', *Béaloideas*, 62/63 (1994), pp. 147–62 at https://doi.org/10.2307/20522445 (accessed 1 May 2021).

Oeur, F.B., 'The Children of the Sun: Celebrating the One Hundred-Year Anniversary of *The Brownies' Book*', *Journal of the History of Childhood and Youth*, 14:3 (2021), pp. 329–44.

Ohlmeyer, J., 'Ireland Has Yet to Come to Terms with its Imperial Past: Some Celebrate and Some Excoriate Connections with the British Empire', *The Irish Times*, 29 December 2020, Dublin at www.irishtimes.com/opinion/ireland-has-yet-to-come-to-terms-with-its-imperial-past-1.4444146 (accessed 24 September 2022).

Ó hÓgáin, D., '"Béaloideas": Notes on the History of a Word', *Béaloideas: The Journal of the Folklore of Ireland Society*, 70 (2002), pp. 83–98 at www.jstor.org/stable/20520794 (accessed 1 May 2018).

Online Manx Dictionary at www.mannin.info/Mannin/fockleyr/e?m.php (accessed 1 January 2020).

O'Sullivan, N., *Coming Home: Art and the Great Hunger* (Hamden, CT: Quinnipiac UP, 2018).

Ò Tuathaigh, G., *I mBèal an Bhàis: The Great Famine and the Language Shift in Nineteenth-Century Ireland* (Hamden, CT: Quinnipiac UP, 2015).

The Oxford Companion to Fairy Tales, J. Zipes, ed. (Oxford: Oxford UP, 2015).

Oxford Dictionary National Biography (ODNB) (Oxford: Oxford UP, 2022) at www.oxforddnb.com (accessed 1 January 2019).

Oxford English Dictionary (OED) Online (Oxford: Oxford UP, 2022) at www.oed.com (accessed 1 January 2019).

Porter, M., '*Tales in a Tent': John Sampson's Representations of Romanies*, thesis (Memorial University of Newfoundland, 2011) at https://research.library.mun.ca/11271/1/Porter_Michelle.pdf (accessed 1 January 2022).

Ragan, K., 'What Happened to the Heroines in Folktales?: An Analysis by Gender of a Multicultural Sample of Published Folktales Collected from Storytellers', *Marvels & Tales*, 23:2 (2009), pp. 227–47 at muse.jhu.edu/article/369130 (accessed 1 May 2021).

Ramazani, J., 'Louise Bennett: The National Poet as Transnational?', *Journal of West Indian Literature*, 17:2 (2009), pp. 49–64 at www.jstor.org/stable/23019948 (accessed 2 November 2022).

Reddock, R.E., 'Women and Slavery in the Caribbean: A Feminist Perspective', *Latin American Perspectives*, 12:1 (1985), pp. 63–80 at www.jstor.org/stable/2633562 (accessed 15 July 2022).

Reid-Salmon, D., *Burning for Freedom: A Theology of the Black Atlantic Struggle for Liberation* (Jamaica: Ian Randle Publishers, 2012).

Reilly, C., 'Feasting in the Time of Famine: Dublin Castle and the Great Hunger', *Coming Home: Art and the Great Hunger*, Niamh O'Sullivan, ed. (Hamden, CT: Quinnipiac UP, 2018).

Richardson, B.C., 'Depression Riots and the Calling of the 1897 West India Royal Commission', *NWIG: New West Indian Guide/Nieuwe West-Indische Gids*, 66:3/4 (1992), pp. 169–91 at www.jstor.org/stable/41849444 (accessed 5 June 2022).

Rodis, K.V., 'Vernacular Literacy and Formal Analysis: Louise Bennett-Coverley's Jamaican English Verse', *Journal of West Indian Literature*, 18:1 (2009), pp. 60–72 at www.jstor.org/stable/23019904 (accessed 1 January 2022).

The Romani Cymru website (2019) at www.valleystream.co.uk/romhome.htm (accessed 1 January 2021).

Salwen, M.B. and B. Garrison, *Latin American Journalism* (New York: Routledge, 2013).

Sampson, A., 'John Sampson and Romani Studies in Liverpool', *Role of the Romanies: Images and Counter Images of 'Gypsies'/Romanies in European Cultures*, Nicholas Saul and Susan Tebbutt, eds. (Liverpool: Liverpool UP, 2004), pp. 15–20 at https://doi.org/10.2307/j.ctt5vjjv0.6 (accessed 28 October 2022).

Schacker, J., *National Dreams: The Remaking of Fairy Tales in Nineteenth-Century England* (Philadelphia: U Pennsylvania P, 2003).

Schacker, J., and D. O'Quinn, eds., *The Routledge Pantomime Reader 1800–1900* (New York: Routledge, 2022).

——— *Staging Fairy Land: Folklore, Children's Entertainment, and Nineteenth-Century Pantomime* (Detroit: Wayne State UP, 2018).

——— 'Unruly Tales: Ideology, Anxiety, and the Regulation of Genre', *The Journal of American Folklore*, 120:478 (Fall 2007), pp. 381–400 at www.jstor.org/stable/20487576 (accessed 1 June 2020).

Schanoes, V., 'Thorns into Gold: Contemporary Jewish American Responses to Antisemitism in Traditional Fairy Tales', *The Journal of American Folklore*, 132:525 (2019), pp. 291–309 at www.jstor.org/stable/10.5406/jamerfolk.132.525.0291 (accessed 1 June 2020).

Simpson, J., and S. Roud, 'Introduction', *A Dictionary of English Folklore* (New York and Oxford: Oxford UP, 2000).

Sio, A.A., 'Race, Colour, and Miscegenation: The Free Coloured of Jamaica and Barbados', *Caribbean Studies*, 16:1 (1976), pp. 5–21 at www.jstor.org/stable/25612729 (accessed 13 July 2022).

Smith, K.C., *Children's Literature of the Harlem Renaissance* (Bloomington: Indiana UP, 2004).

Sullivan, J.A., *The Politics of the Pantomime: Regional Identity in the Theatre, 1860–1900* (Hatfield, UK: U Hertfordshire P, 2011).

Sumpter, C., *The Victorian Press and the Fairy Tale* (London: Palgrave Macmillan, 2008).

Talairach-Vielmas, L., 'Beautiful Maidens, Hideous Suitors: Victorian Fairy Tales and the Process of Civilization', *Marvels & Tales*, 24:2 (2010), pp. 272–96 at www.jstor.org/stable/41388956 (accessed 1 May 2016).

——— 'Forms of the Marvelous', *A Cultural History of Fairy Tales in the Long Nineteenth Century*, Naomi J. Wood, ed., vol. 5 (London: Bloomsbury Academic P, 2021), pp. 25–42.

Talley, T.W., *The Negro Traditions* (Knoxville: U Tennessee P, 1930).

Tatar, M., 'Introduction: Recovering a Cultural Tradition', *The Annotated African American Folktales*, H. Gates and M. Tatar, eds. (New York: W.W. Norton and Co., 2018), pp. liii–xcii.

Tees Valley Museums, 'Lady Florence Bell' (2022) at https://teesvalleymuseums.org/blog/post/lady-florence-bell/ (accessed 5 November 2022).

Thompson, B., 'Watah Come a Me Eye', *Beth's Note* (2022) at www.bethsnotesplus.com/2015/09/watah-come-a-me-eye.html (accessed 1 November 2022).

Tikkanen, A., 'Manx Language', *Encyclopaedia Britannica*, 25 October 2013 at www.britannica.com/topic/Manx-language (accessed 15 November 2022).

Turner, D.T., 'Langston Hughes as Playwright', *CLA Journal*, 11:4 (June 1968), pp. 297–309 at www.jstor.org/stable/4432787 (accessed 1 June 2020).

Üther, H.J., et al., *The Types of International Folktales: A Classification and Bibliography Based on the System of Antti Aarne and Stith Thompson* (Helsinki, Finnland: Suomalainen Tiedeakatemia Academia Scientiarum Fennica, 2011).

Valente, J., 'The Myth of Sovereignty: Gender in the Literature of Irish Nationalism', *ELH*, 61:1 (1994), pp. 189–210 at www.jstor.org/stable/2873438 (accessed 1 January 2018).

Vas de Silva, F., 'Why Cinderella's Mother Becomes a Cow', *Marvels and Tales*, 28:1 (2014).

A Vocabulary of the Anglo-Manx Dialect (London: Oxford UP, 1924) at www.isle-of-man.com/manxnotebook/fulltext/am1924/index.htm.

Wagner, B., *The Tar Baby: A Global History* (Princeton: Princeton UP, 2017).

Warner, M., *From the Beast to the Blonde: On Fairy Tales and Their Tellers* (New York: Farrar, Straus and Giroux, 1996).

———. *Once Upon a Time: A Short History of Fairy Tale* (Oxford: Oxford UP, 2016).

Weihman, L., 'Celtic Revival', *The Routledge Encyclopedia of Modernism* (New York: Routledge, 2016) at www.rem.routledge.com/articles/celtic-revival (accessed 7 October 2022).

Whelan, Mrs, Storyteller, 'Cul-fin, Cul-din, and Cul-corrach', Leland Duncan, recorder and David Nutt, ed., *Folklore: A Quarterly Review*, 5 (1894).

White, H., 'Moore, Thomas', *Dictionary of Irish Biography* (2012) at https://doi.org/10.3318/dib.005948.v1 (accessed 1 June 2022).

'Wife of de Valera Marks 94th Birthday', *The Portsmouth Times*, Ireland, 1 June 1972, p. 11 at https://news.google.com/newspapers (accessed 10 June 2022).

Williams, G.J., 'Pughe, William Owen (1759–1835), Lexicographer, Grammarian, Editor, Antiquary, and Poet', *Dictionary of Welsh Biography* (1959) National Library of Wales at https://biography.wales/pdf/s-PUGH-OWE-1759.pdf (accessed 23 September 2022).

Williams, L.A., *Daniel O'Connell: The British Press and the Irish Famine: Killing Remarks* (New York: Routledge, 2003; 2019).

Wilmot, S., 'The Politics of Protest in Free Jamaica – The Kingston John Canoe Christmas Riots, 1840 and 1841', *Caribbean Quarterly*, 36:3/4 (1990), pp. 65–75 at www.jstor.org/stable/23050439 (accessed 13 July 2022).

Winstedt, E.O., 'The Norwood Gypsies and Their Vocabulary', *The Journal of the Gypsy Lore Society* 9 (1915–16), pp. 1129–65 at https://babel.hathitrust.org/cgi/pt?id=mdp.39015024078373&view=1up&seq=193&q1=cinderella (accessed 1 June 2022).

Wood, N.J., 'Introduction: Fairy Tales and the Long Nineteenth Century', *A Cultural History of Fairy Tales in the Long Nineteenth Century*, vol. 5 (London: Bloomsbury Academic P, 2021), pp. 1–24.

Woodham-Smith, C., *The Great Hunger: Ireland 1845–1849* (London: Penguin Group, 1962).

Yolen, J., 'America's Cinderella', *Children's Literature in Education*, 8 (1977), pp. 21–9.

Young, J.L., et al., 'Even Cinderella Is White: (Re)Centering Black Girls' Voices as Literacies of Resistance', *The English Journal*, 107:6 (2018), pp. 102–8 at www.jstor.org/stable/26610202 (accessed 1 May 2021).

Ziolkowski, J., 'Beauty and the Beast in the Middle Ages', *The Greenwood Encyclopedia of Folktales and Fairy Tales* (London: Greenwood Press, 2008), p. 625.

Zipes, J., *Fairy Tales and the Art of Subversion: The Classical Genre for Children and the Process of Civilization* (New York: Routledge, 2006).

Zipes, J., trans., 'Introduction: Rediscovering the Original Tales of the Brothers Grimms', *The Complete First Edition of the Original Folk and Fairy Tales of the Brothers Grimm* (Princeton, NJ: Princeton UP, 2014).

——— 'The Meaning of Fairy Tale within the Evolution of Culture', *Marvels & Tales*, 25:2 (2011), pp. 221–43 at www.jstor.org/stable/41389000 (accessed 1 May 2020).

———— 'Remaking "Bluebeard," or Good-bye to Perrault', *The Irresistible Fairy Tale: The Cultural and Social History of a Genre* (Princeton, Princeton UP, 2012), pp. 41–54 at www.jstor.org/stable/j.ctt7sknm.8 (accessed 29 November 2022).

———— *Revolt of the Fairies* (New York: Routledge, 1984).

———— 'Speaking the Truth with Folk and Fairy Tales: The Power of the Powerless', *The Journal of American Folklore*, 132:525 (Summer 2019), pp. 243–59 at www.jstor.org/stable/10.5406/jamerfolk.132.525.0243 (accessed 1 June 2021).

———— 'The Triumph of the Underdog: Cinderella's Legacy', *Cinderella Across Cultures: New Directions and Interdisciplinary Perspectives* (Detroit: Wayne State UP, 2016), pp. 358–402.

Zobel Marshall, E., '"Nothing but Pleasant Memories of the Discipline of Slavery": The Trickster and the Dynamics of Racial Representation', *Marvels and Tales: Journal of Fairy-Tale Studies*, 32:1 (2018), pp. 59–75 at http://doi.org/10.13110/marvelstales.32.1.0059 (accessed 1 June 2022).

VOLUME 2 INTRODUCTION
Fairy-Tale Revival Dramas

When Irish actor, playwright and social activist George Bernard Shaw visited Jamaica in 1911, he told a reporter at the *Daily Gleaner* that Jamaica needed a theatre that only permitted local actors performing plays by local dramatists to begin a Jamaican cultural renaissance.[1] Although Shaw's comments were both biased and uniformed by the rich local theatrical traditions in Jamaica, like John Canoe and the ring ding,[2] they reflect his experience of cultural colonialism and the nationalistic potential of drama in Ireland. Theatre was central to literary revivals and renaissances between 1850 and 1950, and the fairy-tale pantomime became a site of both protest and nationalism in Ireland, Scotland, Wales, the Isle of Mann, New York, Jamaica and the British Caribbean.

Fairy-tale dramas, or pantomimes, were ubiquitous in the United Kingdom during the Christmas holidays by the nineteenth century. Charles Dickens claimed these popular pantomimes were the financial backbone of London theatres throughout the nineteenth century.[3] These dramas, ostensibly for children, were multimedia productions based on canonical fairy tales from Perrault, the Grimms and *1001 Nights*, such as 'Little Red Riding Hood', 'Cinderella', 'Jack and the Beanstalk', 'Aladdin', 'Beauty and the Beast' and 'Bluebeard'. These dramas included music, dance, harlequinades and even equestrian showmanship.[4] British pantomimes travelled along with British acting troupes and all the paraphernalia of the London theatre, inundating colonial audiences with hegemonic fairy-tale messages from Great Britain.

The dramas included here speak back to the mainstream pantomime tradition, merging regional and ethnic fairy tales, fairy lore and dramatic tropes with the imported British pantomime. These pantomimes disrupt expectations of happy endings and challenge the fairy-tale trope of supernatural helpers as part of a critique of imperial fairy-tale expectations.

Content warning: Although these pantomimes make important critical interventions, they contain material that may be triggering or offensive. The dramas use extensive tropes from the traditions they critique, including comic treatment of sexist and racist situations. All the material here is original to the source texts. The editorial material in this collection deals critically with the long history of colonial exploitation in the Anglophone fairy-tale tradition. Uncovering and interrogating this history and the mediations made by revival and renaissance authors is essential to maintaining a critical approach to fairy-tale studies and expanding our understanding of the diverse uses of this genre.

PART 1: BLUEBEARD DRAMAS

The first part includes two 'Bluebeard' fairy-tale pantomimes that write back to the imperialistic orientalism on the traditional British 'Bluebeard' drama, including the landmark Caribbean pantomime, often identified as the first[5] by Jamaican authors: *Bluebeard and Brer Anancy* (1949).

PART 2: CINDERELLA DRAMAS

The two tragic Cinderella dramas included here offer a meta-critique of the fairy-tale expectations of the mainstream Cinderella pantomime tradition along with a critique of empire. This is particularly apparent in the context of the Scottish author Barrie's *A Kiss for Cinderella* (1916); reviews for the play appear beside headlines listing the heavy losses being taken by British soldiers in the Great War (see Appendices). Barrie incorporates the global conflict into his pantomime.

PART 3: WONDER TALES AND FAIRY LORE

Harlem Renaissance artist Langston Hughes creates a new fairy-tale tradition entirely in his debut play, *A Gold Piece* (1921) in *The Brownies' Book Magazine*.[6] There is no explicit magic in this drama, but the fairy-tale wonder that defines the genre is recreated with the actions of the children, who end the drama pondering the potential good of the future.

This section also includes photographs from *The Brownies' Book Magazine* of children playing fairies and two tragic fairy dramas. Unlike the Cinderella and Bluebeard pantomimes in this collection, there is no indication that these dramas were intended to be part of the Christmas pantomime tradition. In fact, it seems that these dramas were intended for Mid-Summer's Eve or All-Hallows Eve celebrations.

NOTES

1 Hill, E., *The Jamaican Stage, 1655–1900: Profile of a Colonial Theatre* (Amherst: U Massachusetts P, 1992) pp. 1–10.

2 Also called Jonkonnu and rink-a-dinks (*Miss Lou and Early Jamaican Theatre*, National Library of Jamaica, 2017).

3 Dickens, C., 'On the Decadence of Pantomime', *The Theatre*, 1 January 1896, p. 22; Schacker, J., *Staging Fairy Land: Folklore, Children's Entertainment, and Nineteenth-Century Pantomime* (Detroit: Wayne State UP, 2018), pp. 175–80.

4 Schacker, *Staging Fairy Land*, pp. 28–34; Schacker, J., and D. O'Quinn, eds., 'Introduction', *The Routledge Pantomime Reader 1800–1900* (New York: Routledge, 2022).

5 *Soliday and the Wicked Bird* (1943) by Jamaican author Vera Bell premiered at the Little Theatre six years before *Bluebeard and Brer Anancy* (1949). Bell's pantomime was actually the first pantomime written by a Caribbean author, and two subsequent pantomimes at the Little Theatre included Caribbean content ('The Little Theatre Movement – The Early History', *LTM Pantomime: Over 70 Years of Jamaican Theatre* (2004)). However, contemporary reviews in 1949 identify *Bluebeard and Brer Anancy* as the first Caribbean pantomime. Current cultural and scholarly authorities in Jamaican theatre continue to identify Bennett-Coverley's pantomime as the watershed work that began a truly Jamaican pantomime tradition ('The Little Theatre Movement – The Early History'; *Miss Lou and Early Jamaican Theatre*, National Library of Jamaica, 2017).

6 See the General Introduction for background on *The Brownies' Book Magazine*.

Part 1

BLUEBEARD DRAMAS

The orientalism associated with Bluebeard pantomimes in Great Britain began with *Blue-Beard, or Female Curiosity!* (1798)[1] written by George Coleman the Younger, with music by Michael Kelly.[2] Coleman's play resituates Charles Perrault's tale in Turkey and was the first of Perrault's tales to gain popularity in Great Britain. Coleman's narrative became a staple of English 'Bluebeard' productions in the nineteenth century, along with the orientalism of his drama which 'exploits a fantasy of otherness' (Schacker, *Staging Fairy Land*, p. 40) and melds it with fairy-tale wonder.

Part 1 includes two 'Bluebeard' pantomimes that write back to this imperialistic orientalism of the traditional British 'Bluebeard' drama. Both dramas shift the traditional critique of excess centred in the Ottoman Empire to a critique of the ruling landed elite in the Anglophone world, emphasizing food rights. Both dramas conclude with the death of the title villain rather than his comic punishment in traditional Victorian pantomimes. However, only Bennett-Coverley's *Bluebeard and Brer Anancy* (1949) addresses the institutionalized and systemic colonial exploitation inherent in this injustice, setting her play just after the end of slavery in the British Caribbean.

NOTES

1 Colman's pantomime was inspired by Andre Gretry's 1798 opera *Raoul Barbe-bleue*. See Schacker, J., *Staging Fairy Land: Folklore, Children's Entertainment, and Nineteenth-Century Pantomime* (Detroit: Wayne State UP, 2018), pp. 40–2.
2 Wood, N. J., 'Introduction: Fairy Tales and the Long Nineteenth Century', *A Cultural History of Fairy Tales in the Long Nineteenth Century*, vol. 5 (London: Bloomsbury Academic P, 2021), p. 12; Schacker, *Staging Fairy Land*, pp. 39–42; Hermansson, C. E., *Bluebeard: A Reader's Guide* (Jackson: UP Mississippi, 2009), p. 71.

DOI: 10.4324/9781003034643-1

Editorial Headnote

Bell, F. E. E. O., 'Bluebeard', *Fairy Tale Plays and How to Act Them* (London: Longmans, Green, and Co., 1896).

Lady Florence Olliffe Bell (1851–1930) was born in Paris to a British mother and an Irish father. Bell identified with the Irish Ascendancy and spent most of her life in Great Britain. She married into Thomas Hugh Bell's political industrialist family in northern England and wrote a detailed study of working-class life in a steel mill. Bell is noted for her worked as an anti-suffragist, attempting to prevent women from gaining the vote.[1]

Bell's collection of children's plays simplifies mainstream trends in the pantomime genre. Bell follows the basic Bluebeard pantomime plot without the harlequinade, dance and traditional cross-dressing roles.[2]

Bell seems to lightly critique the orientalism of the English Bluebeard pantomime tradition, setting the play in feudal Western Europe with a Western European villain: Baron Barbazure Bluebeard (Bell, p. 335). Bell even suggests this European characterization of the villain is historic. Bell's critique of excess was part of the comic Bluebeard tradition in the nineteenth century.[3] However, Bell explicitly shifts this social criticism to the behaviour of nobility in Western Europe and food rights: The impoverished noble Penylesse family's desire to restore the family fortunes by 'killing and slaying their neighbours and taking their possessions from them' (Bell, p. 339) makes Bluebeard's villainy and subsequent death a comic exchange between unsympathetic characters. However, like Bell's documentation of working-class life in a steel mill, which details the exploitation and inadequate wages of workers and then unconvincingly blames poverty on alcohol, her intentions here are unclear.

Content warning: The Victorian Bluebeard pantomime tradition has a troubling history. This play includes ethnocentric and sexist language. It also includes comic violence. All of the language and situations here are original to the source text.

NOTES

1 See Tees Valley Museums 'Lady Florence Bell' (2022).
2 Schacker, J., *Staging Fairy Land: Folklore, Children's Entertainment, and Nineteenth-Century Pantomime* (Detroit: Wayne State UP, 2018), pp. 21–2.
3 Schacker, J. and D. O'Quinn, eds., *The Routledge Pantomime Reader 1800–1900* (New York: Routledge, 2022).

1

'BLUEBEARD', *FAIRY TALE PLAYS AND HOW TO ACT THEM*

F. E. E. O. Bell

Source: (London: Longmans, Green, and Co., 1896)

BLUEBEARD IN TWO ACTS

CHARACTERS (7 Male, 2 Female)

BARON BARBAZURE, surnamed BLUEBEARD
SIR SIMON DE PENYLESSE, *an impoverished Noble*
GUY ⎫
BRIAN ⎭ *His Sons*
ROBERT, *an old Seneschal*
FATIMA ⎫
ANNE ⎭ *Daughters of Sir Simon*
FIRST HUNTSMAN
SECOND HUNTSMAN

HUNTSMEN, RETAINERS, &C.

N.B. – If necessary, the sentences given respectively to the First and Second Huntsman in Act II. can both be spoken by the First Huntsman, and that part played by the same person who plays Robert in Act I. differently dressed and made-up.

⚹ The scene of this play is laid, contrary to the usual tradition, in the fourteenth century, in Western Europe, where a counterpart of the Oriental Bluebeard is believed (by the writer) to have resided in feudal times.[1]

BLUEBEARD. COSTUMES

Bluebeard. – Breastplate; long loose coat edged with fur, with hanging sleeves; high leather collar reaching to shoulder; stiff cap with curling feather; long stockings to thigh; pointed shoes. He must have a bright blue pointed beard, and bright blue moustaches, fiercely turned up. His hair may be of the natural colour.

Sir Simon. – Cloth tunic reaching to knee, edged with fur. Leather belt. Long stockings, pointed shoes.

Guy and *Brian*. – Cloth sleeveless tunics, reaching half way down thigh, over coloured woollen shirts, of which sleeves and neck show; long stockings, pointed shoes.

Seneschal. – Costume Chaucer period: cloth tunic reaching half way down thigh; hood coming over shoulder, with pointed piece falling behind; long stockings, pointed boots, reaching half way up calf and turned over at top.

Fatima and *Anne* – Closely fitting long dresses, low in front, with loose hanging sleeves. Fur trimming *ad lib*. down front and at edge of sleeves. Head dress and white veil.

Huntsmen and *Retainers*. – Variations of above male costumes. See illustration at end of Act II.

ACT I

SCENE. – *A Room in a Feudal Castle. A door, C. Window, L., half-way up stage. Vaulted roof, tapestries, &c.* FATIMA *sitting at an embroidery frame, R.C. A table up stage to her*

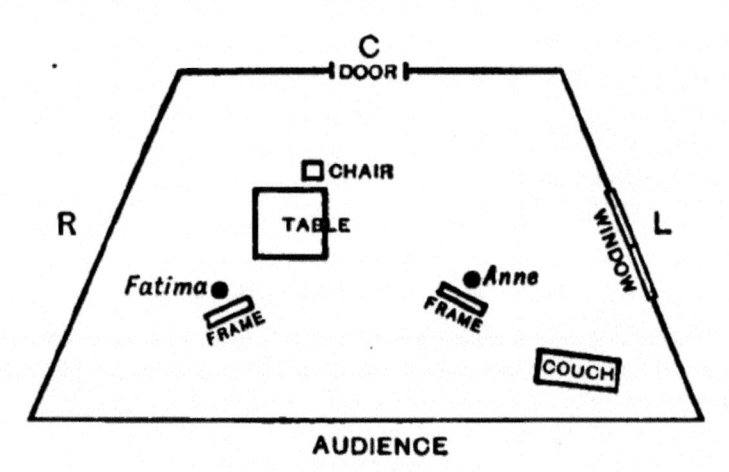

left. ANNE *sitting at another frame, L. C. The frames a little slanted, so that the sisters are somewhat facing each other. A table, R. C., above* FATIMA, *a little to left of her. Seat or couch, L., down stage.*

[*When the curtain goes up they work for a moment in silence, putting their needles in and out, cutting the threads, &c., before* ANNE *speaks.*

Anne (*pushing away her embroidery frame with an impatient gesture*). Oh, I'm so sick of this horrid old embroidery!

Fatima. Oh, fie, Sister Anne, it is a charming occupation!

[*Puts her head on one side and looks at embroidery.*

Anne. Charming, do you call it? It is repulsive. [*Gets up and comes down, L.*] To stick a needle in, and pull it out again, hour after hour, day after day! It is the most deadly existence in the world. That's the worst of living in the Middle Ages – women have nothing to do but to embroider.[2]

Fatima. Oh, sister! I wish you were contented with your lot.

Anne. Contented! I have nothing to be contented with.

Fatima (*shocked*). Nothing!

Anne. No, nothing. First of all, we're as poor as church mice – in fact, I'd much rather be a church mouse, then at least I should see people coming in and out; here I see no one.

[*Goes to window, L.*

Fatima. We have this beautiful castle to live in.

Anne (*turning round to her*). What's the good of that? I want fine clothes, plenty to eat, carriages to drive in, horses to ride. We can't spend the castle, or wear it, or eat it, or drive about in it. Of course for our father, or our brothers Guy and Brian, it is different. They can go out, if they choose, with a hawk on their wrist, and bring us back something for dinner.

Fatima. I shouldn't at all like to have a hawk on my wrist.

Anne (*with contempt*). You! Of course not. You scream if you have a fly on it. But for my part I should welcome a fiery dragon – it would, at any rate, be something to think about!

[*She leans listlessly against the wall at side of window down stage, and looks out.*

Fatima. Come, sister, divert your thoughts by looking out of the window.

Anne. That makes me still angrier than before, for then I see that magnificent castle on the hill opposite us, belonging to Baron Bluebeard, overflowing with riches and luxury, and everything he can possibly want.

Fatima. Everything, they say, but peace and kindness.

[*Working.*

Anne. Oh, bother peace and kindness! [*Comes down, C.*] Besides, who can tell if the tales the travelling minstrels tell are true? And, after all, they merely say that the Baron has had six wives one after another. It need not be his fault if they keep on dying. Perhaps the air of the castle doesn't agree with wives.

Fatima (*significantly*). So it would seem, certainly.

Anne. I declare I shouldn't mind being the seventh, and ruling over the castle and all the land we see.

Fatima (*shuddering*). Oh, fie, sister! How can you think of such a thing?

Anne. And then I should have a splendid dinner every day – roast peacock, fat capon, boar's head, pasties, and who knows what else! Oh, I wish I had them now! [*Comes down, L.; sits on seat, L. corner.*] Surely it is time for a meal! Why does not that doddering old Robert come in and bring us something?

Enter SENESCHAL, *old and grey-bearded, carrying a tray on which are a dish with bread, a bottle of water and some glasses, and some flowers.*

Anne (*jumping up*). Joy! What have you got for us to eat Robert?

Sen. Some excellent bread, my lady, and a flagon of water from the spring.

[*Puts it down on table by* FATIMA, *who has continued to work since beginning of scene.*

Anne (*looks at it*). Bread and water! Good Heavens! Is that all? [*Turns away in disgust. Comes down L. again.*

Fatima. It makes a delicious meal in this hot weather.

[*Drinks water.*

Sen. (*standing up stage, C.*) Perhaps when my master and the young gentlemen come in they will bring something from the chase.

Fatima. Is my father gone out too, then?

Sen. Yes, my lady, he is gone out riding.

Anne. Poor father! I do wish he had a horse a little less than twenty-seven years old to ride upon.

Sen. Perhaps some day, my lady, the young masters will bring back the family prosperity by killing and slaying their neighbours, and taking away their possessions from them. Then the house of Penylesse will be rich again.

Fatima. Nay, Robert, that would be wicked.[3]

Anne (*impatiently*). Oh, Fatima! you are enough to provoke a saint – I'm sure no saint could stand another one as saintly as you!

Sen. (*at window*). Here are the young masters returning from the chase.

Anne (*eagerly*). Let me see! [*Gets up and looks out.*] Yes, so it is! [*Waves to them.*] How joyful they look!

THE SENESCHAL

Sen. Perhaps that means they have brought home something for the spit.

Anne. Yes, indeed, let us hope so. [*Throws door open.*] Make haste!

Enter GUY, *C., followed by* BRIAN.

Guy. Well, here we are! We've had the most glorious day!

Sen. And what sport, my masters, what sport?

9

Guy (*sits on table, R. C., with right leg, his left leg hanging down, and eats a bit of bread from tray*). The most splendid!

[ANNE *claps her hands; goes back, L.;* BRIAN, *L. C.*

Sen. (*up stage, C., eagerly*). Where is it, then?

Brian. In the forest, about six miles from here.

Sen. (*his face falling*). Six miles!

Anne. And what is it?

Guy. It's a wolf.

Sen. A wolf! Mercy on us, we cannot eat that!

Brian. Well, no, I don't think that was the arrangement the wolf contemplated.
[*He strolls up to window, laughing.*

Sen. Then what is there to go on the spit?

Guy. Shall I go and steal a sheep from Baron Bluebeard?

Anne. Oh, do – I should so love to see what would happen!

Brian (*at window*). Well, something is going to happen now, at any rate. Here is my father coming in, and looking as if he had the weight of the universe on his shoulders.

[FATIMA *gets up and puts frame against wall. R.*

Guy (*getting off table and going to window too*). I wonder what is the matter with him?

Sen. He is hungry, I should think. Hunger is the worst care of all.

Enter SIR SIMON.

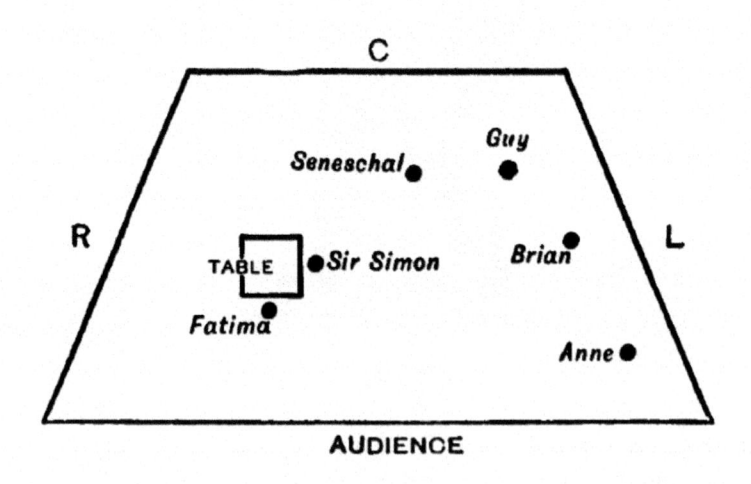

Fatima (*going up, C., to meet him*). Well, father dear, you have been a long time away to-day.

[SEN. *advances seat from back of table, L. Then he stands at back, C.*

Sir Simon (*sits down wearily L. of table, R. C., and passes his hand over his brow*). I have – yes.

[FATIMA *sits on the chair she was on before, which she draws a little nearer to* SIR SIMON.

Anne. What is the matter, father?

Sir Simon. I will tell you presently.

[*The others look from one to the other.*

Anne (*joyfully, aside*). Something is going to happen at last, I believe.

Sir Simon (*to* ROBERT). Is all ready in the kitchen to prepare a meal?

Sen. (*advancing, L. C.*) All is ready, sir, except the principal thing – there is nothing to cook. That is, the fire is burning, the plates and dishes are ready –

Brian. And so are our appetites.

Sir Simon. That is well. [*To* ROBERT.] You will find downstairs two fat capons, a boar's head, and a haunch of venison.

[*The rest look at each other with increasing surprise as he speaks.*

Sen. (*holding up his hands*). Capons – a boar's head, and venison! [*Rushes out.*

Anne. Father, can I believe my ears?

Brian. What fairy tales are these?

Guy. Where do all these splendours come from?

Sir Simon (*after a pause, as though making up his mind painfully to speak*). They are a present from – our neighbour, Baron Barbazure.

All. Baron Barbazure!

Guy. He must have guessed that I was just proposing to steal one of his sheep for our dinner.[4]

Sir Simon (*hastily*). You must do nothing of the kind.

Guy. Why are you so neighbourly all of a sudden, father?

Anne. And why is he? What made him send it, father? Do you know?

Sir Simon. I will tell you. It is best you should all know, that we may consider the question. He has asked me for the hand of one of my daughters.

All. What!

Fatima. No, no, it is impossible!

Anne. One of your daughters, father! Which?

Sir Simon. He has not said which.

Anne. Does he mean us to draw lots for him, then, or how are we to decide?

Fatima. Oh, Anne, there will be no need to decide! The idea is too terrible to be even considered.

Anne. I don't agree with you at all.

Fatima (*anxiously*). Dear father, what did you say?

Sir Simon. He asked if he might come here to pay his respects to you both. I told him he might.

Fatima. You did?

Brian. I'm glad of it. Otherwise we should have had to send the capons back again.

Guy. Do you know, this really is rather amusing. Fancy one of you two chits being the mistress of that great castle up yonder!

Anne. Oh, it would really be delightful!

Brian. You'll give me a mount sometimes, won't you?

[*A loud bell heard.* SIR SIMON, FATIMA, *and* ANNE *get up.*

Guy. What, already!

[*They all stand listening.* SENESCHAL *rushes in perturbed.*

Sen. Master, master! Do you know who is at the door?

Sir Simon. I know. Come, my sons, we will go and receive him.

Sen. Receive him! Are you going to receive him?

[SIR SIMON, GUY, *and* BRIAN *go out, followed by* SENESCHAL.

Fatima (*coming down, R. C.*) Oh, how terrible it is that our father and brothers should be so ready to sell us to the first bidder!

Anne (*L. C.*). My dear girl, that's just it! He is the first bidder who has ever presented himself, and, as far as I can see, he is likely to be the last.

Fatima. Think of marrying a man who has had all those wives already!

Anne (*lightly*). Well, perhaps when he gets them of a better quality they will last longer.

[*The door opens, and* Sir Simon *appears ushering in* Baron Barbazure.

Sir Simon. These, Baron, are my daughters.

[Bluebeard *bows first to* Fatima, *then to* Anne. *They make deep curtseys.*

Anne (*vivaciously*). Oh, we are so delighted to become acquainted with you, Baron. I can't tell you how delighted we are!

Bluebeard (*in a deep, solemn voice*). Oh!

Sir Simon. Where will you sit, Baron?

Bluebeard. Between your two daughters.

[SIR SIMON *advances chair that was L. of table.* FATIMA *sits where she was at first, R. C.* ANNE *draws out chair from behind her frame, which she pushes back a little. They sit down,* GUY *and* BRIAN *standing at window, L. A silence.* BLUEBEARD *rolls his eyes ferociously first at one, then at the other.* FATIMA *casts down her eyes;* ANNE *simpers at him.*

Sir Simon (*sitting, L.*). It's charming weather for the time of year. [*A silence.*] Don't you think so, Baron?

Bluebeard. No, most unpleasant. But we needn't dwell on it now, Sir Simon, I am busy. I wish to speak with your daughters.

Sir Simon. Certainly, Baron.

Guy (*R., up stage to* BRIAN, *R. C., at back*). Our brother-in-law has charming manners.

Bluebeard (*aloud*). Ahem!

[*The two girls start.* FATIMA *keeps her eyes down.*

Anne. We can see your castle from the window quite well.

Bluebeard (*in a deep voice*). Oh!

Anne. Oh, yes, we very often look at it.

Bluebeard. Ah!

Anne. It looks most imposing standing up there on the hill.

Bluebeard. Oh! [*A pause.*] [*To* FATIMA.] And you, madam, do you also see my castle from the window?

Fatima. Yes, Baron.

[*She speaks timidly, with her eyes cast down.*:

Anne (*with a shrill giggle*). Oh yes, the castle is just in the same place when she looks out of the window too! He, he, he!

Bluebeard. Oh!

Anne. You are very fond of the chase, I believe?

Bluebeard. Yes.

Anne. I thought so! We so often see you starting with your retainers in the morning, and then we see you coming back at the close of the day laden with your spoils.

Bluebeard. Ah, indeed! [*To* FATIMA.] And you, madam, do you see me starting for the chase?

'THESE, BARON, ARE MY DAUGHTERS'

Fatima (same action as before). Yes, Baron.

Anne. Oh yes; when she looks that way at the right moment, she can see you just as well as I can!

Bluebeard. Ah, indeed!

[*A pause.*

Anne. And even when you don't go to the chase, there always seems to be something going on at your castle – some feasting, entertainment, or enjoyment. I sometimes almost fancy I hear the sound of your revelry from here.

Bluebeard. Oh!

Anne. You certainly seem to spend your days most agreeably, whether out of doors or in.

Bluebeard. Yes. [*A pause.*] [*To* FATIMA.] And you, madam, how do you spend your days?

Fatima (*eyes cast down*). I sew, my lord.

Anne. Yes, indeed she does. She sits and sews the whole day long. He, he! You can't imagine what a quiet little mouse she is; she never wants to go anywhere, or see anything, or hear anything. She hasn't the slightest curiosity about what is going on in the world outside.

Bluebeard (*with peculiar emphasis*). No curiosity! Ah, ha! Indeed?

Anne. Now, my tastes are much the same as yours, Baron. I should imagine; I like movement, action, revelry, feasting.

Bluebeard (*interrupting her. To* FATIMA). And so you have no curiosity?

Fatima (*as before*). No, my lord.

Bluebeard. Ah, indeed! [*A pause, then he pushes back his chair with a great noise, saying as he does so 'Ahem!' very loud, then gets up. All start, and get up as he does. Pause.*] Sir Simon de Penylesse, I have the honour to ask you for the hand of your daughter.

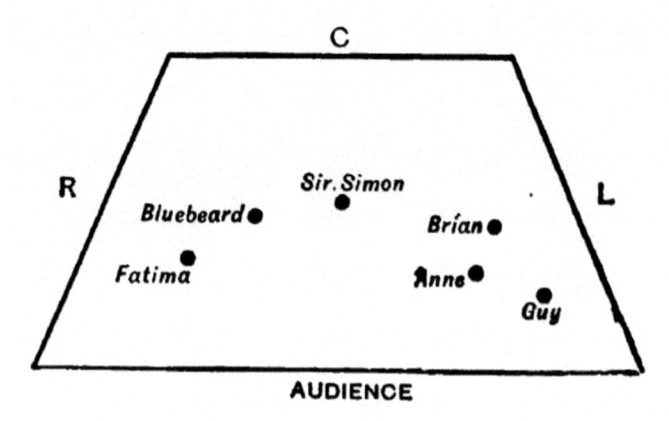

Sir Simon (*crosses in front of* ANNE, *who moves down into L. corner.* GUY *and* BRIAN *come down, L., and stand in a group with* ANNE). Which one, Baron?

Bluebeard. The one who doesn't chatter.

Sir Simon (*taken aback*). What! My daughter Fatima!

Bluebeard (*indicating* FATIMA). Your daughter Fatima, if that is her outlandish name.[5]

Sir Simon. I am sorry her name displeases you, my lord; she is called after her great-grandmother, whom Sir Stephen de Penylesse wedded in the East at the time of the Crusades.

Bluebeard. In the East? That sounds well. Eastern women do as they are told, and hold their tongues. That is what I like.

[*Glaring at* ANNE.

Anne (*vexed*). If only I had known that!

[*Half aside.*

Sir Simon. Baron, you do us too much honour.

Bluebeard. Yes, I feel that, but that's not the point. Do you accept, madam?

Fatima. Oh, my lord, you will forgive me –

Bluebeard (*in a terrible voice*). You are not going to refuse?

Fatima. Father, what must I say?

Sir Simon. You must do as you like, my child.

Bluebeard. Certainly not. She must do as I like. [*To* FATIMA.] I must tell you that if you refuse, I shall besiege the castle and carry you off by main force.

Anne. Oh, how exciting that would be!

Bluebeard (*looking sternly at* ANNE). And very probably hang all your family up to the battlements.

Guy (*to* ANNE). Here, let's make her accept him!

Bluebeard. Whereas, if you accept me, I will treat your family well as long as you give me satisfaction. Your father's table shall be supplied from my own, and I shall occasionally allow your brothers to follow me to the chase, mounted on my horses.

Guy (*to* ANNE, *looking anxiously across at* FATIMA). She surely can't hesitate.

Sir Simon. Come, my daughter, you have heard the Baron's arguments – what is your answer?

Anne (*to* BRIAN). The argument about the battlements was the best.

Fatima (*with an effort*). Very well, my lord, I accept.

Bluebeard (*with a grim laugh*). I thought you would. Farewell, then, madam, for to-day. We will be married this day week at noon.

Fatima (*startled*). This day week, at noon!

Bluebeard. Unless you prefer half-past eleven.

Fatima. No, no, my lord – no.

Bluebeard. This day week, then, at noon.

[*Bows to* FATIMA. FATIMA *makes a curtsey.* ANNE *trips forward and curtseys too. The* BARON *gives her a curt nod then he strides out,* BRIAN *standing R. of door,* GUY *L. of it as he goes out;* SIR SIMON *following him up, C.* SIR SIMON *turns back from door and holds out his arms to* FATIMA, *who flies into them; they come down together.*

Fatima. Father, dear father, why did I say yes?

[SIR SIMON *caresses her.*

Anne. Because it would have come to just the same if you had said no.

Guy. And you would have made things very unpleasant for the rest of us.

Fatima. But fancy marrying a man whose beard is bright blue!

Anne. Is it really so blue, after all? Yes, now I think of it, I see what you mean – just a tinge, perhaps. I thought it becoming.

Sir Simon. Besides, my child, the colour of a man's beard doesn't matter, as long as his heart isn't blue.

Fatima. How do I know it isn't? And oh! I feel most dreadfully blue at the mere thought of going to his castle. You will all come with me, won't you? You won't leave me there alone?

Brian. Come with you? To be sure we will.

Anne. Of course we'll come with you. We will cheerfully share everything with you.

Fatima. Oh, kind, kind friends!

FATIMA sings.

FINALE. *Tune – Italian popular song.*

Oh, my friends, my heart will break
   When I say farewell –
When my way from hence I take,
   The home I love so well!
And when, alas! I'm far away,
   As I too soon shall be,
I shall think of you the livelong day,
   And, pray you, think of me.
     I shall think of you the livelong day,
      And, pray you, think of me.

All together, repeating last six lines to same music.

And when, alas! $\left\{ \begin{array}{l} \text{you're} \\ \text{I'm} \end{array} \right\}$ far away,

  As $\left\{ \begin{array}{l} \text{you} \\ \text{I} \end{array} \right\}$ too soon will be,

$\left\{ \begin{array}{l} \text{We} \\ \text{I} \end{array} \right\}$ will think of you the livelong day,

$\left\{ \begin{array}{l} \text{Whom we no longer see.} \\ \text{And, pray you, think of me.} \end{array} \right\}$

[*During these six lines the performers must form in a line facing audience,* SIR SIMON *in the middle,* FATIMA *on his right, then* BRIAN; ANNE *on* SIR SIMON'S *left, then* GUY. *They must all join hands, and, as they sing, come down stage in time to music, marking time with balancé step as curtain falls. (See Note at end of Dances, at beginning of book.)*

ACT II.

SCENE. – *A Hall in* BLUEBEARD'S *Castle. If there are any possibilities of somewhat elaborate scenery, it would be effective to have a turret or bay window at the back, slanting R. C.*

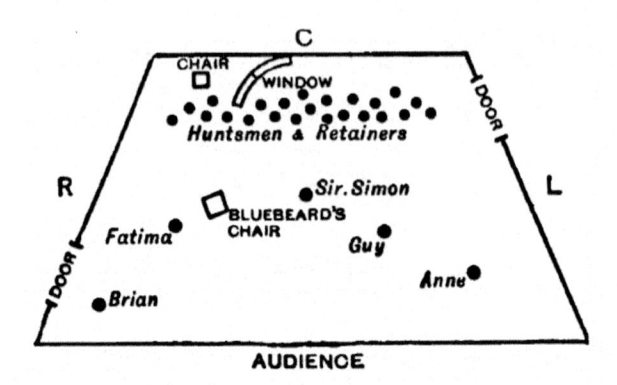

as in diagram. If no such scenery is possible, then simply a large window, R. C. Door, L., up stage. Small door, R., down stage. Large carved armchair half-way down stage,

R. C., in which BLUEBEARD *is sitting when the curtain goes up.* SIR SIMON *sitting on another chair to his left, C.* FATIMA *on a lower seat close to* BLUEBEARD, *on his right,*

'DRINK TO HIM WHO GOES TO THE CHASE'

a little further down stage. ANNE *sitting on a small couch or settee, L.* GUY *is standing, L. C., singing.* BRIAN *standing R. corner down stage.* HUNTSMEN, RETAINERS, &c., *in mediæval costume, ranged at back, as many as available. A chair R. of window at back, with some hangings on it. Singing (chorus of drinking song given below) heard before rise of curtain. Before the chorus comes to an end the curtain goes up; at end of chorus solo, verse, then chorus again.* GUY *has a drinking cup in his hand, so have* BLUEBEARD, SIR SIMON, *and* BRIAN.

GUY *sings.*

Tune – French popular song.

Fill your bumpers, all,
Fill them three times three,
While a toast I call
Which you must drink with me:
'The chase! the chase! the cure for every ill!'

Chorus. Drink to him who goes to the chase!
   Drink to him who joins in the race!
   Drink to him who presses the pace
   Across the breezy hill!

A A

[*At conclusion of chorus all rise.*
Bluebeard. And now, for the chase!
All the Men. Yes, now for the chase!
[*They all go towards door, some sling on horns, others adjust their weapons, &c.*
    BLUEBEARD, C.; ANNE *and* FATIMA *down stage.*
Anne. Oh, I wish we could go too!
Bluebeard (*standing, C.; adjusting horn, &c.*). A woman's place, madam, is at
    home. She should use no weapon but her needle.
Anne. Oh, I'm so sick of needles!
Bluebeard. Your sister, I'll warrant, does not wish to go to the chase.
Fatima (*meekly*). No, my lord.
Guy (*up stage at door.* SIR SIMON, HUNTSMEN, *and* BRIAN *have gone out*). Ha, ha!
    Fancy Fatima going hunting! Why, she would not know a stag from a boar!
Anne. I should know, though! A boar has his horns in quite a different place.
Bluebeard (*to* FATIMA). I shall not return till sunset. What will you do during my absence?
Fatima (*meekly*). I shall sew, my lord.

Anne (*goes up, L.*). What! more sewing? I should like to drown all the needles in the moat.

Bluebeard (*to* FATIMA, *affecting to speak lightly*). Would you like to go over the castle?

Anne. Oh, yes!

Fatima. Very much, my lord, if it pleases you that we should.

Guy (*L. C., to* ANNE). He has got our sister in good order, I must say.

Anne. Never mind, I'll see if I can't cure her of that.

[GUY *goes out, laughing.* ANNE *comes down again, L.*

Bluebeard (to FATIMA, *giving her a bunch of keys*). Before I go, I will give you the keys of the castle. This is the key of the armoury, that of the library, this one of the long picture gallery. The other doors are open.

Anne (*peeping at the keys which* FATIMA *has taken*). But there are four keys on that bunch, brother-in-law. What is the fourth?

Bluebeard (*sternly*). You are more curious than your sister. She did not ask that question. That key belongs to a door you are not to unlock – the door of a room into which you are not to go.

Fatima (*holding up key*). This one? Very well, I will remember. Tell me, my lord, where that room is, that we may avoid it.

Bluebeard. It is there. [*Pointing to a small door, R.*

Fatima (*a little startled*). There? So near!

Anne. Oh, how exciting!

Bluebeard (*looking at her coldly*). Exciting? Why?

Anne. Because I love wondering what is inside there.

Bluebeard. You may spare yourself the trouble. [*Seizes* FATIMA *by the arm.*] Fatima, if you look into that chamber, you shall pay for your curiosity with your life.

Fatima (*startled*). With my life, my lord?

Bluebeard. Yes, with your life. So now you are warned.

Anne (*aside*). Well, that is taking a heavy line, I must say.

Bluebeard. Farewell. [*Looks out of the window.*] The chase has already assembled.

Anne. Come, Fatima, we will see them start.

[BLUEBEARD *goes out, L.;* ANNE *and* FATIMA *looking out of window, R. C. They look off, R., where the hunters are supposed to be assembled.*

Anne. There are Guy and Brian! How well they look on horseback! And my father, too, on his beautiful palfrey! [*Comes down from window.*] Oh, Fatima, what a good thing it was that you became the mistress of this castle! [*Seizes her round waist and dances round with her, humming hunting song, then sinks laughing into big chair, R. C.*] Now, then, let's go all over the castle from top to bottom!

Fatima (*standing C.*). Very well – shall we begin by the armoury, the library, or the picture gallery?

Anne. I know exactly which room I am going to begin with.

Fatima (*unsuspecting, with a smile*). Which one, then?

Anne (*sits up deliberately in chair, looks round at door.* FATIMA *starts.* ANNE, *pointing to door, R.*). That one.

Fatima (*starting back*). That one! Never! Never!

Anne (*lightly*). Upon my word, Fatima, you are too absurd. You don't mean to tell me you are really not going into that room?

Fatima. Of course I am not. It is my duty to obey my husband. How can you think I should go into it the very moment his back is turned?

Anne. My dear girl, not the very moment, of course. We must give him time to get well away. [*Gets up and goes to window.*] Oh, yes, it's all right. Look! [Fatima *joins her at window.*] You can see his back from here – that is the view of him I like best – just going over that hill.

Fatima (*looks through the window, then turns away shuddering. She comes down, C.*). It is no good, Anne, I can't do it. We will unlock any other door you like, only not that one.

Anne (*following her*). You *are* a faint-hearted creature!

Fatima (*lightly*). Never mind if I am. [*Looking at bunch and holding it up by one key after another.*] Now, then, which is it to be? The library? the armoury? or the picture gallery?

Anne (*snatching the bunch from her and holding it behind her back*]. None of them! Neither the library, the armoury, nor the picture gallery.

[*Goes R.*

Fatima (*trying to hold her back*). Anne, Anne! give me back those keys! What are you going to do?

Anne. My dear, it is no use. I shall never be happy till I have been inside that room, so we will go and see it first, and then it will be off my mind. So don't make any more fuss over it. Look here, you go to the window and see that that bluebearded husband of yours is not coming back again, and I will look into his store cupboard and see what he keeps there.

[*Goes to door, R.*

Fatima (*hurriedly following her*). No! no! Anne, you really must not! Don't, don't, I beg of you! [*Tries to take key away from her.* Anne *seizes* Fatima's *right wrist with her left hand and unlocks the door, which opens inwards. They both stand transfixed for a minute, then* Fatima *gives a scream,* Anne *drops the keys with a crash; they rush away, L., to other corner.* Fatima, *L., horror-stricken, clutching* Anne's *arm.*] Anne, did you see?

Anne (*L. C., right of* Fatima, *in a horrified whisper*). Yes, yes, I saw –

Fatima. – lying on the ground, all in a heap –

Anne. Wives!

Fatima (*covering her face*). Yes, that is where he keeps them – the others!

Anne (*stealing another horrified look*). It is a hanging cupboard! Look, there are three of them hanging on pegs at the back by their hair!

Fatima. Ah! It is too horrible! Anne, shut the door quickly, don't let us see it – don't let us think of it again!

Anne (*crosses stage to R., with her hand held up in front of her face so that she shall not see the closet; goes to door*). Where are those miserable keys? [*Looks round and picks up the keys.*] The floor is dark red, horrible! [*Pulls door to again and locks it.*] There now!

Fatima (*looking round with relief as* ANNE *bangs door*). Oh, I wish we had not looked into it!

Anne (*recovering herself, R. C.*). After all, there is no harm done; he will never be the wiser for it. Come, now, let us go and see the ancestors' armour, or the monks' manuscripts, or something cheerful to make us forget all these horrors. We will take a key haphazard, and see which door it opens. [*Looks at bunch.*] Fatima [*goes to* FATIMA], there is a stain on this key!

Fatima (*anxiously*). A stain? [*Looks at it.*] A dark red stain! Was that there before?

Anne (*anxiously; looking at it*). I don't think so.

Fatima. Then he will see when he looks at the key where we have been. Oh! Anne, why were you so imprudent?

Anne. Come, we needn't discuss that all over again. Let us rub this off, that is the simplest plan. Give me your handkerchief.

[FATIMA *takes out a lace handkerchief and rubs the key, then* ANNE *rubs it.*

Anne. That's right! It is going! It is going away! One more rub, and it will be gone. There now!

Fatima (*joyfully*). Is it – is it really gone? [*Turns over key.*] Look, it is stained on the other side!

Anne. Very well then, we will rub the other side. [*Takes it.*] There, no deception, the stain is gone! [*Turns it over.*] What is this? It has gone back again on to this side. I wonder what that means?

Fatima (*takes key*). It means that we shall not be able to get it off, and when he comes back he will know everything.

Anne (*recovering herself*). Tut, tut! We will rub both sides at the same time if necessary, and both ends too, so that the stain won't have any place to fly to. I will take one of those hangings off the chair to do it.

[FATIMA *comes down, L., looking sadly at key.* ANNE *is hurrying towards chair, up R., when the door is thrown open and* BLUEBEARD *strides in.*

Fatima, L. My lord!

[*She folds her hands quickly over keys.*

Bluebeard (*coming down, C.*). Yes, I have returned sooner than I meant.

Anne (*coming down, R., jauntily*). What a delightful surprise!

Bluebeard. I encountered several evil omens directly I got outside the walls, so I determined to come back.

Anne (*gaily*). Evil omens! Indeed, Baron? What were they?

Bluebeard. We met an old woman coming towards us as we left the drawbridge, and my horse knocked her down with his left foot instead of his right: that was a bad omen. Then a little further on we met a wild bull, which tossed one of my huntsmen four times into the air. Four is an unlucky number. I determined to return. And what have you been doing? Have you visited the castle?

Fatima (*stammering*). Not yet.

Anne (*gaily*). We were just going to start on our rounds, but we could not make up our minds where we should begin – by the armoury, or the library, or the picture gallery. Which do you recommend?

Bluebeard. The armoury lies nearest. Come, I will take you myself. Where are the keys?

Fatima (*holding her hands folded over them*). The keys, my lord?

Bluebeard (*sternly*). Where are the keys?

Anne (*affecting to look round*). The keys? Let me see now, where did I see them? There is nothing one loses so often as a bunch of keys. Are you sure you left them with us, my lord?

Bluebeard (*advancing to* FATIMA *and taking her suddenly by the wrist*). Where are the keys? Answer me. [*As he shakes her wrist the keys fall to the ground. He picks them up, and looks at them one after another. A silence.*] There is a dark red stain on this key. What, are even you like all the rest? [*To* FATIMA. FATIMA *falls on her knees, R. of* BLUEBEARD, *and covers her face with her hands.*] Have you unlocked that secret door, and seen what is within?

Anne (*falls on her knees, R. of* BLUEBEARD). Alas, my lord! It was my doing; I snatched the key from her and unlocked the door.

Bluebeard (*motioning her away*). Go away! You don't count.

Anne (*springing up. Aside*). Monster!

Bluebeard (*to* FATIMA, *drawing his sword*). I told you what would happen if that door were opened.

'WHAT, ARE EVEN YOU LIKE ALL THE REST?'

25

Fatima (*springing up*). No, no, you surely wouldn't kill me for a little thing like that!

Bluebeard. A little thing! The ladies whom you will presently join in that room died for the same reason.

Fatima (*entreatingly*). Give me a few minutes longer!

Bluebeard. You may have five minutes, not an instant more, while I sharpen my sword just outside.

[*Pointing significantly to door to show that he is not going far off, he goes out.* ANNE *and* FATIMA *rush to one another, C.*

Anne (*looking round*). Is there no way of escape from here?

Fatima. No, no. I know too well there is none.

Anne. If only Guy or Brian would come back!

Fatima (*anxiously*). Look and see if they are coming, I cannot. [*Sinks into chair, L.*

Anne (*going hurriedly to window*). Ah! There is someone coming over the brow of the hill! A cloud of dust is rising from the road. Who can it be?

Fatima. Sister Anne, Sister Anne, do you see anyone coming?

Anne. Wait, there is a gust of wind blowing the dust about. There now, it has cleared away. Alas! no, it is only a flock of sheep.

Fatima. Then I am lost!

Anne. No, no; don't lose hope yet, our brothers may still come.

Fatima. Oh, Sister Anne, Sister Anne, look and see if they are coming.

Anne. I believe I see someone!

Fatima (*anxiously*). Do you? Do you really?

Anne. Yes, yes, I see two horsemen coming over the hill.

Fatima. Two horsemen? Are they our brothers? [*Eagerly.*

Anne (*looking eagerly*). Wait, wait. They are drawing nearer. Yes, yes, it is! They are coming! They are coming fast!

Fatima (*springing up*). We are saved!

Enter BLUEBEARD. FATIMA *gives a cry and flies into R. corner, down stage.*

Bluebeard (*R.*). Now, madam, the time is over – I am going to cut off your head.

[*His hand on the hilt of his sword as though about to draw it.*

Fatima. Oh, my lord, the five minutes are not over, surely. Give me one more – only one – that I may tell my sister how to bestow my few poor possessions when I am gone! That at least you will not deny me?

Bluebeard (*with a laugh, pushing his sword, which he had drawn out a little, back with a bang*). That won't take you long, I imagine, as I don't suppose you have much to leave. If you had obeyed me, you would at my death have been the mistress of this castle, and of all my vast wealth.

Anne (*at window*). Oh, if that time had come!

Fatima. Anne, dear Anne, come hither – you remember the gold clasp that I had when I was a child?

Anne (*anxiously, looking furtively at window; she comes forward a little*). Yes, yes, the gold clasp? I remember, I always longed for it.

[*Standing at window; waves when* BLUEBEARD *is not looking.*

Fatima. It must belong to you, dear. I should like you to wear it for my sake.

Anne. Yes, yes, I will with great pleasure, dear sister – I mean, with the deepest grief.

[FATIMA, *R.;* BLUEBEARD, *C.;* ANNE, *up stage, L.*

Bluebeard (again with right hand on sword-hilt). Now, madam, are you ready? I will wait no longer.

Anne (L., up stage, looking furtively at window). There they are, clattering into the courtyard! [*Makes signs to them; comes down again hurriedly, L.*] One moment, my lord! Fatima, you have not mentioned that knot of gaily coloured ribbons you had – they will become me well. I should like to wear them sometimes, and think of you.

Fatima. Yes, yes, sister, have them, they are yours; they are in the press in my chamber.

Anne (goes back to look out of window furtively, and then comes back again). And what about the embroidered head-dress, the coif you used to wear before you were married?

Fatima. That, if I remember rightly, you will find in the same place. And old Robert, too – he must have some recollection of me – to him I will leave – [*Tries to think of something.*

Bluebeard. You will leave nothing, madam. I will wait no longer.

[*Draws his sword. He is standing, R. C., and has made a step towards* FATIMA, *who rushes forward and falls at his feet. He seizes her with his left hand while he lifts his sword with the right, and drags her round him to his left hand.* ANNE *flies to door, L., and throws it open.*

Anne (calling through door). Quick! Quick!

[GUY *and* BRIAN *rush in.*

Brian. Why, what is happening?

[GUY *rushes in between* BLUEBEARD *and* FATIMA. BRIAN *on the other side of* BLUEBEARD. *They struggle.* GUY *takes* BLUEBEARD'S *sword from him and throws it away.*

Anne (has rushed into R. corner, FATIMA *to L., down stage, as* BLUEBEARD *falls).* Kill him first, dear brothers, pray! I'll explain afterwards.

Brian. Certainly.

Guy. At once.

[GUY *drags him up stage and throws him to ground with head to R., so that the big chair conceals what exactly happens.* GUY *draws knife and stabs him;* BRIAN *standing up stage above* BLUEBEARD. *This must all be done very quickly.*

Guy (coming down). There, he is slain!

[BLUEBEARD *lies motionless.* FATIMA *falls into* GUY'S *arms, L.;* ANNE *into* BRIAN'S, *R.*

Fatima. Oh, my dear brothers, how can I thank you?

Guy. I had an instinct he had come back for no good, and we followed him.

Anne (with relief). It is well you did.

Enter SIR SIMON *and* HUNTSMEN, *L.*

Sir Simon. My horse fell lame, and I was forced to return, and these good fellows came back with me as their master had left us also. Where is the Baron? Has he not returned yet?

Guy. There he is. [Sir Simon *and the others rush forward.*

All. What! The Baron killed?

Brian. Yes, by our hand. And if we had not killed him you would have found your daughter lying there instead.

[Sir Simon *comes forward, C.*

First Huntsman (at back, R. C.). Ay, you would, sir. I know that from experience.

Second Huntsman (at back, L. C.). Yes, my lord always killed his wife when he came in as early as this.

Fatima (shuddering, and clinging to Sir Simon). Oh, what an escape I have had!

Anne. Fatima, do you remember what he told you just now? That at his death you would be the mistress of this castle and of all his wealth? How delightful! It all belongs to you.

Sir Simon. To be sure it does. [*To* Retainers, *who are standing, L. C., at back.*] Let me present you to your mistress, the Baroness Barbazure.

RETAINERS

28

All. Long live Lady Barbazure!

Fatima. My dear father, sister, and brother, I have much pleasure in inviting you to spend the rest of your lives with me in my castle.

All. We shall be delighted.

Fatima (to HUNTSMEN*).* And I hope that you and all the people about the castle will show what good retainers you are by retaining your situations.

Huntsmen (waving hats). Long live Lady Bluebeard!

Finale. *Ensemble. Tune – German popular air.*

Sing ho! and sing hey day!

For Bluebeard is dead,[6]

And now { your / our } liege lady

Shall reign in his stead.

Farewell, apprehension! The tyrant is gone!

No more we need tremble before his dread frown!

[*All dance (*see Dances in Introduction*) while repeating chorus from beginning.*

29

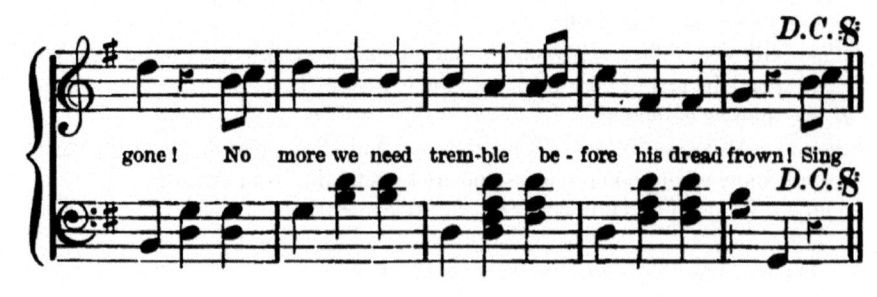

gone! No more we need trem-ble be - fore his dread frown! Sing

Curtain.

NOTES

1 This is a reference to the tradition of orientalism associated with Bluebeard panto-mimes that began with *Blue-Beard, or Female Curiosity!* (1798) by George Coleman the Younger, with music by Michael Kelly. The pantomime was inspired by Andre Gre-try's 1798 opera *Raoul Barbe-bleue.* Coleman's play was the first of Charles Perrault's tales to become popular on the English stage. The character of Fatima is a carry-over from Coleman drama, although the name of the new European villain has changed. This orientalism 'exploits a fantasy of otherness' (Schacker, *Staging Fairy Land*, p. 39). See Wood, N. J., 'Introduction: Fairy Tales and the Long Nineteenth Century', *A Cultural History of Fairy Tales in the Long Nineteenth Century*, 5 (London: Bloomsbury Aca-demic P, 2021), p. 12; Schacker, *Staging Fairy Land*, pp. 39–42; Hermansson, C. E., *Bluebeard: A Reader's Guide* (Jackson: UP Mississippi, 2009), p. 71 for more reading.
2 This 'winking knowledge' (Schacker, *Staging Fairy Land*, p. 179) of the medieval set-ting enables the drama's 'self-reflexive commentary' (p. 179).
3 This critique of imperial conquest as 'wicked' further distinguishes this tale from the ori-entalism of the English *Bluebeard* tradition. The threat in this drama is distinctly local.
4 The hunger of the impoverished noble family is a stark contrast to the feasting that con-tinued in Dublin Castle after the Great Irish Potato Famine. See Reilly, C., 'Feasting in the Time of Famine: Dublin Castle and the Great Hunger', *Coming Home: Art and the Great Hunger*, Niamh O'Sullivan, ed. (Hamden, CT: Quinnipiac UP, 2018), pp. 38–40.
5 Identifying 'Fatima' as an 'outlandish' name is a winking critique of the orientalism of the traditional Bluebeard heroine (Schacker, *Staging Fairy Land*, p. 40).
6 Bluebeard is not typically killed in Victorian Bluebeard pantomimes because he is a relatively comic villain (Schacker and Quinn, ed., *The Routledge Pantomime Reader*).

Editorial Headnote

Bennett-Coverley, The Rt Hon Dr L. and N. Vaz
Bluebeard and Brer Anancy, MS National Library
of Jamaica (NLJ), 1944.

Although two authors are included on the playbill, this script is primarily attributed to Bennett-Coverley with the support of director and producer Noel Vaz. Caribbean Renaissance author the Rt Hon Dr Louise Bennett-Coverley (1919–2006) went by 'Miss Lou' for most of her artistic career.[1] Her Jamaican vernacular poetry, stories, songs and performances were nothing short of revolutionary in colonial Jamaica:

> [Her vernacular] language . . . in fact defied the Eurocentric dictates of colonial life. And without firing a shot, without being violent, without resorting to polemics, Louise Bennett has been herself a symbol of a kind of cultural revolution in Jamaica and the Caribbean.[2]

This revolutionary art has made Bennett-Coverley: 'without a doubt Jamaica's definitive national poet'.[3] The National Library of Jamaica's special collection dedicated to her work rightly identifies her as 'legendary'.

The West Indies Review identified *Bluebeard and Brer Anancy* (1949) as the first pantomime ever written and produced by Caribbean authors when it first premiered, 26 December 1949 (1949).[4] The Little Theatre Movement (LTM) in Jamaica identifies this play as the beginning of the Caribbean pantomime culture.[5] Despite multiple productions, this drama has never before appeared in print. Permission to print it here for the first time has been obtained from the Louise Bennett-Coverley Estate (LBCE) as well as the National Library of Jamaica (NLJ) by the editor; thank you for making this possible. The manuscript printed here includes a complete thirteen-page version of the play. It is followed by an expanded script with gaps in the numbered pages. It is unclear if the missing pages were deliberately cut before production or lost afterwards.

Bennett-Coverley reworks the exoticized Turkish villain as a British agent or authority of imperial violence abroad. *Bluebeard and Brer Anancy* (1949) is set in Jamaica in the 1840s, roughly a decade after the official end of slavery in the British Caribbean. Busha Bluebeard, the white planter who owns Cinnamon Hill Estate, perpetuates the violence and exploitation of the Jamaican slave plantation. Bennett-Coverley shifts the traditional critique of excess in Bluebeard pantomimes to an exposé of systematic colonial exploitation which has deprived the local community of land and food rights. Bennett-Coverley's addition of the character Anancy to the traditional European 'Maiden Killer' (ATU 312) fairy was a new intervention in the imported British pantomime tradition in Jamaica.[6]

Anancy and the rest of the community in *Bluebeard and Brer Anancy* speak in Jamaican vernacular, also known as Patois or Patwa. Bennett-Coverley's consistent use of Jamaican vernacular for her working-class protagonists made a 'profound'[7] impact on her Jamaican audience, inspiring pride in the beauty of Jamaican linguistic traditions.

Vernacular speech is not simply a class marker for Bennett-Coverley, it is essential to the aesthetic of her work as well as her comedic message. In an interview with Daryl Dance, Bennett-Coverley stated:

> The nature of the Jamaican dialect is the nature of comedy, I feel. . . . You can twist it, you can express yourself so much more strongly and vividly than in standard English.[8]

In *Bluebeard and Brer Anancy*, vernacular language endows the working-class trickster-hero Anancy with the verbal versatility to evade the rigid colonial power of Busha Bluebeard, the colonial judicial system and the colonial police. These colonial authorities are limited to standard British English (St. BrE) and easily tricked by Anancy's vernacular double *entendres*, puns and word play.

The role and importance of the community expands in the second version of the pantomime, included here. Anancy and the other members of the community have more songs and longer dialogue, while the interaction between the romantic pair is cut to a few lines and a Jamaican ring ding dance. Although, this deletion may not be deliberate, pages may have been lost instead of cut.

Bluebeard and Brer Anancy combines the imported British pantomime tradition with two Jamaican theatrical traditions: the ring ding and the John Canoe.[9] In a documentary on early Jamaican theatre created by the National Library of Jamaica, Bennett-Coverley identifies the Jamaican ring ding dances as central to Jamaican theatrical traditions. The cathartic dancing, music and performances made ring dings essential to both funerals and celebrations.

John Canoe is a subversive Christmas masquerade carnival that developed in Jamaica. In 1841, just after the end of slavery, colonial authorities used the police to suppress the subversive Christmas carnival, but their efforts were overruled by the Jamaican magistrate at the time.[10] Flaunting colonial oppression, policemen were incorporated as stock characters in the traditional John Canoe masquerade in the nineteenth century. Bennett-Coverley's pantomime, set in the 1840s, recalls the historical power and importance of Jamaican theatrical traditions. Busha Bluebeard's attempt to suppress the initial ring ding in the first act and the John Canoe celebration in the final scene does more than replace the traditional harlequinade at the end of the Victorian British pantomime. It adds a historic critique of empire to Bennett-Coverley's landmark pantomime.

According to the *Little Theatre Movement (LTM) Pantomime* website, the 1949–1950 cast of *Bluebeard and Brer Anancy* was:

Cast of Characters
Miss Sarah: Laura Murray
Miss Clare: Cynthia Leon
Miss Marta: Louise Carter
Sammy: John Elliot
Toby: Vivian Mullings
Jack: Keith Sasso
Primrose: Shirley Wood
Sister Ann: Robert Verity
Mr Crumple: Guy Poolman
Nana Lou: Louise Bennett
Anancy: Ranny Williams
Busha Bluebeard: Harold Brownlow
Reporter: Lee Gordon
Big Tom: Lee Parris
Spirit of the Ganga Garden: Florence Reid
Ganga Nannie: Laura Murray
Sergeant: Leslie Gabbay
Pages: B. Johnson, A. Johnson, C. Minott, C. Phillips

The Chorus:
Winifred Doran, Marjorie Dunlop, Ingrid Cobb, Cynthia Lee, Alma Hylton, Monica Whyte, Linda Kennedy, Gloria Harris, Enid Goode, Constance McDonald, Xebbia Ellington, Sydney Matcham, Leila Beckett, Dorothy Lumsden, Millie Smith, Sybil Bowers, Eda Taylor, Edith Muschette, Polly Webb, Dorritt Bent, George Taylor, Vivian Mullings, Robert Ghisays, Lloyd Reckord, Horace Forbes, Joel Baker, Robert Dunbar, Rudolph Dumbar, Ronald Nazralla, Harrington Southwood-Smith, Simeon Shepherd, L. G. Parris John Canoes: Leo Fairweather, N. Fairweather, E. Delfosse, J. Forest

Written by
Louise Bennett and
Noel Vaz

Directed by
Noel Vaz

Music by
Barbara Ferland

Lyrics by
Orford St. John

Additional lyrics by Louise Bennett and Barbara Ferland

Musical Direction by
Barbara Cover and Major R. G. Jones

Designed by
Gloria Escoffery

Choreography by
Anatoly Soohih

In the NLJ's documentary *Miss Lou and the Early Jamaican Theatre* (2017), Bennett-Coverley sums up pantomimes in Jamaica prior to 1949 with the statement: 'The pantomime was a very white pantomime' (29:50–30:08). The cast of *Bluebeard and Brer Anancy* (1949–1950) sets this pantomime apart. This is the first pantomime to cast local Jamaican actors in leading roles, including comic actor Ranny Williams, who plays the lead role of Anancy.[11] It was also the first pantomime to include a cast of John Canoe characters.

Content warning: Although *Bluebeard and Brer Anancy* (1949) challenges and intervenes in the racist and xenophobic messages of the Victorian Bluebeard pantomime tradition, the content here may still be offensive or triggering. This text still uses the tropes of the tradition as a part of the critique. The setting may also be triggering: a former slave plantation in the decade after the end of slavery in Jamaica. The pantomime depicts institutionalized colonial injustice, including racist and sexist language, occasionally used in comic ways. It also includes marijuana use. All the language and situations here are original to the source text. Bennett-Coverley's landmark pantomime is an essential addition to pantomime history and the field of fairy-tale studies.

NOTES

1 The hyphenation of Dr Bennett-Coverley's name here follows the example in the two volumes of the *Journal of West Indian Literature* devoted to critical approaches to her work: volumes 17 and 18 (2009).
2 Prof. Rex Nettleford in the NLJ's *Miss Lou and Early Jamaican Theatre*, YouTube, 7 September 2017, 45:05–46:00.
3 Nwankwo, I. K., 'Introduction (Ap)Praising Louise Bennett: Jamaica, Panama, and Beyond', *Journal of West Indian Literature*, 17:2 (2009), p. 8.
4 'Soliday and the Wicked Bird' (1943–1944) by Jamaican author Vera Bell premiered at the Little Theatre a few years before *Bluebeard and Brer Anancy* (1949–1950). Jamaican tropes and references were also included in 'Aladdin' (1945–1946). However, *Bluebeard and Brer Anancy* is still identified as the first Jamaican pantomime by reviewers, actors and producers in Jamaica because this drama changed the pantomime

tradition. See 'The Little Theatre Movement – The Early History' (2004) and NLJ, *Miss Lou and Early Jamaican Theatre*, YouTube, 7 September 2017.

5 According to LTM Pantomime: Over 70 Years of Pantomime in Jamaica (2004):

> The Little Theatre Movement (LTM) has the distinction of being Jamaica's longest surviving theatre company of contemporary times. It was founded in 1941 by Henry Fowler and Greta Bourke (later Fowler) to raise funds for the building of a Little Theatre, and to help in the development of drama in Jamaica. From its inception, the LTM committed itself to a vigorous policy of serving the public.

6 This trope is repeated in Bennett-Coverley's literary fairy tales with a similar effect.

7 Nwankwo, I. K., 'Introduction (Ap)Praising Louise Bennett', p. 9.

8 Bennett, L, and D. Scott, 'Bennett on Bennett', *Caribbean Quarterly*, 14:1/2 (1968) p. 97.

9 Also spelled Jonkannu.

10 Hill, E., *The Jamaican Stage, 1655–1900: Profile of a Colonial Theatre* (Amherst: U Massachusetts P, 1992), p. 248.

11 *The West Indian Review* was critical of the producer's decision not to use Jamaican pantomime veterans, who were exclusively white expatriates living in Jamaica. In the NLJ's *Miss Lou and Early Jamaican Theatre*, Ranny Williams identifies the casting of *Bluebeard and Brer Anancy* (1949) as a watershed in the Jamaican pantomime tradition.

2

BLUEBEARD AND BRER ANANCY

The Rt Hon Dr L. Bennett-Coverley and N. Vaz

Source: MS National Library of Jamaica (NLJ), 1944

Bluebeard and Brer Anancy Transcript
Handwriting in italics.

"BLUEBEARD & BRER 'NANCY"[1]

Music: Rookoombine[2] – The Chorus

Announcer (*Noel*):[3] "Bluebeard & Brer 'Nancy" – A Jamaican Pantomime Script by Louise Bennett & Noel Van, Music by Barbara Ferland and Lyrics by Orford St. John *in the parish of Old St. James.*

Music: Rookoombine – The Chorus

Anancy: Everytime bad luck ketch oonoo[4] you sey is Bredda Anancy mek it – Sister Pig sey is me mek she have long mout' – but her mout' long fe true especially at Christmas time – Bredda Goat sey it me mek him caan' stop sey 'baah' – Bredda Politician sey is me mek him lose him seat – next t'ing you gwine hear sey is me mek Busha Bluebeard wife dem . . . but stop oonoo don' know nothing 'bout dat yet – All right I gwine tell oonoo –

Once upon a time there was a very rich man who lived in a big big big house, top of a high hill – him have a whole heap a wife – every minute him married – so him married so him . . . but ah won' badda tell you no more I gwine mek you hear fe youself . . . oonoo waan hear? Do mek a hear . . .[5]

Music: Evening Time – Soprano, Bass and Chorus

First Man: De food cook Miss Marta?

Miss Marta: De pot a bwoil[6] me son.

Second man: How de breadfruit[7] stan Miss Sarah?

Miss Sarah: Soon the off man.

First Man: Well den time fe everybody come.

Miss Marta: Yes, call all dem bwoys[8] and gal fe me. Tell dem fe come.

Music: Call all dem gal come – Chorus

DOI: 10.4324/9781003034643-3

Music: Zuzuma – Solo[9]

Miss Marta: Come Toby, you is a bang belly man.

Others: Come Jamsey – Come Toby, see fe you own yah. Give me nuff banana . . . mine you share me out . . .

Old Lady: No rice an peas market dyah. Patience man . . .

Sound Effect: Pig squealing

Old Lady: Oonoo stop likkle. . . .

Voice: (from distance) Hog inna me coco.

Miss Marta: Oonoo hear dat? Mass Jacky a come. A Jacky bwoy. Mass Jacky a come. Me sweet bwoy a come . . .

[S]ound Effect: Pig squealing (nearer this time)

– 2 –

Voices: What a nice hog. Watch de hog. What a meaty pig. Nice fe roas'. . .

Old Lady: Massa, wheh you get him from? But is who for hog?

Jack: Whose you think? Who owns hogs around here? And cows and horses and houses and fields?[10]

Crowd: Busha Bluebeard[11]

Old Lady: Me pickney, tek care you get eena trouble.[12] Him is a big man.

Sammy: Is Bluebeard hog fe true?

Jack: Yes, not only a hog but a trespasser.

Second Man: Which part him trespass?

Jack: Clear into me cocoa field. My dear sir I was coming down the hill to join you ring ding.[13] As I ketch longside Caleb fence I hear Mass Toby bawl out, Mass Jacky! Hog eena you cocoa.

Music: Hog eena de cocoa – Chorus

Narrator: While the villagers have been [singing] Primrose has entered along with her Uncle, Mr. Crumple, Bluebeard's Overseer, her sister Anne, followed by their Nana.

Primrose: Delightful! I enjoyed it so much. Please sing us another.[14]

Uncle: Dear Primrose. It is time we were getting along back to the barracks.

Primrose: Oh Uncle, I so wanted to hear them sing again.

Uncle: There'll be plenty of time for that. These natives will persist in their noisy revelry all night.

Primrose: Oh but please Uncle, delay a while.

Uncle: We must not incur the displeasure of Mr. Bluebeard. I hardly think he approves of these carryings on.

Primrose: Oh Uncle! It's been such a lovely day. I feel so happy I think I'll sing a little song.

Music: Now that it's Spring – Solo

Jack: If the ladies find our music entertaining, perhaps they would like to join in the dance.

Nana: Go on me pickney, enjoy youself.

Jack: What shall it be?

All: Rocky Road . . . get your partners.

Nana: Come Mr. Crumple my love, come partner me.

Music: Rocky Road (one verse)

– 3 –

Narrator: (during music) While they engage in dancing Busha Bluebeard is driving up the hill in his kittereen[15] . . . Anancy, who throughout the performance, contrives to turn up in the most unexpected places and each time a different character is the coachman . . . Here comes Busha Bluebeard . . .

Music: Fade in Bluebeard song. (along margin).

Bluebeard: What is the meaning of all this noise and vulgarity on my property? Mr. Crumple, how many times must I tell you not to allow this undisciplined behaviour . . . Look at this mess . . . disgusting.[16]

Sound Effect: Pig squeals

Bluebeard: Is that a pig I hear?

Sound Effect: Pig squeals again

Bluebeard: Not only carousing but thieving as well, eh? Who stole my pig?

Jack: No one stole your pig sir. It was trespassing on my property destroying my field.

Bluebeard: Did you say your property boy?

Jack: Yes, my property, considerably lessened since you impoverished my parents, but a property none the less.

Bluebeard: Insolent trash. Get off these grounds at once. Do you hear me? At once!

Old Lady: Gwan Mass Jacky, fe hinda trubble, gwan me pickney.[17]

Anancy: Bwoy, you no hear de gentleman sey yuh fe come off a him property? (Aside) Stay whey you deh (aloud) I saw gwan, ggwan . . .

Jack: I will not be driven off. To whom does this ground rightfully belong?

Crowd: A fe you, a fe him own. A fe him puppa.[18]

Bluebeard: Insolent rascal, begone I say . . . Be gone!

Primrose: Stop sir, stop . . . I'm sure he means no harm.

Bluebeard: A charming young lady. I have not had the pleasure.

Uncle: Sir, she is my niece, but lately arrived.

Bluebeard: Staying with you?

Uncle: Yes, spending time with me.

Bluebeard: I am sure such a charming lady is unable to enjoy the benefits of refined society in the dismal circumstances of Mr. Crumple's quarters . . . have your nieces baggage transferred to the Great House immediately . . .

Uncle: Certainly Sir, immediately . . .

Primrose: But really sir.

Nana: Thank you very much sir. We ready to come now.[19]

Uncle: This is my nieces nurse.

Bluebeard: Coachman take charge of the baggage and Nana. Crumple, you instruct the headman that if they see this rascal on the property any longer to turn the hounds on him. As for you, fellow. Remove yourself altogether. If you value your skin it would be better to leave at once. To the Great House. . . . Come along my dears.

Music: Bluebeard Theme

Nana: But them kaan go widout me. Das not proper

Anancy: Is who invite dis old woman.

Nana: After me no older dan you. You no hear Massa sey fe look afta de luggage.

Anancy: (mimics Crumple in best English). I must ask you my good woman to refrain from using such a familiar manner of conversation and from address-ing me in the vernacular.

Nana: Dont mek me leggo me tongue pan you . . . *Se[e] yah man.*

Music: "What I mean" – Solo

Nana: (after song) All tight come on you old Buggu Yagga[20]

Jack: This man Bluebeard means no good – least of all to these young ladies.

Old Lady: You right Mass Jacky. Ah memba poor Miss Suzy daughter.

Jack: Miss Suzy daughter?

Old Lady: You wouldn't memba me bwoy.

Nan: Memba Sarah Gal

Woman: An de tree foreign lady dem.

Old Lady: An de nice lady him bring from St. Jago

Woman: An Liza

Music: "Water come a me yeye" – Chorus[21]

Jack: My friends . . . the time has come for me to go from this property. Bluebeard's words were no idle threats. He will set his hounds on my tracks as soon as night falls. Goodbye Grannie – Miss Sarah – Mass Toby – Mass Sammy – Goodbye.

Old Lady: Yes Mass Jack – is betta yuh go dan get eena trouble. Gwan me son . . . God go with you. Sammy walk part way wid him . . . Mek him gwan . . . some funny ting happen up a dis Cinnamon Hill yah.

Toby: If dem funny . . . you no memba

Music: "Lass Caan Fine"

Narrator: (speaking over music) so we leave the villagers and go to the haunted Bamboo grove where Jack and Sammy are parting company.

Sound effect: (night noises)

Music: "Water come a me yeye" – Piano

Sammy: Good night Mass Jack

Jack: Good night Sammy . . . Bluebeard means no good to his guests. If he gets them under the spell of his evil charm they will disappear like his other wives . . . (fade music). To go to the Great House to help would be madness. Yet I must go. But how? . . .

Sound Effect: Noise

JACK: What was that?

Anancy: Sings – (Song). See me Nancy coming down (repeat)
Me da come fe help you
See me nancy coming down.

Jack: Anancy, what can this mean?

Anancy: Sings song again

Jack: Spider, Spider, what do you say? . . . Oh it is the coachman . . . for a moment I thought I saw a Spider.

Anancy: You see a spider yes. You see Anancy . . . Anywhey trouble dey Anancy dey me son.[22]

Jack: But how can you be Anancy?

Anancy: Me can be anyting me want. Me can be dog an bite enemy. Me can be puss an tief. Me can be a johncrow. Me can be your enemy but me can be you frien'. Me can be dis me can be dat. Me can be Coachman of course for me is Anancy.

Anancy sings: Me can be a native
Me can be a foreigner
Me can be a worker
Me can be de Governor
Me can federate one
Can devaluate one
Give you what you fancy
For me is Anancy

Jack: Then you can help me. I am anxious to get word to the young ladies staying up at the Great House for I believe they are in danger. But I have been driven out of the district as you know.

Anancy: As cordin as[23] how it look to me you don't want send the message to the young woman, you wan' go look the woman. But mind, I warnin you, "De same sinting wha' sweet man mout wi' hut him belly".[24] All de same I caan'[25] blame you, de young lady really nice. I going help you.

– 6 –

Jack: Thank you, but how?

Anancy: You did hear say dat Bluebeard going give a bigtime Ball fe celebrate him engagement to Miss Primrose?

Jack: No . . . that cant be true. Oh, how can we save her.

Anancy: Yes is true yes. Bluebeard going have a big time ball fe celebrate him engagement. Me hear say him sen go invite all de dignitaries of the parish from Eas' and' Wes'. You'd a like go?[26]

Jack: How can I? I have no clothes for such an occasion . . . and what's more I should be recognized.

Anancy: Don't watch dat, watch results. You wan' go?

Jack: I should be more than grateful if you could help me.

Anancy: Tek you time. Tek you time. You can't get someting fe nutten. If you scratch my back I will scratch fe you . . .

Jack: But I am penniless. All my family's wealth has been taken from me – even my mother's jewels.

Anancy: Jewels! you know whey dem dey?[27]

Jack: It has been rumoured they form part of Bluebeard's treasure at the Great House.

Anancy: Come we meck a bargain. I will get you into de Great House. You do you little business wi' de young lady, we find out whey do jewels deh. An we split . . . You gree?[28]

Jack: Agreed.

Music: Song (Jack and Anancy)

(Plus second Verse)

> I agree fe help you
> You agree fe help me
> Anyting we scuffle
> Me and you will share it

Jack: If I see the lady

> Life will be so sunny

Anancy: You can keep the lady

> Meck me keep the money.

Music: A Polka

Narrator: At the Great House, the Ball is in progress at which Bluebeard has just announced his engagement to Primrose and the Guests, replete with suckling pig and Planters Punch, are now toasting the newly-betrothed in the popular drink Sangares.[29]

Music: Sangares

Narrator: Jack enters in disguise and meets Anancy who is now in the garb and position of doorman. Anancy has contrived to steal the jewels from Bluebeard and now he slips them into Jack's pocket unknown to Jack, who

– 7 –

Narrator (cont'd.): finds an opportunity to speak to Primrose alone.

Jack: Could these be yours?

Primrose: Why Jack, how did you get here? I never thought I would have seen you again. You shouldn't have come back . . . it's dangerous . . . Bluebeard dislikes you. I beg you to go quickly before he discovers your identity.

Jack: Primrose I love you so.

Primrose: Let us just say goodbye and part quickly. Please give me my gloves and my fan.

Music: "Fan and Gloves" – (One verse sung)

Bluebeard: Primrose, I see you are occupied. Am I acquainted with your dancing partner?

Primrosc: You may have met my cousin . . . Mr . . . Mr . . .

Anancy: Mr. Burrowes, Busha, Mr. John Burrowes

Bluebeard: Are you from the Boroughbridge family? Can I tempt you to a game of dice Mr. Burrowes? What do you play?

Anancy: Him will have to play borrows

Jack: Thank you, but I

Anancy: If you fraid fe lizard you caan kill snake[30]

Jack: But I haven't a farthing on me

Anancy: Small matters Mr. Burrowes. Mr. Bluebeard must trust a man of you standing and integrity.

Primrose: Are you lucky in a gamble

Jack: Perhaps I shall be lucky with dice. I'm very unlucky in love.

Bluebeard: Bring the dice Crumple. Order the table to be set up. Primrose my dear, wont it be somewhat distressing to you to watch the game in progress? The consequences might prove disastrous.

Primrose: I shall be most interested to watch such an adept as yourself sir, but my cousin may have beginner's luck.

Bluebeard: What are the stakes?

Jack: Half your possessions against all mine.

Anancy: The boy is heavy. Now gentlemen name your game . . .

Bluebeard: Make it seven eleven

Anancy: You throw first Busha

Sound Effect: Click of dice

Anancy: Five, no luck. You throw now Mr. Burrowes

Sound Effect: Click of dice

– 8 –

Anancy: Three . . . tough luck my boy. Come now Busha

Sound Effect: Click of dice

Anancy: Bar . . . throw again

Sound effect: Click of dice

Bluebeard: Ah! seven

Anancy: Seven yes, but cocked dice

Sound effect: Click of dice

Anancy: Six and five eleven, Mr. Burrowes Win.

Crowd: Applauses

Jack: The game's mine. Half your possessions sir

Bluebeard: So you claim half my property?

Jack: Mine by right, now mine by good fortune.

Anancy: No talk too soon. Ef you no done climb hill no trow way you stick.[31]

Bluebeard: You young rapscallion.

Sound effect: Crash of falling table

Bluebeard: He cheated cleverly. His dice are loaded. Search him.

Jack: You're not going back on your bargain sir. I have no loaded dice, search me
if you wish.

Bluebeard: You have had your fun young man. It's time you dropped your pre-
tence. I know who you are . . . this boy is an idle rascal from the district.

Anancy: Top, you mean him is not Mr. Burrow from Boroughbridge. You mean
his was foolin' me. See ya man, you lef de Busha house yah . . . gwan . . .
gwan . . . I say, gwan right now. Out wid you or you gwine sorry. Come.[32]

Bluebeard: Stop. I demand that the culprit be searched.

Anancy: Oh yes your honor I was forgetting. I will search him for you.

Bluebeard: No. Let Mr. Crumple do it. . . . Crumple.

Mr. Crumple: (searching) nothing here . . . this pocket empty . . . nothing here . . .
wait a minute what have we here?. . . aha . . . jewels Busha Bluebeard.

Bluebeard: Jewels . . . jewels . . . thieving rascal . . . take him away. Have him
locked up in the Parish Jail . . . *rascal.*[33] Primrose, do not be put out by the actions of your so-called cousin . . . Let us all make merry. On with the Dance!

Music: Polka

– 9 –

Narrator: The Day of the wedding of Primrose to Busha Bluebeard has arrived.
There is much bustle as preparatio[n]s are under way in the Great Hall and
in the Kitchen. . . . Primrose, asleep in an enormous four-poster, is awakened
by Nana.

Nana: Morning light me love. Time you get up.

Primrose: Oh Nana, I had the most dreadful dream. I dreamt I was lost in a garden of terrible things. It was overgrown with weeds and there were strange
creatures, insects and snakes, and I tried to get to something that looked like
a door, but I couldn't. Everywhere I turned I was pursued and menaced.

Nana: Must be all de black crab you eat las' night me chile. Today is your wedding
day, you no have to tink pon nightmare. As for me me hands full o work . . .
me have cake fe go decorate.

Sound effect: Rap at door

Primrose: Come in

Sound effect: Door opens

Bluebeard: Good morning my dear . . . it's going to be a busy day for all. Nana go and see that the gold candlesticks are placed at the entrances and the servants are all properly attired . . .

Nana: Yes sir

Sound effect: Door opening and closing

Bluebeard: There is something I must say to you Primrose. I have to go off to court immediately.

Primrose: The Court sir?

Bluebeard: Yes. To attend the trial of that imposter who stole my jewels – your jewels I should say. While I'm away I want you to take charge of my household. Here are the keys.

Primrose: Thanks for the honour sir, but I do not

Bluebeard: You may use them as you require. Except this one. This key belongs to my personal vault. Guard it with your life and refrain from using it. Goodbye my dear I shall be back soon to wed you.

Sound effect: Door opening and closing.

Primrose: Jack . . . Jack . . . what dreadful fate awaits you . . . my heart is locked in a cell with you . . . whatever be your lot I can never forget you.

Music: Song – They are You – sung by Primrose

Primrose: I don't understand it. Why has Bluebeard given me these keys? He is

– 10 –

Primrose (cont'd): gone to Jacky's trial, to have him imprisoned or worse. Oh Jacky, is there nothing I can do to help you.

Anancy: Of course you can help him

Primrose: Pardon me, but who are you

Anancy: I am Anancy

Primrose: What did you say sir?

Anancy: A say you can hinder de young fellow you love from go to prison.

Primrose: But . . . but

Anancy: Awright no bodder but but. I know de whole story. I been following you career. Jacky is a nice bwoy an Bluebeard is a wicked man. I don't like see advantage so I going help you help him.[34]

Primrose: How sir?

Anancy: You see de key wha Bluebeard caution you not fe use at all at all?[35]

Primrose: This key sir?

Anancy: Hear what I tell you. Dat is de key to Bluebeard secret room. People say de room is full up a ghost and duppy.[36] You fraid?

Primrose: Oh no sir.

Anancy: Well dis room no eena de house. It under de ground. You walk so go dung trough de weed garden, den you see one door. I always see do door. Plenty people see de door, but nobody ever see de key.[37]

Primrose: And this is it?

Anancy: Yes. Is it. Chile, you know de power you have in you han dem?

Primrose: Tell me. What shall I do?

Anancy: Now if you promise me to go eena de secret room an take out what evidence you can fine against Bluebeard not forgetting to remove a sizeable quantity of gold for me, ah wi go to court house an make young Jacky get way.[38]

Primrose: Oh sir, you have my promise. I will do anything for that. But are you sure you can get him off?

Anancy: If you do fe you part, I will do fe me. But you have fe trus' me.[39]

Primrose: I trust you sir and I will do my part.

Anancy: Is not a nice place you gwine you know[40]

Primrose: Nothing can be too hard for me to do.

Anancy: For love?

Primrose: For love.

– 11 –

Music: Song – Shy White Bird – sung by Primrose

Narrator: The scene changes to outside the Court House where Jack's friends – the villagers – are warning the Constable that he better see that Jack is treated with justice . . .

Music: Song "Court a Call"

Narrator: Anancy arrives from nowhere in their midst ready with a plan for Jack's escape which he relates to the excited crowd.

Anancy: You see what a mean[41]

Crowd: Yes, yes, we see

Anancy: Wait, bide you time. Me going inside the Court House fe see how de case progressing. You watch the window I will come tell you how things going.[42]

Sammy:[43] Make we sing fe cheer up Jacky bwoy[44]

Music: Song "See Water"

Anancy: Five witnesses gone already. De man wont listen to a soul.

Crowd: How Mass Jacky a take it?

Anancy: Ah proud a de bwoy. Him siddown wid innocency jus bran all over his face. Now and den when dem tell bad lie pon him him smile.[45]

Sammy: Make sign to him tell him fe go on same way. No make dem frighten him . . .[46]

Anancy: Awright a will try[47]

Reporter: Am I late. Am I late. Has the case started

Crown: Shhh. Shhh stop you nize . . .[48]

Reporter: My good man I

Anancy: Hi little man, what's matter? Wha kine a ructions dat you making eena de court yard? You dont know that the Court is in Session?[49]

Reporter: My good man I am a reporter. Cant I come up there?

Anancy: No you stay whey you dey and I wi issue bulletin an you report to de people dem.[50]

Reporter: Awright . . .[51]

Narrator: Soon Anancy appears at the window, beckens to the Reporter, whispers in his ear and bobs out of sight.

Reporter: He says Mr. Jacky is making a speech. Ah kaan hear de speech, but Lawd ah can just picture him saying[52] "Your Honour I stand before you falsely, unjustly, treacherously, maliciously, atrociously, deliberately and calculatingly accused of a crime of which I am

– 12 –

Reporter (cont'd) innocent as a babe. I fear no foe. I am dauntless and undaunted. My head is hatless and unbowed. Your Honour I am certain and without a doubt that you have no alternative but to immediately and without delay admonish and discharge me of this ridiculous crime". . . after such a speech, what can a Judge do but acquit him, yes, acquit him. Let him go. Das what dem have fe do.[53] Let him go.

Crowd: Reacts to this

Anancy: (loudly) Dem sentence him . . . Dem sentence him . . .[54]

Crowd: Reacts to this

Reporter: (bursting into tears) Dat Poor fellow, dat nice young boy. Dem sentence him. wail'.[55]

Anancy: Oonoo memba what a did tell oonoo?[56]

Crowd: Yes . . . we memba awright . . . we memba[57]

Anancy: Good . . . now is de time . . . dem bringing him out now.[58] *MARCH* [may indicate music]

Crowd: (shouting) Murder! Police! Police! Murder! Marshal law . . . help . . . murder . . . (general commotion)

Narrator: And so Anancy's plan succeeds. The Police are caught up the crowd. Their attention distracted from the prisoner and Jack jumps on a mule and escapes. Bluebeard is infuriated and issues orders that every hut in the village is to be searched until Jack is found.

Music: Song – Zoza Mule[59]

Narrator: Back in the Bamboo Grove where he is hiding from the Police Jack considers the next move. There is a noise from the bushes and Anancy appears.

Anancy: Alright dont frighten is me[60]

Jack: Glad to see you sir. I cant thank you enough. Sam told me it was you who laid the scheme for my escape.

Anancy: Simple matematics sah. It was a pleasure. But what happen? You don't look too happy?[61]

Jack: Well, in point of fact I was wondering if . . . Have you seen Miss Primrose?

Anancy: Well, ah dont see her from this morning and I have a grave suspicion . . .

Jack: I cant bear to think that I am safely here and she may be in danger at this moment whenever she is.

Anancy: According to parangles,[62] she should a reach de weed garden by now.

– 13 –

Jack: Surely you don't mean Bluebeard's ganja garden?[63] Come man we must go to her at once.

Anancy: Bide yo time me friend. I wouldn't advise you to try to find her wid dem handcuff pon you hand. She have fe do a few little things for me before we can see her, an perhaps for you too.

Jack: But today she is going to be married to that villain. I must get word to her right away.

Anancy: Calm yourself down me son and trust me. Everything is working according to Anancy plan. I going look bout her all de same, for I dont too like dat weed garden. Keep you spirits up me son, the worst is bound to happen. Tataa.

Music: ? Song *Garden of Weeds*

Narrator: Primrose enters the Forbidden Garden and spies the mysterious door which leads into Bluebeard's sanctum. As she opens it there flies out from the darkness of the dungeon bats and weird creatures who menace her. She manages to escape into the dungeon . . . there she meets the sympathetic spirits of Bluebeard's part seven wives who lead her to an old trunk where she finds a document. Bluebeard enters by means of an underground passage. Primrose hides in the nick of time. He smokes his ganja pipe and falls asleep. Primrose steals the pipe and escapes. He awakes to see her ascending the stairs. He pursues her to her bedroom where Sister Ann and The Nana are frantically packing to leave the house. When they realize the fate in store for poor Primrose they jump into her bed and cover their heads. Bluebeard enters and is shout to strangle[64] Primrose in a fit of fury when Jack and Anancy come to the rescue. Bluebeard is overwhelmed by the power of his own ganja pipe and is turned into a rolling calf.[65] . . Everyone is jubilant.

Music: Song – Sea Water

Narrator: Marriage is in the air. Jack gets Primrose and everybody is happy as they celebrate with a waltz by the Gentry and a John Canoe[66] by the Peasantry.

Music: Waltzing at Weddings

Music: Rookoombine

Announcer: Gives credits and signs off Production.

BLUEBEARD *[AND BRER ANANCY]*[67]
ACT I SCENE I

Scene: Cinnamon Hill Estate, 100 years ago. Outside the estate gates. In the distance can be seen sky line of factory,[68] book keeper's quarters, barracks and the great house on the hill. It is late afternoon. Some loungers listen while a man strums on his guitar as he sings "Evening Time."[69] This is developed by chorus off stage. Presently 8 or 10 women come over small bridge bringing with them cooking utensils, wood, water, food. They proceed to build a fire and cook as they sing "Mek we cook we bittle on the way."[70] Presently 8 men and 8 girls enter in a creative dance built on traditional movements of digging, cutting etc. They sing about their jobs. At the end of song "Evening Time" general patter ensues.

FIRST MAN
De food cook Miss Marta?

MISS MARTA
De pot a bwoil[71] me son

SECOND MAN
How de breadfruit stan Miss Sarah

MISS SARAH
Soon tek off man.

FIRST MAN
Well den time fe everybody come.

MISS MARTA
Yes, call all dem bwoy and gal fe me. Tell dem fe come.

Chorus sings "Call All dem gal . . . come", during which general entry from off stage. Sammy, a burly looking head man, comes down to pots to investigate. Sings "Gal, you cook de food" at end of which there is the last chorus of "Evening Time" and food is shared out. General patter.

MISS MARTA
Come Toby, you is a bang belly[72] man.

OTHERS
Come Jamesy – Come Toby, see fe you own yah. – Gie me nuff bananas –

Mind you share me out etc.

One of the loungers has come down to fireplace and starts to molest woman and scuffle food. A little quarrel ensues, during which the call "Hog in a me cocoa" is heard off stage. Old lady, molested by boy

OLD LADY
No rice an peas market dyah.[73] Patience man. Oonoo stop little.
("Hog in a me cocoa" is repeated)

MISS MARTA
Oonoo hear dat? Mass Jacky a come.

2.[74]

CROWD
A Jacky bwoy. Mass Jacky a come. Me sweet bwoy a come etc.

General interest towards off stage. Loud squealing of pig head. Jack enters pulling
pig, repeating theme.

VOICES
What a nice hog. Watch de hog. What a meaty pig. Nice fe roas'.

OLD LADY
Massa, wheh you get him from? But is who for hog?

JACK
Whose you think? Who owns hogs around here? And cows and horses and houses
and fields?

CROWD
(Warily). Busha Bluebeard.

OLD LADY
Me pickney, tek care you get eena trouble. Him is a big man.

SAMMY
Is Bluebeard hog fe true?

JACKY
Yes, not only a hog but a trespasser.

SECOND MAN
Which part him trespass?

JACKY
Clear into me cocoa field. My dear sir I was coming down de hill to join you ring
ding. As I ketch alongside Caleb fence I hear Mass Toby bawl out, "Mass
Jacky! Hog eena you cocoa."

_____

Chorus join in song. During the singing the girls and their Uncle, Bluebeard's
attorney[75] enter. They are followed by their Nana. They applaud and move
through gateway.

PRIMROSE
Delightful! I enjoyed it so much. Please sing us another.

UNCLE
Dear Primrose. It is time we were getting along back to the barracks.

PRIMROSE
Oh Uncle, I so wanted to hear them sing again.

UNCLE
There'll be plenty of time for that. These natives will persist in their noisy revelry all night.

3.

SISTER ANN
Oh but please Uncle, delay awhile.

UNCLE
We must not incur the displeasure of Mr. Bluebeard. I hardly think he approves of these carryings on.

JACKY
If the ladies find our songs entertaining, perhaps they would like to join in a dance.

SISTER ANN
I'm not proficient enough for that, I'm sure, but I should love to try.

———

Jack gives her the go by, crosses to Primrose.

SISTER ANN
(Flummoxed). Well! The nerve of some people's children.

SAMMY
Come chile – You can skimmy down an bessy up?

SISTER ANN
No. But I can shimmy up an bessy down. (Changing her tune.). Young man, do you know who I am.

SAMMY
(In best Oxford). That's all right old girl, I'm not a snob.

UNCLE
Children, children, what are you thinking of? This isn't quite the thing, I must say.

NANA
Go on my pickney. Enjoy oonooself.

JACKY
What shall it be?

ALL
Rocky Road. Get you partners. Toby, you be singer man.

NANA
Come Mr. Crumple my love, come partner me.

4.

During the dance Primrose & Jack come down stage.

PRIMROSE
Oh this is fun. I've never danced to such a wonderful rhythm.

JACK
It's your dancing that's wonderful. You learn so quickly.

PRIMROSE
You flatter me sir.

JACK
No flattery at all Mam. You dance like the queen of the fairies. (Holds her to him.)

PRIMROSE
(Gently disengaging herself.) Then you must not crush my wings.

The dance is stopped by entry of a small boy shouting "Busha Bluebeard! Busha Bluebeard a come!" Coach enters. Uncle rushes up to coach.

BLUEBEARD
(Stepping down). What is the meaning of all this noise and vulgarity on my property? Mr. Crumble, how many times must I tell you not to allow this undisciplined behaviour? (Coming down to fire). Look at this mess. Disgusting!

Anancy, the coachman, has been following Bluebeard around gesturing and posing like him.

BLUEBEARD
Have this place cleared immediately.

Anancy has picked up a big dumpling and is about to eat it when Bluebeard turns around and catches him. Crowd laughs.

ANANCY
(Pretending to be disgusted) Look yah sah. What a disgraceful looking dumplin. (Holding his nose.)

CRUMPLE
Allow me Mr. Bluebeard to go carefully into this matter. (He goes across to investigate. Anancy slaps the dumpling into Crumple face).

ANANCY

Is who jerk me hand sah? You see how dem people yah wan' get me eena trouble? No min' Mr. Crumple. Ah sorry sah.

5.

ANANCY

(Takes outsized kerchief and wipes Crumple's face. Much bustle as people clear fire props, pots etc. Pig squeals loudly offstage).

BLUEBEARD

Is that a pig I hear? (Squealing heard again.) Not only carousing but thieving as well eh? Who stole my pig?

JACK

No one stole your pig sir. It was trespassing on my property destroying my field.

BLUEBEARD

Did you say your <u>property</u> boy?

JACK

Yes, my property, considerably lessened since you impoverished my parents, but a property none the less.

BLUEBEARD

Insolent trash. Get off these grounds at once. Do you hear me? At once

OLD LADY

Gwan Mass Jacky, fe hinda trouble gwan me pickney.

ANANCY

Bwoy, you no hear de gentleman say yuh fe come off a him property? (Aside). Stay whe you deh . . . I say gwan, gwan.

JACK

I will not be driven off. To whom does this ground rightfully belong?

CROWD

A fe yuh, a fe him own. A fe him puppa

BLUEBEARD

(Going towards Jack). Insolent rascal, be gone I say. Be gone! (Raises his stick to strike)

PRIMROSE

Stop Sir, stop. I am sure he means no harm.

BLUEBEARD

A charming young lady. I have not had the pleasure.

UNCLE

Sir she is my niece, but lately arrived.

BLUEBEARD
Staying with you? (Eyeing her)

6.

UNCLE
Yes spending some time with me

BLUEBEARD
I am sure such a charming lady is unable to enjoy the benefits of refined society in the dismal circumstances of Mr. Crumple's quarters.

PRIMROSE
(Gestures to Sister Ann)

BLUEBEARD
Oh, you mean your maids?

SISTER ANN
Maid? I'm not a maid – not any longer! (Then annoyed) I'll have you know I'm her elder sister – by a few weeks, you understand. Dear Papa rest his soul, gave us girls a thorough grounding in things.

NANA
Behave yourself Miss Ann. You like show off too much.

SISTER ANN
Dear Papa was a Sea Captain – He took his little daughter – that's me – to keep him company at sea. The sailors used to call me Queenie Queenie of the Coast. (Sings "Queenie")

BLUEBEARD
Crumple, have your nieces baggage transferred to the great house immediately.

UNCLE
Certainly Sir, immediately.

PRIMROSE
But really Sir.

NANA
Thank you very much Sir. We ready to come now.

UNCLE
This is my nieces' nurse.

BLUEBEARD
Coachman take charge of the baggage and Nana. Crumple. You instruct the headman that if they see this rascal on the property any longer to turn the hounds on him. As for you, fellow. Remove yourself altogether. If you value your skin it would be better to leave at once. To the Great House. Come along my dears. (Exit with girls.)

7.

NANA
But dem kean go widout me. Das not proper.

ANANCY
Is who invite dis old woman?

NANA
After me no older dan you. You no hear Massa say fe look after de luggage.

ANANCY
(Mimics Crumple in best English). I must ask you my good woman to refrain from using such a familiar manner of conversation and from addressing me in the vernacular.

NANA
(Pulling off Anancy by his coat). Shut up you mout you old and come on!

JACK
This man Bluebeard means no good – least of all to these young ladies.

OLD LADY
Yuh right Mass Jacky. Ah memba poor Miss Suzy daughter.

JACK
Miss Suzy daughter?

OLD LADY
You wouldn't memba me bwoy.

MAN
Memba Sarah gal.

WOMAN
An de tree foreign lady dem.

OLD WOMAN
An de nice lady him bring from St. Jago.

WOMAN
An Liza

———————————

Song – "Water Come a Me Yeye."

———————————

JACK
(Mounts bridge). My friends. I am afraid the time has come for me to go from this property. Bluebeard's words were no idle threats. He will set his hounds on my tracks as soon as night falls. Good-bye Grannie –

8.

JACK
– Miss Sarah – Mass Toby – Mass Sammy – goodbye.

OLD LADY (MISS MARTHA)
Yes Mass Jack – is betta yuh go dan get eena trouble. Gwan me son. God bless you.

CHORUS
Goodbye Mass Jack

GRANNY
Sammy walk part way wid him. (They exit). Mek him gwan. Some funny ting happen up a dis Cinnamon Hill yah.

TOBY
If them funny! You no memba . . .

––––––––––––––––

Song: "Lass Can' Fine."

CURTAIN

9.
ACT I SCENE II
Cut Scene (Lines Through Page)

Front of curtain. The Bamboo Grove. Bamboo trellis across stage with a curtain of leaf designs behind. Dark stage. Orchestra plays refrain "Wata Come a Me yeye" softly. Enter Sammy holding storm lantern.

SAMMY
Night dark fe true Mass Jack. Look as if ah haffe turn back.

JACK
Where are we Sammy?

SAMMY
This is bamboo Grove Mass Jack. Dem say duppy dyah. You can res here tell mornin ef you don' fraid – for not a soul gwine put dem foot dyah.

JACK
All right Sammy – thank you for the company. I'm not afraid. You better turn back. Good night Sammy.

SAMMY
Good night Mass Jack (exit)

JACK
(sitting) Perhaps its just as well I'm going away. My parents are dead. . . my home and property taken from me, and my whole life menaced by the power of

56

an evil enemy. What hope is there? And yet I know this is my home and the people my friends, and there is a greater need for me to stay. I know that Bluebeard means no good to his guests. If he gets them under the spell of his evil charm they will disappear like his other wives. They are constantly in my mind but how can I help them? To go to the great house would be madness. Yet I must go. But how? (Sits down on the ground and hold his head, deep in thought.) The spider crawls into the centre of the web with sinister laughter and chuckling)

JACK
What noise is this?

ANANCY
(Sings)
See me Nancy coming down (repeat)
Me da come fe help you.
See me Nancy coming down.

JACK
(Getting up & looking around) Anancy, what can this mean! (First half of song is repeated. On second half of song Jack sees spider & speaks)

END

24.

[Includes handwritten directions and dialogue with typed text marked through.]

BLUEBEARD
Enter Bluebeard: (shouting) Primrose Primrose my dear! Ah! there you are, there is something I must say to you.

PRIMROSE
What is it Sir.

BLUEBEARD
You will be the most handsome and envied woman in the land. I shall shower my riches on you. Everything will be yours for the asking. (He takes her hand and is about to kiss it when she withdraws it.) Now to business. I have to go off to court right away.

PRIMROSE
To court sir?

BLUEBEARD
Yes. To attend the trial of that imposter who stole my *pig* ~~jewels your jewels I should say~~. While I'm away I want you to take charge of my household. Here are the keys.

PRIMROSE

Thanks for the honour sir *but I do not understand. I did not know Jack was arrested*

BLUEBEARD

Oh yes I sent a police after him as soon as I got home, they tell me he was trying to run away.

You may use them as you require. Except this one. This key belongs to my personal vault. Guard it with your life and refrain from using it. Goodbye my dear. I shall be back soon to wed you. (Exit Bluebeard, to 2 or four bars of march. Girl moves forward soliloquizing.)

25.
ACT I SCENE II
(Strike Through Correction – May Have Meant
Act II Scene I)

Front of curtain. Bluebeard has gone off and curtain falls behind him as Primrose moves up front.

PRIMROSE

I don't understand it. Why has Bluebeard given me these keys? He is gone to Jacky's trial, to have him imprisoned or worse. Oh Jacky, is there nothing I can do to help you!

ANANCY

(suddenly appearing from behind curtain) of course you can help him.

PRIMROSE

(surprised) Pardon me, but who are . . . Oh, the ~~hairdresser~~ *footman*

ANANCY

So you tink.

PRIMROSE

What did you say sir?

ANANCY

Ah say you can hinder do young fellow you love from go to prison.

PRIMROSE

But, but.

ANANCY

Awright, no bodder <u>but</u> <u>but</u>. I know de whole story. I been followin you career. Jacky is a nice bwoy an Bluebeard is a wicked man. I don't like see advantage so I going help you help him.

PRIMROSE

How sir?

ANANCY

You see de key wha Bluebeard caution you not fe use at all at all?

58

PRIMROSE
Yes sir.

ANANCY
Well is _it_ you mus use.

PRIMROSE
But . . .

ANANCY
Don't but, me tell you. Hear what I tell you. Dat key is de key to Bluebeard secret
   room. People say de room full up a ghost an duppy. You fraid?

26.

PRIMROSE
Oh No sir.

ANANCY
Well dis room no eena de house. It under de cellar. You walk so go dung through
   de weed garden, den you see one door. I always see de door. Plenty people
   see de door, but nobody ever see the key.

PRIMROSE
Could this be it sir?

ANANCY
Yes. Is it. Chile you know de power you have in you han dem?

PRIMROSE
Tell me. What to do with it.

ANANCY
Now if you promise to go eena de secret room and take out what evidence you can
   fine gainst Bluebeard, not fegetting fe remove a sizeable quantity of gold for
   me, ah wi go to court house an make young Jacky get way.

PRIMROSE
Oh Sir, you have my promise. I will do anything for that. But are you sure you
   can get him off?

ANANCY
If you do fe you part, I will do fe me. But you have fe trus me.

PRIMROSE
I trust you sir, and I will do my part.

ANANCY
Is not a nice place you gwine you know.

PRIMROSE
Nothing can be too hard for me to do.

ANANCY
For love?

PRIMROSE
For love. Song: "Love is the Sweetest thing".

27.
ACT II SCENE II
(Strike Through Correction)

Outside court house. Chorus discovered. "Chorus a Call" to the tune of "Day dah Light". Crumple enters from court house.

CRUMBLE
Constable, you would be advised to keep order outside the court. His honour will be here directly and these people must be disciplined.

MAN'S VOICE
Him face favour discipline. (laughter)

WOMEN
A wheh him a say doah?

MAN
Make we crumple up Mr. Crumple.
(Crumple moves up to go off and collides with Sammy.)
Song: Womens Voices "Hol him Sammy hol him"

              "   "   "   "   "

    Mens Voices. "Wheel him Janie wheel him"
The court bell is rung and Mr. Crumple sits down with a thud. Bluebeard enters in riding breeches etc.

BLUEBEARD
What is the meaning of your undignified position Crumple? Get up at once Sir and brush you[r] britches.

CRUMPLE
Certainly your Honour. Is your Honour ready to try the prisoner? He awaits your pleasure within.

BLUEBEARD
To the business Crumple. I must despatch the matter. I have more important matters to attend to today.

POLICE
Maker way for his Honour Busha Bluebeard. (Little march played)

CROWD
Boo! Boo!

OLD LADY
Lard. Poor Mass Jacky. Busha Bluebeard going make it hard fe you today bwoy.

MAN
Him wi never get off.

28.

(Anancy suddenly appears in crowd.)

ANANCY
My friends. You are aware of the predicament of young Jack.

ALL
Yes Sah, yes.

ANANCY
You would like to see him get off, wouldn't you?

ALL
But things look bad fe true sah.

ANANCY
You can help him if you wish.

ALL
Would love to. Tell we. ect.

ANANCY
Come here then and I will tell you a plan. (They all gather around him with much mime and waving of hands.

ALL
Yes, yes, ah see etc.

ANANCY
Wait. Bide you time. Me going inside the court house fe see how de case progressing. You watch me. (Exit.)

MAN
Make we sing so cheer up Jacky bwoy.
Song: ~~Brown Gawn a Court~~ *Sea water*. At end of song window opens and Anancy appears.

ANANCY
Five witnesses come an gawn already. De man won't listen to a soul.

ALL
How Mass Jacky a take it?

ANANCY

Ah proud a de bwoy you see. Him siddown calm wid innocency jus bran all over him face. Now an den when dem tel a lie pon him him smile.

MAN

Make sign to him tell him fe go on same way. No make dem frighten him.

29.

ANANCY

Alright, ah will try. (Enter reporter.)

REPORTER

am I late! am I late, am I in time!

CROWD

SHH!

ANANCY

Hi little man, what's matter? Wha kine a ructions dat you making eena de court yard? You don't know court is in session?

REPORTER

My good man I am a reporter. Can't I come up there?

ANANCY

No, you stay whe you deh an I we report to you and you report to people dem.

REPORTER

Den what about my paper?

ANANCY

You can tell dem too.

REPORTER

Good, good. Now about de case of Rex Bluebeard versus Jacky –

ANANCY

Dat's well under way my frien. Wait little. (Ducks inside then reappears, beckoning the reporter to come closer to window. Much mime. Reporter rushes down back to crowd gesticulating etc.)

REPORTER

He say that Mr. Crumple is in the witness box going witness when all of a sudden, suddenly, Mr. Jacky the prisoner, springs out of his chair, jumps up and gives tongue. He says, pointing like this, (using right hand) no, he is handcuffed, so pointing like this, (using both hands), "It's a lie.". (Murmurs from crowd.)

Then his Honour says, "Prisoner at the bar sit down". You will get the chance to
speak in your defence later. "Jacky open his mout to speak again (with great
excitement), constables rush at him. (Limply). He sit down.

ANANCY
(Appearing at window) Pst! Come here. (to reporter)

REPORTER
(Runs to window, listens to Anancy who whispers to him).

30.

REPORTER
He says Mr. Jacky is making a speech. Ah kaan hear de speech, but Lawd ah
can jus picture him saying, "Your Honour I stand before you falsely, unjustly, treacherously, machion . . . atrociously, deliberately and calculatingly
accused of a crime of which I am innocent as a babe. I fear no foe. I am
dauntless and undaunted. My head is hatless and unbowed. Your Honour I am
certain and without a doubt that you have no alternative but to immediately
and without delay admonish and discharge me of this ridiculous crime." After
such a speech what can a judge do but acquit him, yes, acquit him. Let him
go. Das what dem have fe do. Let him go.

ANANCY
(Appearing at window, speaks in loud voice). Dem sentence him, dem sentence
him, dem sentence him!

REPORTER
(bursting into tears). Dat poor fellow, dat nice young bwoy. Dem sentence him
Whai!

ANANCY
Oonoo memba what ah did tell oonoo?

CROWD
Yes sah, awright, yes.

ANANCY
Good. (Anancy[76] [Jack, not Anancy] handcuffed and 2 policemen with basket
shields appear starch. Anancy shouts from window). Murder! Police! Police!
Murder!

CROWD
(looking up). Murder! Dem gwine kill him. Marshall-law! Murder! (Policeman
looks up and Jack is grabbed by a man and rushed off stage. Commotion
ensues. Enter Bluebeard from archway shouting and Crumple shivering
behind.)

BLUEBEARD
What is the meaning of all this commotion? Where is the prisoner?

CONSTABLE
The prisoner? (in great agitation.)[77]

CROWD
Him gone.

31.

BLUEBEARD
Sergeant!

SERGEANT
(saluting). Yessir.

BLUEBEARD
You and your men have been duped by the prisoner and his gang of ruffians. You've allowed him to escape. Now find him, do you hear me? Find him. Scour the countryside, search every nook and corner, every peasant hut in the vicinity and find him or it will be very hard for you.

SERGEANT
Yessir, we will set about it sir. At once sir. (Bluebeard stalks out.). Right turn, quick march! (Police march out.)

WOMAN
Dem wi never ketch him.

CROWD
(Sings) Jack gawn, Jack gawn
Mass Jack get weh
Jack ride zoza mule etc.

CURTAIN

36.
ACT II SCENE II
(Strike Through And Pencilled Correction)

Front of curtain. Enter Anancy looking for someone.

ANANCY
But top whe dat young woman deh sah?[78] Time a go you know.

PRIMROSE
Oh Mr. Anancy, is it true?

ANANCY
If what is true Miss Primrose?

PRIMROSE
What I heard the people saying as I came along the road – that Jacky had escaped.

ANANCY
Oh yes, true enough. Him escape but still a prisoner, poor bwoy.

PRIMROSE
How is that?

ANANCY
Him got on handcuff an him can' get them off, an police all over the district a
search fe him.

PRIMROSE
And if they find him?

ANANCY
Prison fe him. Life sentence. Excep' of course him can prove something against
Bluebeard fe counteract.

PRIMROSE
Oh but he can. Look at this pipe. In it Bluebeard smokes what he calls his weed.
I saw him at it in the dungeon. "Twas a fearful experience sir, more like a
terrible dream. There I saw the spirits of seven dead women, Bluebeard's
former wives. Then Bluebeard himself entered and started to smoke his pipe
and conjured all kinds of gruesome spirits. Then he fell asleep. I stole his pipe
and ran out of the room.

ANANCY
That's right. What else you tief?

PRIMROSE
I found this document, which states that fifty acres of Cinnamon Hill

37.

PRIMROSE
lands plus a great house and many costly jewels are the property of Erasmus
Dermott, and should go to his only son Jack Dermott. That's Jacky isn't it?

ANANCY
Oh yes, that's him. But wait, you don't tief no money?

PRIMROSE
Oh, I had almost forgotten. There were stacks of gold in the dungeon but I could
only manage to take this small bag. That's for you Mr. Anancy.

ANANCY
Now you talking. Tenk you mah.[79] Den you not marrying Bluebeard again?

PRIMROSE
Oh no. I am only going back to the great house to warn my sister and guardian. We must leave here before Bluebeard awakens. Will you take me to see Jacky? When I get back, shall I meet you here?

ANANCY
Yes, if we don't meet somewhere else.

PRIMROSE
What do you mean?

ANANCY
Maybe something, maybe nutten.

PRIMROSE
I must go now. Give Jacky my love.

ANANCY
Alright Miss Primrose, alright. Good go wi you. (Exit Primrose.)

POLICE
(rushing in). Have you been here long? See anybody pass?

ANANCY
Wha kin' a smady?[80]

POLICE
A man wid handcuff on.

ANANCY
Handcuff? Mus be dangerous criminal.

38.

POLICE
Escaped convict. Escape from justice on his way to prison.

ANANCY
Den how you know dat him still have on handcuff?

POLICE
I don't know for certain, but after him can' take off de handcuff widout key.

ANANCY
Den supposing you ketch him an him don' got on Handcuff. You got anoder handcuff to handcuff hin wid?

POLICE
Oh yes (producing open handcuff from pocket) We always travel with handcuff.

ANANCY
(examining handcuffs) but it open!

POLICE
Yes.

ANANCY
Den how you lock it? (Police snaps handcuffs close). Das grand, den how you open it back?

POLICE
(producing keys from pocket and opening handcuff) like dis.

ANANCY
Look at dat ee. Good gosh. Gi'e me a try. Make me see if ah could a lock it an open it back as nice as you. (Takes handcuff from police and snaps it on his wrist.). Tenk you corpie. Alright. Ah gawn yah. Tata. (Whistles tune while he throws key in the air and catches it. Exit dancing with police calling after him.

ACT III SCENE II

Primrose's bedroom[81] in great house. Sister Ann discovered. Enter Primrose

SISTER ANN
At last Primrose. Where have you been? Don't you realize the gravity of the situation child? It's time you started dressing for your wedding.

PRIMROSE
There isn't going to be any wedding. Sister Ann, Mr. Bluebeard is a dangerous thief, a murderer, and a worker of witchcraft. We must leave this house at once, the three of us.

SISTER ANN
Leave the house? Child you must be mad. The excitement has gone to your head.

PRIMROSE
Nothing's the matter with me, but I have been in the garden of weeds and the secret chamber. I have seen the seven dead women, his former wives. I have seen Bluebeard himself smoking his devilish weed and conjuring up spirits. I tell you we are not safe here. We must go now Sister Ann, right now.

SISTER ANN
(ranting) Poor dear Primrose, poor child. Nana, come here quickly. Primrose is out of her mind. (enter Nana)

PRIMROSE

Nana I am not crazy, I am all right. Please believe that. Do you remember the dream
I told you this morning about the dreadful garden? Well it has become a reality.
There is such a place right here in Bluebeard's grounds. I have been there and
seen the most frightening things. I know it sounds unbelievable but it's true.

NANA

Me poor pickney. Lay down an rest youself. De poor little head can' stan de stress
an strain.

PRIMROSE

How can I convince you that I am sane? How can I prove . . .? Ah (taking keys from
pocket.). Here's the key to the mysterious room. I have still got it. I dropped
while I was in the dungeon and it fell in blood. There are the stains. I tried and
tried to wipe them off but they won't come off. There it is. See for yourself.

40.

SISTER ANN

Blood! There is blood on it Nana.

NANA

Yes. Blood fe true.

PRIMROSE

Take it Nana. Try to wipe the blood off.

NANA

(Taking key and rubbing it with skirt). It can' come off. All de rubah de rub de
blood get brighter an brighter. Lawd Miss Primrose. Wha kin' a trouble we
eena so!

SISTER ANN

WE must get out of here at once. Come Primrose dear. Assemble your things.
(Frantic packing. They are going towards the door when there is a loud
knocking and Bluebeard is heard calling. Primrose turns the key in the lock
and leans against the door. Sister Ann goes towards the opposite door, opens
it, and is held by Big Tom. There is a tussle. She escapes into room and slams
door, turning key in lock.)

BLUEBEARD

Let me in, or I'll break the door down!

PRIMROSE

Sister Ann, Sister Ann, do you see anyone coming?

SISTER ANN

No sister. Only a cloud of dust.
(More knocking and shouting from Bluebeard.)

PRIMROSE
Sister Ann, Sister Ann, do you see anyone coming now?

SISTER ANN
No sister. Only a cloud of dust.
(The door is broken in & Bluebeard rushes in. Primrose falls to the ground. He
stands over her with fingers curled as if to strangle her.)

BLUEBEARD
So you think you can disobey me and live?

41.

BLUEBEARD
my secret room and discover the horrors there and run and tell the world? Oh No,
my little one. You'll go the way of all curious and disobedient women. You
will go and join your predecessors in the dungeon. Seven and one are eight,
Madam. (Laughs terribly grabs her up from the floor. She struggles on to her
knees. He drags her to her feet, still laughing)

PRIMROSE
Sister Ann, anybody coming?

SISTER ANN
Yes sister.
(Bluebeard clasps hands around Primrose's throat as if to strangle her when Jacky,
followed by Anancy enter through window. They rush towards Bluebeard
and girl. There is a tussle and swaying of figures. Jack & Bluebeard all over
room. Bluebeard is overpowered and Primrose runs to Jack)

ANANCY
(To Bluebeard). So Massa Bluebeard to tink you was a bad man, roun yah no sah?
You always take up you wood too. As you get a chance you gawn eena you
secret room wid you pipe. See it yah. An you puff an blow. So you take big
puff (drawing on pipe) so you blow (blowing out smoke into Bluebeard's
face. There is a big cloud of smoke, a great clanging of chaings. Anancy stag-
gers back. The cloud clears. Bluebeard appears as a rolling calf.)

THE END

NOTES

1 *Brer* and *Bredda* are Jamaican colloquial for 'Brother'. 'Nancy and Anancy are used
interchangeably in this play for the character of Anancy.
2 *Rookoombine* is a popular Jamaican folksong.
3 Noel is handwritten beneath "Announcer". This notation may indicate that Dir Noel
Vaz was the announcer and narrator; neither role is included in the cast.
4 *Oonoo* is Jamaican colloquial for anyone or everyone or you all.

5 Jamaican vernacular: but I shouldn't tell you anymore, I'm going to make you hear for yourself. . . . Anyone want to hear? Do you want to hear . . . ?
6 Jamaican vernacular: boil.
7 Breadfruit, similar to large jackfruit, is a staple of the Jamaican diet that grows on trees throughout the Caribbean. According to the Government of Jamaica website, 'Breadfruit is a common food tree in Jamaica. It was introduced from Tahiti in about 1792 by Captain William Bligh, and soon became an important food source for slaves'. It is an excellent source of carbohydrates. It is now popular with locals and visitors, and it is exported to cultural centres with West Indian migrants outside the Caribbean. It can also be used to provide shade for crops such as cocoa, which is grown on the fictional plantation on Cinnamon Hill in the pantomime. See 'Marketing and Business Profile: Breadfruit (*Artocarpus Altilis*)' (2019), *RADA: People, Land and Opportunity* website, Rural Agricultural Development Authority.
8 Jamaican colloquial for boy.
9 *Ay-Zuzuma* was a written by Bennett-Coverley for this pantomime, and it remained an extremely popular song outside the pantomime.
10 The social inequities and exploitation of slavery continued with little change after the official end of slavery in 1834. The 1897 West India Royal Commission officially recognized local farmers' need for land as the first inequity in the British Caribbean. (Report 1897:70.) See Richardson, 'Depression Riots and the Calling of the 1897 West India Royal Commission', p. 171.
11 The term 'Busha' indicates a Caribbean planter or overseer: 'In the Caribbean: the manager or overseer of a plantation or estate. Frequently as a title or form of address. Cf. overseer *n*. 1a(a)'. *OED Online*.
12 The *OED Online* identifies it as an offensive term for a child of colour. However, Bennett-Coverley seems to be using the term here as it is defined in the *Dictionary of Jamaican English* (2002): 'child'. Afro-Jewish Jamaican author Herbert DeLisser (1878–1944) similarly defines the term as children: 'corruption of "piccanninies," which is itself a corruption of two Spanish words: pequeñeos niños' which mean, little children' (DeLisser, *Jane's Career*, 1913).
13 Bennett-Coverley defines a 'ring ding' as a big party complete with singing, dancing and even theatrical performances (*Miss Lou and Early Jamaican Theatre*). Both before and after slavery, ring dings were frequently shut down by colonial authorities. 'Ring-Ding' (1968–1980) is also the name of the Jamaican Broadcasting Company (JBC) show produced by Miss Lou.
14 Bennett-Coverley shifts between Jamaican vernacular and standard English for different characters in the play, reflecting different colonial Caribbean identities. Primrose and Anne have recently arrived from Great Britain (although they seem to have a Jamaican nanny, suggesting they were born on the island).
15 Kittereen: 'In the West Indies: a kind of one-horse chaise or buggy'. See *OED Online*.
16 In *Miss Lou and the Early Jamaican Theatre*, Bennett-Coverley states: 'If you were respectable, you didn't have ring dings' (7:50–8:03). Bennett-Coverley explains upper class prejudice against these dance performances stating: 'anything that's Jamaican is not too good' (8:11–9:45).
17 Jamaican vernacular: Go on Mr. Jack, stay away from trouble, go on my child.
18 Crowd affirms that the land belonged to Jack and his father in Jamaican vernacular.
19 This is the character that Bennett-Coverley played in the pantomime.
20 According to the *Urban Dictionary*, the phrase Bugga Yagga seems to have both positive and negative connotations. Bugga literally means bag of or a lot of something. Bugga can be a relatively neutral term for a woman, but a Yagga Bugga can be any kind of insult.
21 'Water Come a Me Yeye' is a traditional Jamaican folk song that begins: 'Every time I 'membah Liza,/Watah come a me eye'.

22 Jamaican vernacular for 'You see a spider, yes. You see Anancy. . . . Anywhere there is trouble, there is Anancy my son'.

23 Jamaican vernacular for according to.

24 Jamaican proverb in Jamaican vernacular: 'The same something that is sweet in a man's mouth will hurt his belly'.

25 Jamaican vernacular: can't.

26 Jamaican vernacular: Yes, it is true, yes. Bluebeard is going to have a big time ball to celebrate his engagement. I heard him say he is going to invite all the dignitaries of the parish from the east to the west. You'd like to go?

27 Jamaican vernacular: Jewels! You know where they are?

28 Jamaican vernacular: Come, we will make a bargain. I will get you into the Great House. You do your little business with the young lady, we find out where the jewels are. And we split. . . . You agree?

29 Planters Punch, also called Sangree, is a rum punch that originated in Jamaica, according to the first known Planters Punch recipe in *Fun Magazine* (1878).

30 Jamaican vernacular: If you are afraid of the lizard, you cannot kill a snake.

31 Jamaican vernacular: Don't talk too soon. If you have not finished climbing the hill, don't throw away your stick.

32 Jamaican vernacular: Stop, you mean he is not Mr. Burrow from Boroughbridge? You mean he was fooling me? See here man, you leave the Busha's house. Go on . . . go on . . . I say, go on right now. Out with you or you are going to be sorry. Come.

33 May be 'rascal' – handwritten text inserted in pencil is unclear.

34 Jamaican vernacular: Alright, no bother with that. I know the whole story. I have been following your career. Jacky is a nice boy and Bluebeard is a wicked man. I don't like to see advantage, so I am going to help you help him.

35 Jamaican vernacular: You see the key that Bluebeard cautioned you not to use at all?

36 According to the Merriam-Webster dictionary, a duppy is: 'a haunting spirit of the dead conceived in folklore of West Indians as a usually malevolent shadow or immaterial body'.

37 Jamaican vernacular: Well, this room is not in the house. It is under the ground. You walk so, go down through the weed garden, then you see one door. I always see the door. Plenty of people see the door, but nobody has ever seen the key.

38 Jamaican vernacular: Now if you promise me to go in the secret room and take out what evidence you can find against Bluebeard, not forgetting to remove a sizeable quantity of gold for me, I will go to the courthouse and make young Jacky get away.

39 Jamaican vernacular: If you do your part, I will do mine. But you have to trust me.

40 Jamaican vernacular: It is not a nice place you are going, you know.

41 Jamaican vernacular: I mean.

42 Jamaican vernacular: Wait, bide your time. I am going inside the courthouse to see how the case is progressing. You watch the window, and I will come and tell you how things are going.

43 Sammy.

44 Jamaican vernacular: We will sing to cheer up Jacky boy.

45 Jamaican vernacular: I'm proud of the boy. He sits down calm[ly] with innocence just branded all over his face. Now and then when they tell a bad lie about him, he smiles.

46 Jamaican vernacular: Make a sign to him to tell him to go on the same way. Don't let them frighten him.

47 Jamaican vernacular: Alright, I will try.

48 Jamaican vernacular: Shh. Shhh, stop your noise.

49 Jamaican vernacular: Hi little man, what's the matter? What kind of a ruckus are you making in the courtyard? Don't you know that the Court is in Session?

50 Jamaican vernacular: No you stay where you are and I will issue a bulletin, and you report it to the people.

51 Jamaican vernacular: Alright . . .
52 Jamaican vernacular: He says Mr. Jacky is making a speech. I can't hear the speech, but Lord I can just picture him saying.
53 Jamaican vernacular: That is what they have to do.
54 Jamaican vernacular: They sentenced him. . . . They sentenced him. . . .
55 Jamaican vernacular: That poor fellow, that nice young boy. They sentenced him. Wail.
56 Jamaican vernacular: Everyone remember what I told everyone?
57 Jamaican vernacular: Yes . . . we remember alright . . . we remember.
58 Jamaican vernacular: Good . . . now is the time . . . they are bringing him out now.
59 Text smudged here, the letters are unclear. May also be 'Yaga Mule' or 'Zase Mule'.
60 Jamaican vernacular: Alright, don't be frightened, it is me.
61 Jamaican vernacular: Simple mathematics, sir. It was a pleasure. But what has happened? You don't look too happy?
62 Term unknown, seems to mean plans.
63 According to the *OED Online*, ganja is 'a preparation of Indian hemp (*Cannabis sativa*, variety *indica*), strongly intoxicating and narcotic'.
64 Shouts he will strangle.
65 According to folktales collected in 1896 by students of colour at Mico College, a rolling calf is the spirit of a person who was too evil to go either to heaven or to hell. Instead, the rolling calf must roam the earth with a chain from Satan around its neck as a warning to the living. See 'The Folklore of the Negroes of Jamaica', *Folklore*, 15:1 (1904), p. 92.
66 According to *About Jamaica* (2017), a John Canoe, also known as a Jonkonnu or Junkanoo, is a traditional Jamaican Christmas carnival (which may have its roots in French or English Christmas carnival traditions). Processions of masqueraders dance and engage in theatrical performances. Masquerade bands include set characters, such as a king, a queen, the John Canoe or Actor Boy, the devil and the Belly Woman. Also see Hill (1992).
67 This is the beginning of the extant pages of the extended script. It is unclear if the missing pages were cut before the performance or lost afterwards.
68 This reference is to a rum distillery on the plantation.
69 According to Louise Bennett's article on *Jamaicans.com*, 'Evening Time' was composed specifically for *Bluebeard and Brer Anancy* (1949), lyrics by Louise Bennett and music by Barbara Ferland. It has taken on a life apart from the pantomime and is often mistaken for a traditional Jamaican folksong. It describes the action in the first scene, people gathering to eat after a long day of work ('Evening Time' 2003).
70 Jamaican vernacular: Let us cook a bittle (term unknown, perhaps 'little') on the way.
71 Bwoil is Jamaican vernacular for boil. The addition of a 'w' to 'oi' or 'oy' in standard English words is common in Bennett-Coverley's spelling.
72 Jamaican vernacular for a large stomach that hangs over the waist.
73 Rice and peas were a special meal for Sunday in Jamaica. It was a traditional dish of rice and red beans that originated in West Africa; slaves brought it to Jamaica and cooked it on Sunday when they were traditionally given some rest from work.
74 See endnotes in abbreviated play earlier.
75 In Jamaica, 'attorney' can be the term for someone who manages land for an absentee owner.
76 Anancy seems to be a typographical error here; this should be 'Jack'.
77 The policeman is a stock character in the Jamaican John Canoe Christmas masquerade.
78 Jamaican vernacular: what's that young woman over there?
79 Jamaican address for a woman, like ma'am.
80 Jamaican vernacular for someone or somebody. Also spelled smaddy.
81 May be a "room in the Great House": "Primrose's bed" may be struck through.

Part 2

CINDERELLA DRAMAS

A review of mainstream British pantomimes from *Illustrated London News*, 'The Pantomimes and Burlesque' (31 December 1859) states that tragic pantomimes fell out of fashion by the middle of the century (p. 640).[1] Bibliographies of mainstream Cinderella pantomimes demonstrate the pervasive nature of the comic Cinderella coming out of London during the nineteenth and early twentieth century. Within this relatively comic framework, performers and audience members engage in a process that is often transgressive and carnivalesque, offering 'opportunities for social commentary' (Schacker, *Staging Fairy Land*, p. 28).

By contrast, both the Scottish playwright J. M. Barrie's' *A Kiss for Cinderella* (1916) and the Welsh playwright and actor Emlyn Williams's *Cinderella* (1924) chose to move from comic to tragic Cinderella pantomimes. The heroines are doomed by their own fairy-tale expectations, and they end the drama clinging to a dream that will never materialize because they lack supernatural helpers who are powerful enough to truly impact reality. The context of each play makes Cinderella's romantic disappointment a broader critique of empire.

Although pantomime was often trivialized by its association with children, the spectacle and experience of fairy-tale dramas, particularly Cinderella, permeated a wide variety of social venues for adults across the British Empire (Schacker, *Staging Fairy Land*, pp. 7–8, 46).[2] Reviews of Cinderella dramas and notices for Cinderella parties were printed alongside the texts of Cinderella narratives in periodicals and newspapers. These demonstrate that Cinderella was continually re-enacted in different social modes. These texts, newspaper articles and notices may be found grouped together in Volume 1. The dramas themselves have been separated out into this volume for the sake of space.

NOTES

1 Schacker 2018.
2 Cinderella costumes were a staple of fancy dress costume guides like Arden Holt's *Fancy Dresses Described; or, What to Wear at Fancy Balls* (1887). Notices for Cinderella Dances and Cinderella Parties were featured in newspapers across the British

DOI: 10.4324/9781003034643-4

empire. Like Cinderella's masquerade in the fairy tale, the events ended at midnight. The article 'Cinderella Parties' (1878) in *The Aberystwyth Observer* describes rules for simple dinners and dress, perhaps a reference to Cinderella's impoverished status before the ball, which was also a favourite masquerade costume. Re-enactments of Cinderella through social activities gave this narrative more layers of meaning throughout the nineteenth century. For more information, see Schacker and Quinn, eds., *The Routledge Pantomime Reader 1800–1900* (New York: Routledge, 2021).

Editorial Headnote

Barrie, J. M., *A Kiss for Cinderella: A Comedy* (London: Hodder and Stoughton Ltd, 1916).

'A Kiss for Cinderella' is a Scottish play produced and set during 1916, in the middle of the First World War. It premiered in London on 16 March 1916 at the Wyndham's Theatre, where it was a resounding success. It toured the UK and the US, and it was turned into a full-length film in 1925. War-time conditions in the UK are prominent in the play, including food rationing, blackouts, Zeppelin raids, fear of spies, caring for recovering veterans, and displaced children.

In a review by the *Aberdeen Evening Express* on Friday 6 October 1916, it states:

> If anyone doubts . . . the magic of Sir James Barrie . . . the doubt can be resolved by a visit to this beautiful dream play which the magician has given us. 'A Kiss for Cinderella' will prove as perennially popular as 'Peter Pan'. There is the same quaint whimsical humour in both plays, the same pointed irony, the same tenderness, the same wholly indescribably blending of comedy and pathos.[1]

Set in a snowy December, Barrie's play was written for the Christmas pantomime season in the United Kingdom.

Despite the review praising the play's comedic dream-like drama, the ultimately tragic narrative undermines the assumptions of the ATU 510 Cinderella narrative. The idea of a woman who is the perfect 'fit' for a prince is parodied in the first scene, where Cinderella names the stone statue of Venus 'Mrs. Brodie' (Barrie, p. 10) because the statue is Mr. Bodie's 'ideal' (p. 10). These burlesque dramas act as a counterpart to what critic Richard Henry Horne in *The Contemporary Review* calls the 'real' fairy-tale pantomimes that dominated the stage in the nineteenth century.[2]

Cinderella, originally called 'Miss Thing' (Barrie, p. 12), takes on the persona that Mr. Bodie assigns her. She creates her own backstory of lost nobility (p. 12) in the hopes her Prince Charming will arrive and enable her rise. Ultimately, the audience is always aware that the tubercular Cinderella's impending death will end her fairy-tale hopes as well as the care she that she provides for a rag-tag group of war-time orphans.

Cinderella's ethnic identity is obscured and unclear to the characters around her. Her mix of Scottish and Cockney accents marks her as displaced in this urban drama (Barrie, p. 12). And her identity continues to shift throughout the play. Cinderella is a chameleon, perpetually trying to fit into the hegemonic fairy-tale narrative that has historically excluded her.

The protagonist's belief in the fairy tales she reads is both endearing and fatal (Barrie, p. 14). Like the Lost Boys of Barrie's *Peter Pan*, the children in this tale are doomed because they do not have the means to survive in a harsh, war-time world. Cinderella's godmother never shows up with the invitation to the long-awaited ball where she hopes to meet a prince (p. 13) and in the end she collapses in the snow in her attempt to get to the party herself (pp. 100–1). The final message of *A Kiss for Cinderella* is that there is no fairy godmother powerful enough in 1916 to right the wrongs of war and poverty for the displaced and ethnically marginalized.

Content warning: This drama includes racist and ethnocentric language within the context of its wartime setting.

NOTES

1 See Appendix C.
2 See Horne, R. H., 'The Burlesque and the Beautiful', *Contemporary Review*, 18 (1871), pp. 390–406 and Schacker, *Staging Fairy Land*, 175–80.

3

A KISS FOR CINDERELLA:
A COMEDY

J. M. Barrie

Source: London: Hodder and Stoughton Ltd, 1916

I

The least distinguished person in 'Who's Who' has escaped, as it were, from that fashionable crush, and is spending a quiet evening at home. He is curled up in his studio, which is so dark that he would be invisible, had we not obligingly placed his wicker chair just where the one dim ray from the stove may strike his face. His eyes are closed luxuriously, and we could not learn much about him without first poking our fingers into them. According to the tome mentioned (to which we must return him before morning), Mr. Bodie is sixty-three, has exhibited in the Royal Academy, and is at present unmarried. They do not proclaim him comparatively obscure: they left it indeed to him to say the final word on this subject, and he has hedged. Let us put it in this way, that he occupies more space in his wicker chair than in the book, where nevertheless he looks as if it was rather lonely not to be a genius. He is a painter for the nicest of reasons, that it is delightful to live and die in a messy studio; for our part, we too should have become a painter had it not been that we always lost our paint-box. There is no spirited bidding to acquire Mr. Bodie's canvases: he loves them at first sight himself, and has often got up in the night to see how they are faring; but ultimately he has turned cold to them, and has even been known to offer them, in lieu of alms, to beggars, who departed cursing. We have a weakness for persons who don't get on, and so cannot help adding, though it is no business of ours, that Mr. Bodie had private means. Curled up in his wicker chair he is rather like an elderly cupid. We wish we could warn him that the policeman is coming.

The policeman comes: in his hand the weapon that has knocked down more malefactors than all the batons – the bull's-eye. He strikes with it now, right and left, revealing, as if she had just entered the room, a replica of the Venus of Milo, taller than himself though he is a stalwart. It is the first meeting of these two, but, though a man who can come to the boil, he is as little moved by her as she by

DOI: 10.4324/9781003034643-5

him. After the first glance she continues her reflections. Her smile over his head vaguely displeases him. For two pins he would arrest her.

The lantern finds another object, more worthy of his attention, the artist. Mr. Bodie is more restive under the light than was his goddess, perhaps because he is less accustomed to being stared at. He blinks and sits up.

MR. BODIE (*giving his visitor a lesson in manners*). I beg your pardon, officer.
POLICEMAN (*confounded*). Not that, sir; not at all.
MR. BODIE (*pressing his advantage*). But I insist on begging your pardon, officer.
POLICEMAN. I don't see what for, sir.
MR. BODIE (*fancying himself*). For walking uninvited into the abode of a law-abid-
ing London citizen, with whom I have not the pleasure of being acquainted.
POLICEMAN (*after thinking this out*). But I'm the one as has done that, sir.
MR. BODIE (*with neat surprise*). So you are, I beg your pardon, officer.
(*With pardonable pride in himself* MR. BODIE *turns on the light. The studio, as we can now gather from its sloped roof, is at the top of a house; and its window is heavily screened, otherwise we might see the searchlights through it, show-ing that we are in the period of the great war. Though no one speaks of* MR. BODIE'S *pictures as Bodies, which is the true test of fame, he is sufficiently eminent not to have works of art painted or scratched on his walls, mercy has been shown even to the panels of his door, and he is handsomely stingy of draperies. The Venus stands so prominent that the studio is evidently hers rather than his. The stove has been brought forward so that he can rest his feet on it, whichever of his easy chairs he is sitting in, and he also falls over it at times when stepping back to consider his latest failure. On a shelf is a large stuffed penguin, which is to be one of the characters in the play, and on each side of this shelf are two or three tattered magazines. We had hankered after giving* MR. BODIE *many rows of books, but were well aware that he would get only blocks of wood so cleverly painted to look like books that they would deceive every one except the audience. Everything may be real on the stage except the books. So there are only a few magazines in the studio (and very likely when the curtain rings up it will be found that they are painted too). But* MR. BODIE *was a reader; he had books in another room, and the careworn actor who plays him must suggest this by his manner.*
Our POLICEMAN *is no bookman; we who write happen to have it from himself that he had not bought a book since he squeezed through the sixth standard: very tight was his waist that day, he told us, and he had to let out every button. Nevertheless it was literature of a sort that first brought him into our ken. He was our local constable: and common interests, as in the vagaries of the moon, gradually made him and us cease to look at each other askance. We fell into the way of chatting with him and giving him the evening papers we had bought to read as we crossed the streets. One of his duties was to herd the vagrant populace under our arches during air-raids, and at such times he could be properly gruff, yet comforting, like one who would at once run*

in any bomb that fell in his beat. When he had all his flock nicely plastered against the dank walls he would occasionally come to rest beside us, and thaw, and discuss the newspaper article that had interested him most. It was seldom a war-record; more frequently it was something on the magazine page, such as a symposium by the learned on 'Do you Believe in Love at First Sight?' Though reticent in many matters he would face this problem openly; with the guns cracking all around, he would ask for our views wistfully; he spoke of love without a blush, as something recognised officially at Scotland Yard. At this time he had been in love, to his own knowledge, for several weeks, but whether the god had struck him at first sight he was not certain; he was most anxious to know, and it was in the hope of our being able to help him out that he told us his singular story. On his face at such times was often an amazed look, as if he were staring at her rather than at us, and seeing a creature almost beyond belief. Our greatest success was in saying that perhaps she had fallen in love at first sight with him, which on reflection nearly doubled him up. He insisted on knowing what had made us put forward this extraordinary suggestion; he would indeed scarcely leave our company that night, and discussed the possibility with us very much as if it were a police case.

Our POLICEMAN'S *romance, now to be told, began, as we begin, with his climbing up into* MR. BODIE'S *studio.* MR. BODIE *having turned on the light gave him the nasty look that means 'And now, my man, what can I do for you?' Our* POLICEMAN, *however, was not one to be worsted without striking a blow. He strode to the door, as he has told us, and pointed to a light in the passage.)*

POLICEMAN (*in his most brow-beating voice, so well known under the arches*). Look here, sir, it's that.

MR. BODIE. I don't follow.

POLICEMAN. Look at that passage window. (*With natural pride in language.*) You are showing too much illumination.

BODIE. Oh! well, surely –

POLICEMAN (*with professional firmness*). It's agin the regulations. A party in the neighbouring skylight complains.

BODIE (*putting out the light*). If that will do for to-night, I'll have the window boarded up.

POLICEMAN. Anything so long as it obscures the illumination.

BODIE (*irritated*). Shuts out the light.

POLICEMAN (*determinedly*). Obscures the illumination.

BODIE (*on reflection*). I remember now, I did have that window boarded up.

POLICEMAN (*who has himself a pretty vein of sarcasm*). I don't see the boards.

BODIE. Nor do I see the boards. (*Pondering.*) Can she have boned them?

POLICEMAN. She? (*He is at once aware that it has become a more difficult case.*)

BODIE. You are right. She is scrupulously honest, and if she took the boards we may be sure that I said she could have them. But that only adds to the mystery.

POLICEMAN (*obligingly*). Mystery?

BODIE. Why this passion for collecting boards? Try her with a large board, officer. Extraordinary!

POLICEMAN (*heavily*). I don't know what you are talking about, sir. Are you complaining of some woman?

BODIE. Now that is the question. Am I? As you are here, officer, there is something I want to say to you. But I should dislike getting her into trouble.

POLICEMAN (*stoutly*). No man what is a man wants to get a woman into trouble unnecessary.

BODIE (*much struck*). That's true! That's *absolutely* true, officer.

POLICEMAN (*badgered*). It's true, but there's nothing remarkable about it.

BODIE. Excuse me.

POLICEMAN. See here, sir, I'm just an ordinary policeman.

BODIE. I can't let that pass. If I may say so, you have impressed me most deeply. I wonder if I might ask a favour of you. Would you mind taking off your helmet? As it happens, I have never seen a policeman without his helmet.

(*The perplexed officer puts his helmet on the table.*)

Thank you. (*Studying the effect.*) Of course I knew they took off. You sit also?

(*The* POLICEMAN *sits.*)

Very interesting.

POLICEMAN. About this woman, sir –

BODIE. We are coming to her. Perhaps I ought to tell you my name – Mr. Bodie. (*Indicating the Venus.*) This is Mrs. Bodie. No, I am not married. It is merely a name given her because she is my ideal.

POLICEMAN. You gave me a turn.

BODIE. Now that I think of it, I believe the name was given to her by the very woman we are talking about.

POLICEMAN (*producing his note-book*). To begin with, who is the woman we are talking about?

BODIE (*becoming more serious*). On the surface, she is just a little drudge. These studios are looked after by a housekeeper, who employs this girl to do the work.

POLICEMAN. H'm! Sleeps on the premises?

BODIE. No; she is here from eight to six.

POLICEMAN. Place of abode?

BODIE. She won't tell any one that.

POLICEMAN. Aha! What's the party's name?

BODIE. Cinderella.

(*The* POLICEMAN *writes it down unmoved.* MR. BODIE *twinkles.*)

Haven't you heard that name before?

POLICEMAN. Can't say I have, sir. But I'll make inquiries at the Yard.

BODIE. It was really I who gave her that name, because she seemed such a poor little neglected waif. After the girl in the story-book, you know.

POLICEMAN. No, sir, I don't know. In the Force we find it impossible to keep up with current fiction.

BODIE. She was a girl with a broom. There must have been more in the story than that, but I forget the rest.

POLICEMAN. The point is, that's not the name she calls herself by.

BODIE. Yes, indeed it is. I think she was called something else when she came – Miss Thing, or some such name; but she took to the name of Cinderella with avidity, and now she absolutely denies that she ever had any other.

POLICEMAN. Parentage?

BODIE (*now interested in his tale*). That's another odd thing. I seem to remember vaguely her telling me that her parents when alive were very humble persons indeed. Touch of Scotch about her, I should say – perhaps from some distant ancestor; but Scotch words and phrases still stick to the Cockney child like bits of egg-shell to a chicken.

POLICEMAN (*writing*). Egg-shell to chicken.

BODIE. I find, however, that she has lately been telling the housekeeper quite a different story.

POLICEMAN (*like a counsel*). Proceed.

BODIE. According to this, her people were of considerable position – a Baron and Baroness, in fact.

POLICEMAN. Proceed.

BODIE. The only other relatives she seems to have mentioned are two sisters of unprepossessing appearance.

POLICEMAN (*cleverly*). If this story is correct, what is she doing here?

BODIE. I understand there is something about her father having married again, and her being badly treated. She doesn't expect this to last. It seems that she has reason to believe that some very remarkable change may take place in her circumstances at an early date, at a ball for which her godmother is to get her what she calls an invite. This is evidently to be a very swagger function at which something momentous is to occur, the culminating moment being at midnight.

POLICEMAN (*writing*). Godmother. Invite. Twelve P.M.[1] Fishy! Tell me about them boards now.

BODIE (*who is evidently fond of the child*). You can't think how wistful she is to get hold of boards. She has them on the brain. Carries them off herself into the unknown.

POLICEMAN. I dare say she breaks them up for firewood.

BODIE. No; she makes them into large boxes.

POLICEMAN (*sagaciously*). Very likely to keep things in.

BODIE. She has admitted that she keeps things in them. But what things? Ask her that, and her mouth shuts like a trap.

POLICEMAN. Any suspicions?

(MR. BODIE *hesitates. It seems absurd to suspect this waif – and yet!*)

BODIE. I'm sorry to say I have. I don't know what the things are, but I do know they are connected in some way with Germany.

POLICEMAN (*darkly*). Proceed.

BODIE (*really troubled*). Officer, she is too curious about Germany.

POLICEMAN. That's bad.

BODIE. She plies me with questions about it – not openly – very cunningly.

POLICEMAN. Such as – ?

BODIE. For instance, what would be the punishment for an English person caught hiding aliens in this country?

POLICEMAN. If she's up to games of that kind –

BODIE. Does that shed any light on the boxes, do you think?

POLICEMAN. She can't keep them shut up in boxes.

BODIE. I don't know. She is extraordinarily dogged. She knows a number of German words.

POLICEMAN. That's ugly.

BODIE. She asked me lately how one could send a letter to Germany without Lord Haig knowing. By the way, do you, by any chance, know anything against a firm of dressmakers called *Celeste et Cie*?

POLICEMAN. Celest A. C.? No, but it has a German sound.

BODIE. It's French.

POLICEMAN. Might be a blind.

BODIE. I think she lives at Celeste's. Now I looked up Celeste et Cie in the telephone book, and I find they are in Bond Street. Immensely fashionable.

POLICEMAN. She lives in Bond Street? London's full of romance, sir, to them as knows where to look for it – namely, the police. Is she on the premises?

BODIE (*reluctantly*). Sure to be; it isn't six yet.

POLICEMAN (*in his most terrible voice*). Well, leave her to me.

BODIE. You mustn't frighten her. I can't help liking her. She's so extraordinarily *homely* that you can't be with her many minutes before you begin thinking of your early days. Where were you born, officer?

POLICEMAN. I'm from Badgery.

BODIE. She'll make you think of Badgery.

POLICEMAN (*frowning*). She had best try no games on me.

BODIE. She will have difficulty in answering questions; she is so used to asking them. I never knew a child with such an appetite for information. She doesn't search for it in books; indeed the only book of mine I can remember ever seeing her read, was a volume of fairy tales.

POLICEMAN (*stupidly*). Well, that don't help us much. What kind of questions?

BODIE. Every kind. What is the Censor? Who is Lord *Times*? – she has heard people here talking of that paper and its proprietor, and has mixed them up in the quaintest way; then again – when a tailor measures a gentleman's legs what does he mean when he says – 26, 4–32, 11? What are doctors up to when they tell you to say 99? In finance she has an almost morbid interest in the penny.

POLICEMAN. The penny? It's plain the first thing to find out is whether she's the slavey[2] she seems to be, or a swell[3] in disguise.

BODIE. You won't find it so easy.

POLICEMAN. Excuse me, sir; we have an infall*ay*ble way at Scotland Yard of finding out whether a woman is common or a lady.

BODIE (*irritated*). An infallible way.

POLICEMAN (*firmly*). Infallayble.

BODIE. I should like to know what it is.

POLICEMAN. There is nothing against my telling you. (*He settles down to a mas-
terly cross-examination.*) Where, sir, does a common female keep her valu-
ables when she carries them about on her person?

BODIE. In her pocket, I suppose.

POLICEMAN. And you suppose correctly. But where does a lady keep them?

BODIE. In the same place, I suppose.

POLICEMAN. There you suppose wrongly. No, sir, here. (*He taps his own chest, and
indicates discreetly how a lady may pop something down out of sight.*)

BODIE (*impressed*). I believe you are right, officer.

POLICEMAN. I am right – it's infallayble. A lady, what with drink and suchlike
misfortunes, may forget all her other refinements, but she never forgets that.
At the Yard it's considered as sure as finger-marks.

BODIE. Strange! I wonder who was the first woman to do it. It couldn't have been
Eve this time, officer.

POLICEMAN (*after reflecting*). I see your point. And now I want just to have a look
at the party unbeknownst to her. Where could I conceal myself?

BODIE. Hide?

POLICEMAN. Conceal myself.

BODIE. That small door opens on to my pantry, where she washes up.

POLICEMAN (*peeping in*). It will do. Now bring her up.

BODIE. It doesn't seem fair – I really can't –

POLICEMAN. War-time, sir.

(MR. BODIE *decides that it is patriotic to ring. The* POLICEMAN *emerges from the
pantry with a slavey's hat and jacket.*)

These belong to the party, sir?

BODIE. I forgot. She keeps them in there. (*He surveys the articles with some emo-
tion.*) Gaudy feathers. And yet that hat may have done some gallant things.
The brave apparel of the very poor! Who knows, officer, that you and I are not
at this moment on rather holy ground.

POLICEMAN (*stoutly*). I see nothing wrong with the feathers. I must say, sir, I like
the feathers.

(*He slips into the pantry with the hat and jacket, but forgets his helmet, over which
the artist hastily jams a flower bowl. There were visiting-cards in the bowl
and they are scattered on the floor.* MR. BODIE *sees them not: it is his first
attempt at the conspirator, and he sits guiltily with a cigarette just in time to
deceive* CINDERELLA, *who charges into the room as from a catapult. This is
her usual mode of entrance, and is owing to her desire to give satisfaction.*

Our POLICEMAN, *as he has told us under the arches, was watching her through
the keyhole, but his first impressions have been so coloured by subsequent*

events that it is questionable whether they would be accepted in any court of law. Is prepared to depose that, to the best of his recollection, they were unfavourable. Does not imply by unfavourable any aspersion on her personal appearance. Would accept the phrase 'far from striking' as summing up her first appearance. Would no longer accept the phrase. Had put her down as being a grown woman, but not sufficiently grown. Thought her hair looked to be run up her finger. Did not like this way of doing the hair. Could not honestly say that she seemed even then to be an ordinary slavey of the areas. She was dressed as one, but was suspiciously clean. On the other hand, she had the genuine hungry look. Among more disquieting features noticed a sort of refinement in her voice and manner, which was characteristic of the criminal classes. Knew now that this was caused by the reading of fairy tales and the thinking of noble thoughts. Noted speedily that she was a domineering character who talked sixteen to the dozen,[4] and at such times reminded him of funny old ladies. Was much struck by her eyes, which seemed to suggest that she was all burning inside. This impression was strengthened later when he touched her hands. Felt at once the curious 'homeliness' of her, as commented on by MR. BODIE, *but could swear on oath that this had not at once made him think of Badgery. Could recall not the slightest symptoms of love at first sight. On the contrary, listened carefully to the conversation between her and* MR. BODIE *and formed a stern conclusion about her. Believed that this was all he could say about his first impression.)*

CINDERELLA (*breathlessly*). Did you rang, sir?

BODIE (*ashamed*). Did I? I did – but – I – I don't know why. If you're a good servant, you ought to know why.

(*The cigarette, disgusted with him, falls from his mouth; and his little servant flings up her hands to heaven.*)

CINDERELLA (*taking possession of him*). There you go again! Fifty years have you been at it, and you can't hold a seegarette in your mouth *yet*! (*She sternly produces the turpentine.*)

BODIE (*in sudden alarm*). I won't be brushed. I will not be scraped.

CINDERELLA (*twisting him round*). Just look at that tobaccy ash! And I cleaned you up so pretty before luncheon.

BODIE. I will *not* be cleaned again.

CINDERELLA (*in her element*). Keep still.

(*She brushes, scrapes, and turpentines him. In the glory of this she tosses her head at the Venus.*)

I gave Mrs. Bodie a good wipe down this morning with soap and water.

BODIE (*indignant*). That is a little too much. You know quite well I allow no one to touch her.

(CINDERELLA *leaves him and gazes in irritation at the statue.*)

CINDERELLA. What *is* it about the woman?

BODIE (*in his heat forgetting the* POLICEMAN). She is the glory of glories.

CINDERELLA (*who would be willowy if she were long enough*). She's thick.

BODIE. Her measurements are perfection. All women long to be like her, but none ever can be.

CINDERELLA (*insisting*). I suppose that's the reason she has that snigger on her face.

BODIE. That is perhaps the smile of motherhood. Some people think there was once a baby in her arms.

CINDERELLA (*with a new interest in Venus*). Her own?

BODIE. I suppose so.

CINDERELLA. A married woman then?

BODIE (*nonplussed*). Don't ask trivial questions.

CINDERELLA (*generously*). It was clever of you to make her.

BODIE. I didn't make her. I was – forestalled. Some other artist chappie did it. (*He likes his little maid again.*) She was dug up, Cinderella, after lying hidden in the ground for more than a thousand years.

CINDERELLA. And the baby gone?

BODIE (*snapping*). Yes.

CINDERELLA. If I had lost my baby I wouldn't have been found with that pleased look on my face, not in a thousand years.

BODIE. Her arms were broken, you see, so she had to drop the baby –

CINDERELLA. She could have up with her knee and catched it –

BODIE (*excitedly*). By heavens, that may just be what she is doing. (*He contemplates a letter to the 'Times.'*)

CINDERELLA (*little aware that she may have solved the question of the ages.*) Beauty's a grand thing.

BODIE. It is.

CINDERELLA. I warrant *she* led them a pretty dance in her day.

BODIE. Men?

CINDERELLA. Umpha! (*Wistfully.*) It must be fine to have men so mad about you that they go off their feed and roar. (*She turns with a sigh to the dusting of the penguin.*) What did you say this is?

BODIE (*ignorant of what he is letting himself in for*). A bishop.

CINDERELLA (*nearly choking*). The sort that marries swell couples?

BODIE. Yes.

CINDERELLA (*huskily, as if it made all the difference to her*). I never thought of that.

BODIE (*kindly*). Why should you, you queer little waif. Do you know why I call you Cinderella?

CINDERELLA. Fine, I know.

BODIE. Why is it?

CINDERELLA (*with shy happiness*). It's because I have such pretty feet.

BODIE. You dear little innocent. (*He thinks shame of his suspicions. He is planning how to get rid of the man in the pantry when she brings him back to hard facts with a bump.*)

CINDERELLA (*in a whisper*). Mr. Bodie, if you wanted to get into Buckingham Palace on the dodge, how would you slip by the policeman? (*She wrings her hands.*) The police is everywhere in war-time.

BODIE (*conscious how near one of them is*). They are – be careful, Cinderella.

CINDERELLA. I am – oh, I am! If you knew the precautions I'm taking –

BODIE (*miserable*). Sh!

CINDERELLA (*now in a quiver*). Mr. Bodie, you haven't by any chance got an invite for to-night, have you?

BODIE. What for?

CINDERELLA (*as still as the Venus*). For – for a ball.

BODIE. There are no balls in war-time.

CINDERELLA (*dogged*). Just the one. Mr. Bodie, did you ever see the King?

BODIE. The King? Several times.

CINDERELLA (*as white as the Venus*). Was the Prince of Wales with him?

BODIE. Once.

CINDERELLA. What's he like?

BODIE. Splendid! Quite young, you know. He's not married.

CINDERELLA (*with awful intensity*). No, not yet.

BODIE. I suppose he is very difficult to satisfy.

CINDERELLA (*knitting her lips*). He has never seen the feet that pleased him.

BODIE. Cinderella, your pulse is galloping. You frighten me. What possesses you?

CINDERELLA (*after hesitating*). There is something I want to tell you. Maybe I'll not be coming back after to-night. She has paid me up to to-night.

BODIE. Is she sending you away?

CINDERELLA. No. I've sort of given notice.

BODIE (*disappointed*). You've got another place?

(*She shuts her mouth like a box.*)

Has it anything to do with the Godmother business?

(*Her mouth remains closed. He barks at her.*)

Don't then. (*He reconsiders her.*) I like you, you know.

CINDERELLA (*gleaming*). It's fine to be liked.

BODIE. Have you a lonely life?

CINDERELLA. It's kind of lonely.

BODIE. You won't tell me about your home?

(*She shakes her head.*)

Is there any nice person to look after you in the sort of way in which you look after me?

CINDERELLA. I'm all alone. There's just me and my feet.

BODIE. If you go I'll miss you. We've had some good times here, Cinderella, haven't we?

CINDERELLA (*rapturously*). We have! You mind that chop you gave me? Hey, hey, hey! (*Considering it judicially.*) That was the most charming chop I ever saw. And many is the lick of soup you've given me when you thought I looked down-like. Do you mind the chicken that was too high for you? You give me the whole chicken. That was a day.

BODIE. I never meant you to eat it.

CINDERELLA. I didn't eat it all myself. I shared it with them.

BODIE (*inquisitively*). With them? With whom?

(*Her mouth shuts promptly, and he sulks. She picks up the visiting-cards that litter the floor.*)

CINDERELLA. What a spill! If you're not messing you're spilling. Where's the bowl?

(*She lifts the bowl and discovers the helmet. She is appalled.*)

BODIE (*in an agony of remorse pointing to the door*). Cinderella, quick!

(*But our* POLICEMAN *has emerged and barred the way*).

POLICEMAN (*indicating that it is* MR. BODIE *who must go*). If *you* please, sir.

BODIE. I won't! Don't you dare to frighten her.

POLICEMAN (*settling the matter with the palm of his hand*). That will do. If I need you I'll call you.

BODIE (*flinching*). Cinderella, it's – it's just a form. I won't be far away.

(*He departs reluctantly.*)

POLICEMAN (*sternly*). Stand up.

CINDERELLA (*a quaking figure, who has never sat down*). I'm standing up.

POLICEMAN. Now, no sauce.

(*He produces his note-book. He is about to make a powerful beginning when he finds her eyes regarding the middle of his person.*)

Now then, what are you staring at?

CINDERELLA (*hotly*). That's a poor way to polish a belt. If I was a officer I would think shame of having my belt in that condition.

POLICEMAN (*undoubtedly affected by her homeliness though unconscious of it*). It's easy to speak; it's a miserable polish I admit, but mind you, I'm pretty done when my job's over; and I have the polishing to do myself.

CINDERELLA. You have no woman person?

POLICEMAN. Not me.

CINDERELLA (*with passionate arms*). If I had that belt for half an hour!

POLICEMAN. What would you use?

CINDERELLA. Spit.

POLICEMAN. Spit? That's like what my mother would have said. That was in Badgery, where I was born. When I was a boy at Badgery –

(*He stops short. She has reminded him of Badgery!*)

CINDERELLA. What's wrong?

POLICEMAN (*heavily*). How did you manage that about Badgery?

CINDERELLA. What?

POLICEMAN. Take care, prisoner.

(*The word makes her shudder. He sits, prepared to take notes.*)

Name?

CINDERELLA. Cinderella.

POLICEMAN. Take care, Thing. Occupation, if any?

CINDERELLA (*with some pride*). Tempary help.

POLICEMAN. Last place?

CINDERELLA. 3 Robert Street.

POLICEMAN. Scotch?

(*Her mouth shuts.*)

Ah, they'll never admit that. Reason for leaving?

CINDERELLA. I had to go when the war broke out.

POLICEMAN. Why dismissed?

CINDERELLA (*forlorn*). They said I was a luxury.

POLICEMAN (*getting ready to pounce*). Now be cautious. How do you spend your evenings after you leave this building?

(*Her mouth shuts.*)

Have you another and secret occupation?

(*She blanches.*)

Has it to do with boxes? What do you keep in those boxes? Where is it that these goings-on is going on? If you won't tell me, I'm willing to tell you. It's at A. C. Celest's . . . In Bond Street, W.

(*He has levelled his finger at her, but it is a pistol that does not go off. To his chagrin she looks relieved. He tries hammer blows.*)

Are you living in guilty splendour? How do you come to know German words? How many German words do you think *I* know? Just one, *espionage*. What's the German for 'six months hard'?

(*She is now crumpled, and here he would do well to pause and stride up and down the room. But he cannot leave well alone.*)

What's this nonsense about your feet?

CINDERELLA (*plucking up courage*). It's not nonsense.

POLICEMAN. I see nothing particular about your feet.

CINDERELLA. Then I'm sorry for you.

POLICEMAN. What is it?

CINDERELLA (*softly as if it were a line from the Bible*). Their exquisite smallness and perfect shape.

POLICEMAN (*with a friendly glance at the Venus*). For my part I'm partial to big women with their noses in the air.

CINDERELLA (*stung*). So is everybody. (*Pathetically.*) I've tried. But it's none so easy, with never no butcher's meat in the house. You'll see where the su-perb shoulders and the haughty manners come from if you look in shop windows and see the whole of a cow turned inside out and 'Delicious' printed on it.

POLICEMAN (*always just*). There's something in that.

CINDERELLA (*swelling*). But it doesn't matter how fine the rest of you is if you doesn't have small feet.

POLICEMAN. I never give feet a thought.

CINDERELLA. The swells think of nothing else. (*Exploding.*) Wait till you are at the Ball. Many a haughty beauty with superb uppers will come sailing in – as sure of the prize as if 'Delicious' was pinned on her – and then forward steps the Lord Mayor, and, *utterly disregarding her uppers*, he points to the bottom of her skirt, and he says 'Lift!' and she *has* to lift, and there's a dead silence, and nothing to be heard except the Prince crying 'Throw her out!'

POLICEMAN (*somewhat staggered by her knowledge of the high life*). What's all this about a ball?

(CINDERELLA *sees she has said too much and her mouth shuts.*)

Was you ever at a ball?

CINDERELLA (*with dignity*). At any rate I've been at the Horse Show.

POLICEMAN. A ball's not like a Horse Show.

CINDERELLA. You'll see.

POLICEMAN (*reverting to business*). It all comes to this, are you genteel, or common clay?

CINDERELLA (*pertly*). I leaves that to you.

POLICEMAN. You couldn't leave it in safer hands. I want a witness to this.

CINDERELLA (*startled*). A witness! What are you to do?

(*With terrible self-confidence he has already opened the door and beckoned.* MR. BODIE *comes in anxiously.*)

POLICEMAN. Take note, sir. (*With the affable manner of a conjurer.*) We are now about to try a little experiment, the object being to discover whether this party is genteel or common clay.

CINDERELLA. Oh, Mr. Bodie, what is it?

BODIE (*remembering what he has been told of the Scotland Yard test*). I don't like . . . I won't have it.

POLICEMAN. It gives her the chance of proving once and for all whether she's of gentle blood.

CINDERELLA (*eagerly*). Does it?

BODIE. I must forbid . . .

CINDERELLA (*with dreadful resolution*). I'm ready. I wants to know myself.

POLICEMAN. *Ve* – ry well. Now then, I heard you say that the old party downstairs had paid you your wages to-day.

CINDERELLA. I see nothing you can prove by that. It was a half-week's wages – 1s. 7d. Of course I could see my way clearer if it had been 1s. 9d.

POLICEMAN. That's neither here nor there. We'll proceed. Now, very likely you wrapped the money up in a screw of paper. Did you?

(*She is afraid of giving herself away.*)

Thinking won't help you.

CINDERELLA. It's *my* money.

BODIE. Nobody wants your money, Cinderella.

POLICEMAN. Answer me. Did you?

CINDERELLA. Yes.

POLICEMAN. Say 'I did.'

CINDERELLA. I did.

POLICEMAN. And possibly for the sake of greater security you tied a string round it – did you?

CINDERELLA. I did.

POLICEMAN (*after a glance at* MR. BODIE *to indicate that the supreme moment has come*). You then deposited the little parcel – where?

BODIE (*in an agony*). Cinderella, be careful!

(*She is so dreading to do the wrong thing that she can only stare. Finally, alas, she produces the fatal packet from her pocket. Quiet triumph of our* POLICEMAN.)

BODIE. My poor child!

CINDERELLA (*not realising yet that she has given herself away*). What is it? Go on.

POLICEMAN. That'll do. You can stand down.

CINDERELLA. You've found out?

POLICEMAN. I have.

CINDERELLA (*breathless*). And what am I?

POLICEMAN (*kindly*). I'm sorry.

CINDERELLA. Am I – common clay?

(*They look considerately at the floor; she bursts into tears and runs into the pantry, shutting the door.*)

POLICEMAN (*with melancholy satisfaction*). It's infallayble.

BODIE. At any rate it shows that there's nothing against her.

POLICEMAN (*taking him further from the pantry door, in a low voice*). I dunno. There's some queer things. Where does she go when she leaves this house? What about that ball? – and her German connection? – and them boards she makes into boxes – and A. C. Celest? Well, I'll find out.

BODIE (*miserably*). What are you going to do?

POLICEMAN. To track her when she leaves here. I may have to adopt a disguise. I'm a masterpiece at that.

BODIE. Yes, but –

POLICEMAN (*stamping about the floor with the exaggerated tread of the Law*). I'll tell you the rest outside. I must make her think that my suspicions are – allayed. (*He goes cunningly to the pantry door and speaks in a loud voice.*) Well, sir, that satisfies me that she's not the party I was in search of, and so, with your permission, I'll bid you good evening. What, you're going out yourself? Then I'll be very happy to walk part of the way with you.

(*Nodding and winking, he goes off with heavy steps, taking with him the reluctant* MR. BODIE, *who like one mesmerised also departs stamping.*

MISS THING *peeps out to make sure that they are gone. She is wearing her hat and jacket, which have restored her self-respect. The tears have been disposed of with a lick of the palm. She is again a valiant soul who has had too many brushes with the police not to be able to face another with a tight lip. She is going, but she is not going without her wooden board; law or no law she cannot do without wooden boards. She gets it from a corner where it has been artfully concealed. An imprudent glance at the Venus again dispirits her. With a tape she takes the Beauty's measurements and then her own, with*

90

depressing results. The Gods at last pity her, and advise an examination of her rival's foot. Excursions, alarms, transport. She compares feet and is glorified. She slips off her shoe and challenges Venus to put it on. Then, with a derisive waggle of her foot at the shamed goddess, the little enigma departs on her suspicious business, little witting that a masterpiece of a constable is on her track.)

II

It is later in the evening of the same day, and this is such a street as harbours London's poor. The windows are so close to us that we could tap on the only one which shows a light. It is on the ground floor, and makes a gallant attempt to shroud this light with articles of apparel suspended within. Seen as shadows through the blind, these are somehow very like Miss Thing, and almost suggest that she has been hanging herself in several places in one of her bouts of energy. The street is in darkness, save for the meagre glow from a street lamp, whose glass is painted red in obedience to war regulations. It is winter time, and there is a sprinkling of snow on the ground.

Our policeman appears in the street, not perhaps for the first time this evening, and flashes his lantern on the suspect's window, whose signboard (boards again!) we now see bears this odd device,

Celeste et Cie.
The Penny Friend.

Not perhaps for the first time this evening he scratches his head at it. Then he pounds off in pursuit of some client who has just emerged with a pennyworth. We may imagine the two of them in conversation in the next street, the law putting leading questions. Meanwhile the 'fourth' wall of the establishment of Celeste dissolves, but otherwise the street is as it was, and we are now in the position of privileged persons looking in at her window. It is a tiny room in which you could just swing a cat,[5] and here Cinderella swings cats all and every evening. The chief pieces of furniture are a table and a bench, both of which have a suspicious appearance of having been made out of boards by some handy character. There is a penny in the slot fireplace which has evidently been lately fed, there is a piece of carpet that has been beaten into nothingness, but is still a carpet, there is a hearth-rug of brilliant rags that is probably gratified when your toes catch in it and you are hurled against the wall. Two pictures – one of them partly framed – strike a patriotic note, but they may be there purposely to deceive. The room is lit by a lamp, and at first sight presents no sinister aspect unless it comes from four boxes nailed against the walls some five or six feet from the floor. In appearance they are not dissimilar to large grocery boxes, but it is disquieting to note that one of them has been mended with the board we saw lately in Mr. Bodie's studio. When our policeman comes, as come we may be sure he will, the test of his acumen will be his box action.

The persons in the room at present have either no acumen or are familiar with the boxes. There are four of them, besides Cinderella, whom we catch in the act of adding to her means of livelihood. Celeste et Cie, a name that has caught her delicate fancy while she dashed through fashionable quarters, is the Penny Friend because here everything is dispensed for that romantic coin. It is evident that the fame of the emporium has spread. Three would-be customers sit on the bench awaiting their turn listlessly and as genteelly unconscious of each other as society in a dentist's dining-room, while in the centre is Cinderella fitting an elderly gentleman with a new coat. There are pins in her mouth and white threads in the coat, suggesting that this is not her first struggle with it, and one of the difficulties with which she has to contend is that it has already evidently been the coat of a larger man. Cinderella is far too astute a performer to let it be seen that she has difficulties, however. She twists and twirls her patron with careless aptitude, kneads him if need be, and has him in a condition of pulp while she mutters for her own encouragement and his intimidation the cryptic remarks employed by tailors, as to the exact meaning of which she has already probed Mr. Bodie.

CINDERELLA (*wandering over her client with a tape*). 35–14. (*She consults a paper on the table.*) Yes, it's 35–14.

(*She pulls him out, contracts him and takes his elbows measure.*)

28–7; 41–12; 15–19. (*There is something wrong, and she has to justify her handiwork.*) You was longer when you came on Monday.

GENTLEMAN (*very moved by the importance of the occasion*). Don't be saying that, Missy.

CINDERELLA (*pinning up the tails of his coat*). Keep still.

GENTLEMAN (*with unexpected spirit*). I warns you, Missy, I won't have it cut.

CINDERELLA (*an artist*). I'll give you the bits.

GENTLEMAN. I prefers to wear them.

(*She compares the coat with the picture of an elegant dummy.*)

Were you going to make me like that picture?

CINDERELLA. I had just set my heart on copying this one. It's the Volupty.

GENTLEMAN (*faint-hearted*). I'm thinkin' I couldn't stand like that man.

CINDERELLA (*eagerly*). Fine you could – with just a little practice. I'll let you see the effect.

(*She bends one of his knees, extends an arm and curves the other till he looks like a graceful teapot. She puts his stick in one hand and his hat in the other, and he is now coquettishly saluting a lady.*)

GENTLEMAN (*carried away as he looks at himself in a glass*). By Gosh! Cut away, Missy!

CINDERELLA. I'll need one more try-on. (*Suddenly.*) That's to say if I'm here.

GENTLEMAN (*little understanding the poignancy of the remark*). If it would be convenient to you to have the penny now –

CINDERELLA. No, not till I've earned it. It's my rule. Good night to you, Mr. Jennings.

GENTLEMAN. Good night, Missy.

(*We see him go out by the door and disappear up the street.*)

CINDERELLA (*sharply*). Next.

(*An old woman comes to the table and* CINDERELLA *politely pretends not to have seen her sitting there.*)

It's Mrs. Maloney!

MRS. M. Cinders, I have a pain. It's like a jag of a needle down my side.

CINDERELLA (*with a sinking, for she is secretly afraid of medical cases*). Wait till I pop the therm-mo-mometer in. It's a real one. (*She says this with legitimate pride. She removes the instrument from* MRS. MALONEY'S *mouth after a prudent interval, and is not certain what to do next.*)

Take a deep breath. . . . Again. . . . Say 99. (*Her ear is against the patient's chest.*)

MRS. M. 99.

CINDERELLA (*at a venture*). Oho!

MRS. M. It ain't there the pain is – it's down my side.

CINDERELLA (*firmly*). We never say 99 down there.

MRS. M. What's wrong wi' me?

CINDERELLA (*candidly*). I don't want for to pretend, Mrs. Maloney, that the 99 is any guidance to me. I can *not* find out what it's for. I would make so bold as to call your complaint muscular rheumatics if the pain came when you coughed. But you have no cough.

MRS. M. (*coming to close quarters*). No, but he has – my old man. It's him that has the pains, not me.

CINDERELLA (*hurt*). What for did you pretend it was you?

MRS. M. That was his idea. He was feared you might stop his smoking.

CINDERELLA. And so I will.

MRS. M. What's the treatment?

CINDERELLA (*writing after consideration on a piece of paper*). One of them mustard leaves.

MRS. M. (*taking the paper*). Is there no medicine?

CINDERELLA (*faltering*). I'm a little feared about medicine, Mrs. Maloney.

MRS. M. He'll be a kind of low-spirited if there's not a lick of medicine.

CINDERELLA. Have you any in the house?

MRS. M. There's what was left over of the powders my lodger had when the kettle fell on his foot.

CINDERELLA. You could give him one of them when the eough is troublesome. Good night, Mrs. Maloney.

MRS. M. Thank you kindly. (*She puts a penny on the table.*)

CINDERELLA (*with polite surprise*). What's that?

MRS. M. It's the penny.

CINDERELLA. So it is! Good night, Mrs. Maloney.

MRS. M. Good night, Cinders.

(*She departs. The penny falls into* CINDERELLA'S *box with a pleasant clink.*)

CINDERELLA. Next.

(*A woman of* 35 *comes forward. She is dejected, thin-lipped, and unlovable.*)

MARION (*tossing her head*). You're surprised to see *me*, I dare say.

CINDERELLA (*guardedly*). I haven't the pleasure of knowing you.

MARION (*glancing at the remaining occupant of the bench*). Is that man sleeping? Who is he? I don't know him.

CINDERELLA. He's sleeping. What can I do for you?

MARION (*harshly*). Nothing, I dare say. I'm at Catullo's Buildings. Now they're turning me out. They say I'm not respectable.

CINDERELLA (*enlightened*). You're – that woman?

MARION (*defiantly*). That's me.

CINDERELLA (*shrinking*). I don't think there's nothing I could do for you.

MARION (*rather appealing*). Maybe there is. I see you've heard my story. They say there's a man comes to see me at times though he has a wife in Hoxton.

CINDERELLA. I've heard.

MARION. So I'm being turned out.

CINDERELLA. I don't think it's a case for me.

MARION. Yes, it is.

CINDERELLA. Are you terrible fond of him?

MARION. Fond of him! Damn him!

(CINDERELLA *shrinks.* MARION *makes sure that the man is asleep.*)

Cinders, they've got the story wrong; it's me as is his wife; I was married to him in a church. He met that woman long after and took up with her.

CINDERELLA. What! Then why do you not tell the truth?

MARION. It's my pride keeps me from telling. I would rather be thought to be the wrong 'un he likes than the wife the law makes him help.

CINDERELLA. Is that pride?

MARION. It's all the pride that's left to me.

CINDERELLA. I'm awful sorry for you, but I can't think of no advice to give you.

MARION. It's not advice I want.

CINDERELLA. What is it then?

MARION. It's pity. I fling back all the gutter words they fling at me, but my heart, Cinders, is wet at times. It's wet for one to pity me.

CINDERELLA. I pity you.

MARION. You'll tell nobody?

CINDERELLA. No.

MARION. Can I come in now and again at a time?

CINDERELLA. I'll be glad to see you – if I'm here.

MARION. I'll be slipping away now; he's waking up. (*She puts down her penny.*)

CINDERELLA. I'm not doing it for no penny.

MARION. You've got to take it. That's my pride. But – I wish you well, Cinders.

CINDERELLA. I like you. I wish you would wish me luck. Say 'Good luck to you to-night, Cinderella.'

MARION. Why to-night?

(*The little waif, so practical until now, is afire inside again. She needs a confidant almost as much as* MARION.)

CINDERELLA (*hastily*). You see –

(*The* MAN *sits up.*)

Good evening, Missis.

MARION. Good luck to you to-night, Cinderella.

(*She goes.*)

(*The* MAN *slips forward and lifts the penny.*)

CINDERELLA (*returning to earth sharply*). Put that down.

MAN. I was only looking at the newness of it. I was just admiring the design.

(*The newness and the design both disappear into the box. A bearded person wearing the overalls of a seafaring man lurches down the street and enters the emporium. Have we seen him before? Who can this hairy monster be?*)

POLICEMAN (*in an incredibly gruff voice*). I want a pennyworth.

CINDERELLA (*unsuspecting*). Sit down. (*She surveys the coster.*) It's you that belongs to the shirt, isn't it?

MAN. Yes; is't ready?

CINDERELLA. It's ready.

(*It proves to be not a shirt, but a 'front' of linen, very stiff and starched. The laundress cautiously retains possession of it.*)

The charge is a penny.

MAN. On delivery.

CINDERELLA. Before delivery.

MAN. Surely you can trust me.

CINDERELLA. You've tried that on before, my man. Never again! All in this street knows my rule, – Trust in the Lord – every other person, cash.

(*A penny and a 'shirt' pass between them and he departs.*)

CINDERELLA *turns her attention to the newcomer.*)

What's your pleasure?

POLICEMAN. Shave, please.

CINDERELLA (*quivering before his beard*). Shave! I shaves in an ordinary way, but I don't know as I could tackle that.

POLICEMAN. I thought you was a barber.

CINDERELLA (*stung*). I'll get the lather.

(*She goes doubtfully into what she calls her bedroom.*

He seizes this opportunity to survey the room. A remarkable man this, his attention is at once riveted on the boxes, but before he can step on a chair and take a peep the barber returns with the implements of her calling. He reaches his chair in time not to be caught by her. She brings a bowl of soap and water and a towel, which she puts round him in the correct manner.)

CINDERELLA. You're thin on the top.

POLICEMAN (*in his winding sheet*). I've all run to beard.

CINDERELLA (*the ever ready*). I have a ointment for the hair; it is my own invention. The price is a penny.

POLICEMAN (*gruffly*). Beard, please.

CINDERELLA. I've got some voice drops.

POLICEMAN. Beard, please.

CINDERELLA (*as she prepares the lather*). Is the streets quiet?

POLICEMAN (*cunningly*). Hereabouts they are; but there's great doings in the fashionable quarters. A ball, I'm told.

CINDERELLA (*gasping*). You didn't see no peculiar person about in this street?

POLICEMAN. How peculiar?

CINDERELLA. Like a – a flunkey?[6]

POLICEMAN. Did I now – or did I not?

CINDERELLA (*eagerly*). He would be carrying an invite maybe; it's a big card.

POLICEMAN. I can't say I saw him.

(*Here an astonishing thing happens. The head of a child rises from one of the boxes. She is unseen by either of the mortals.*)

CINDERELLA (*considering the beard*). How do I start with the like of this?

POLICEMAN. First you saws . . .

(*She attempts to saw. The beard comes off in her hand.*)

CINDERELLA (*recognising his face*). You!

POLICEMAN (*stepping triumphantly out of his disguise*). Me!

(*As sometimes happens, however, the one who means to give the surprise gets a greater. At sight of his dreaded uniform the child screams, whereat two other children in other boxes bob up and scream also. It is some time before the policeman can speak.*)

So that's what the boxes was for!

CINDERELLA (*feebly*). Yes.

POLICEMAN (*portentously*). Who and what are these phenomenons?

CINDERELLA (*protectingly*). Don't be frightened, children. Down!

(*They disappear obediently.*)

There's no wrong in it. They're just me trying to do my bit. It's said all should do their bit in war-time. It was into a hospital I wanted to go to nurse the wounded soldiers. I offered myself at every hospital door, but none would have me, so this was all I could do.

POLICEMAN. You're taking care of them?

(*She nods.*)

Sounds all right. Neighbours' children?

CINDERELLA. The brown box is. She's half of an orphan, her father's a blue-jacket,[7] so, of course, I said I would.

POLICEMAN. You need say no more. I pass little bluejacket.

CINDERELLA. Those other two is allies.[8] She's French – and her's a Belgy. (*Calls.*) Marie-Therese!

(*The French child sits up.*)

Speak your language to the gentleman, Marie-Therese.

MARIE. Bon soir, monsieur – comment portezvous? Je t'aime. (*She curtsies charmingly to him from the box.*)

POLICEMAN. Well, I'm – d!

CINDERELLA. Delphine.

(*The Belgian looks up.*)

Make votre bow.

Gladys.

(*The English child bobs up.*)

A friend, Gladys.

(GLADYS *and the* POLICEMAN *grin to each other.*)

GLADYS. What cheer!

CINDERELLA. Monsieur is a Britain's defender.

MARIE. Oh, la, la! Parlez-vous français, monsieur? Non! I blow you two kisses, Monsieur – the one is to you (*kisses hand*) to keep, the other you will give – (*kisses hand*) to Kitch.

POLICEMAN (*writing*). Sends kiss to Lord Kitchener.

CINDERELLA. She's the one that does most of the talking.

POLICEMAN (*who is getting friendly*). I suppose that other box is an empty.

(CINDERELLA'S *mouth closes.*)

Is that box empty?

CINDERELLA. It's not exactly empty.

POLICEMAN. What's inside?

CINDERELLA. She's the littlest.

(*The children exchange glances and she is severe.*)

Couchy.

(*They disappear.*)

POLICEMAN. An ally?

CINDERELLA. She's – she's – Swiss.

POLICEMAN (*lowering*). Now then!

CINDERELLA. She's not exactly Swiss. You can guess now what she is.

POLICEMAN (*grave*). This puts me in a very difficult position.

CINDERELLA (*beginning to cry*). Nobody would take her. She was left over. I tried not to take her. I'm a patriot, I am. But there she was – left over – and her so terrible little – I couldn't help taking her.

POLICEMAN. I dunno. (*Quite unfairly.*) If her folk had been in your place and you in hers, they would have shown neither mercy nor pity for you.

CINDERELLA (*stoutly*). That makes no difference.

POLICEMAN (*was this the great moment?*). I think there's something uncommon about you.

CINDERELLA (*pleased*). About *me*?

POLICEMAN. I suppose she's sleeping?

CINDERELLA. Not her!

POLICEMAN. What's she doing?

CINDERELLA. She's strafing!

POLICEMAN. Who's she strafing?

CINDERELLA. Very likely you. She misses nobody. You see I've put some barb-wire round her box.

POLICEMAN. I see now.

CINDERELLA. It's not really barb-wire. It's worsted. I was feared the wire would hurt her. But it just makes a difference.

POLICEMAN. How do the others get on with her?

CINDERELLA. I makes them get on with her. Of course there's tongues out, and little things like that.

POLICEMAN. Were the foreign children shy of you at first?

CINDERELLA. Not as soon as they heard my name. 'Oh, are you Cinderella?' they said, in their various languages – and 'when's the ball?' they said.

POLICEMAN. Somebody must have telled them about you.

CINDERELLA (*happy*). Not here. They had heard about me in their foreign lands. Everybody knows Cinderella: it's fine. Even her – (*indicating German*) the moment I mentioned my name – 'Where's your ugly sisters?' says she, looking round.

POLICEMAN. Sisters? It's new to me, your having sisters. (*He produces his note-book.*)

CINDERELLA (*uneasily*). It's kind of staggering to me, too. I haven't been able to manage them yet, but they'll be at the ball.

POLICEMAN. It's queer.

CINDERELLA. It *is* queer.

POLICEMAN (*sitting down with her*). How do you know this ball's to-night?

CINDERELLA. It had to be some night. You see, after I closes my business I have chats with the children about things, and naturally it's mostly about the ball. I put it off as long as I could, but it had to be some night – and this is the night.

POLICEMAN. You mean it's make-believe?

CINDERELLA (*almost fiercely*). None of that!

POLICEMAN (*shaking his head*). I don't like it.

CINDERELLA (*shining*). You wouldn't say that if you heard the blasts on the trumpet and loud roars of 'Make way for the Lady Cinderella!'

(*Three heads pop up again.*)

POLICEMAN. Lady?

CINDERELLA (*in a tremble of exultation*). That's me. That's what you're called at royal balls. Then loud huzzas is heard outside from the excited popu-lace, for by this time the fame of my beauty has spread like wild-fire through the streets, and folks is hanging out at windows and climbing lamp-posts to catch a sight of me.

(*Delight of the children.*)

POLICEMAN. My sakes, you see the whole thing clear!

CINDERELLA. I see it from beginning to end – like as if I could touch it – the gold walls and the throne, and the lamp-posts and the horses.

POLICEMAN. The horses?

CINDERELLA. . . . Well, the competitors. The speeches – everything. If only I had my invite! That wasn't a knock at the door, was it?

POLICEMAN (*so carried away that he goes to see*). No.

CINDERELLA (*vindictively*). I dare say that flunkey's sitting drinking in some public-house.

(*Here* MARIE-THERESE *and* GLADYS, *who have been communicating across their boxes, politely invite the* POLICEMAN *to go away.*)

MARIE. Bonne nuit, Monsieur.

GLADYS. Did you say you was going, Mister?

POLICEMAN. They're wonderful polite.

CINDERELLA. I doubt that's not politeness. The naughties – they're asking you to go away.

POLICEMAN. Oh! (*He rises with hauteur.*)

CINDERELLA. You see we're to have a bite of supper before I start – to celebrate the night.

POLICEMAN. Supper with the kids! When I was a kid in the country at Badgery – You've done it again!

CINDERELLA. Done what?

POLICEMAN (*with that strange feeling of being at home*). I suppose I would be in the way?

CINDERELLA. There's not very much to eat. There's just one for each.

POLICEMAN. I've had my supper.

CINDERELLA (*seeing her way*). Have you? Then I would be very pleased if you would stay.

POLICEMAN. Thank you kindly.

(*She prepares the table for the feast. Eyes sparkle from the boxes.*)

CINDERELLA (*shining*). This is the first party we've ever had. Please keep an eye on the door in case there's a knock.

(*She darts into her bedroom, and her charges are more at their ease.*)

MARIE. (*sitting up, the better to display her nightgown*). Monsieur, Monsieur, voilà!

GLADYS. Cinderella made it out of watching a shop window.

POLICEMAN (*like one who has known his hostess from infancy*). Just like her.

MARIE (*holding up a finger that is adorned with a ring*). Monsieur!

GLADYS (*more practical*). The fire's going out.

POLICEMAN (*recklessly*). In with another penny. (*He feeds the fire with that noble coin.*) Fellow allies, I'm going to take a peep into the German trench! Hah!

(*He stealthily mounts a chair and puts his hand into* GRETCHEN'S *box. We must presume that it is bitten by the invisible occupant, for he withdraws it hurriedly to the hearty delight of the spectators. This mirth changes to rapture as* CINDERELLA *makes a conceited entrance carrying a jug of milk and five hot potatoes in their jackets. Handsomely laden as she is, it is her attire that calls forth the applause. She is now wearing the traditional short brown dress of* CINDERELLA, *and her hair hangs loose. She tries to look modest.*)

CINDERELLA (*displaying herself*). What do you think?

POLICEMAN (*again in Badgery*). Great! Turn round. And I suppose you made it yourself out of a shop window?

CINDERELLA. No, we didn't need no shop window; we all knew exactly what I was wearing when the knock came.

GLADYS. Of course we did.

(*A potato is passed up to each and a cup of milk between two. There is also a delicious saucerful of melted lard into which they dip.* GRETCHEN *is now as much in evidence as the others, and quite as attractive; the fun becomes fast and furious.*)

CINDERELLA (*to* POLICEMAN). A potato?

POLICEMAN. No, I thank you.

CINDERELLA. Just a snack?

POLICEMAN. Thank you.

(*She shares with him.*)

CINDERELLA. A little dip?

POLICEMAN. No, I thank you.

CINDERELLA. Just to look friendly.

POLICEMAN. I thank you. (*Dipping.*) To you, Cinderella.

CINDERELLA. I thank you.

POLICEMAN (*proposing a toast*). The King!

CINDERELLA (*rather consciously*). And the Prince of Wales.

GLADYS. And father.

POLICEMAN. The King, the Prince of Wales, and father.

(*The toast is drunk, dipped and eaten with acclamation.* GLADYS, *uninvited, recites 'The Mariners of England.'* MARIE-THERESE *follows (without waiting for the end) with the Marseillaise, and* GRETCHEN *puts out her tongue at both. Our* POLICEMAN *having intimated that he desires to propose another toast of a more lengthy character, the children are lifted down and placed in their nightgowns at the table.*)

POLICEMAN (*suddenly becoming nervous*). I have now the honour to propose absent friends.

GLADYS (*with an inspiration to which* MARIE-THERESE *bows elegantly*). Vive la France!

POLICEMAN. I mean our friends at the Front. And they have their children, too. Your boxes we know about, but I dare say there's many similar and even queerer places, where the children, the smallest of our allies, are sleeping this night within the sound of shells.

MARIE. La petite Belgique. La pauvre enfant!

DELPHINE (*proudly*). Me!

POLICEMAN. So here's to absent friends –

GLADYS (*with another inspiration*). Absent boxes!

POLICEMAN. Absent boxes! And there's a party we know about who would like uncommon to have the charge of the lot of them – (*looking at* CINDERELLA). And I couples the toast with the name of the said party.

CINDERELLA (*giving a pennyworth for nothing*). Kind friends, it would be pretending of me not to let on that I know I am the party referred to by the last speaker – in far too flattersome words. When I look about me and see just four boxes I am a kind of shamed, but it wasn't very convenient to me to have more. I will now conclude by saying I wish I was the old woman that lived in a shoe, and it doesn't matter how many I had I would have known fine what to do. The end. (*After further diversion.*) It's a fine party. I hope your potato is mealy?

POLICEMAN. I never had a better tatie.

CINDERELLA. Don't spare the skins.

POLICEMAN. But you're eating nothing yourself.

CINDERELLA. I'm not hungry. And, of course, I'll be expected to take a bite at the ball.

(*This reminder of the ball spoils the* POLICEMAN'S *enjoyment.*)

POLICEMAN. I wish – you wasn't so sure of the ball.

GLADYS (*in defence*). Why shouldn't she not be sure of it?

DELPHINE. Pourquoi, Monsieur?

CINDERELLA (*rather hotly*). Don't say things like that here.

MARIE. Has Monsieur by chance seen God-mamma coming?

POLICEMAN. God-mamma?

CINDERELLA. That's my Godmother; she brings my ball dress and a carriage with four ponies.

GLADYS. Then away she goes to the ball – hooray – hooray!

CINDERELLA. It's all perfectly simple once Godmother comes.

POLICEMAN (*with unconscious sarcasm*). I can see she's important.

CINDERELLA (*with the dreadful sinking that comes to her at times.*) You think she'll come, don't you?

POLICEMAN. Cinderella, your hand's burning – and in this cold room.

CINDERELLA. Say you think she'll come.

POLICEMAN. I – well, I . . . I . . .

GLADYS (*imploringly*). Say it, Mister!

DELPHINE (*begging*). Monsieur! Monsieur!

MARIE. If it is that you love me, Monsieur!

POLICEMAN (*in distress*). I question if there was ever before a member of the Force in such a position. (*Yielding.*) I expect she'll come.

(*This settles it in the opinion of the children, but their eyes are too bright for such a late hour, and they are ordered to bed. Our* POLICEMAN *replaces them in their boxes.*)

CINDERELLA. One – two – three . . . couchy! (*They disappear.*)

POLICEMAN (*awkwardly and trying to hedge*). Of course this is an out-of-the-way little street for a Godmother to find.

CINDERELLA. Yes, I've thought of that. I'd best go and hang about outside; she would know me by my dress.

POLICEMAN (*hastily*). I wouldn't do that. It's a cold night. (*He wanders about the room eyeing her sideways.*) Balls is always late things.

CINDERELLA. I'm none so sure. In wartime, you see, with the streets so dark and the King so kind, it would be just like him to begin early and close at ten instead of twelve. I must leave before twelve. If I don't, there's terrible disasters happens.

POLICEMAN (*unable to follow this*). The ball might be put off owing to the Prince of Wales being in France.

CINDERELLA. He catched the last boat. I'll go out and watch.

POLICEMAN (*desperate*). Stay where you are, and – and I'll have a look for her.

CINDERELLA. You're too kind.

POLICEMAN. Not at all. I must be stepping at any rate. If I can lay hands on her I'll march her here, though I have to put the handcuffs on her.

GLADYS (*looking up*). I think I heard a knock!

(*The* POLICEMAN *looks out, shakes his head, and finally departs after a queer sort of handshake with* MISS THING.)

CINDERELLA. He's a nice man.

GLADYS. Have you known him long?

CINDERELLA (*thinking it out*). A longish time. He's head of the secret police; him and me used to play together as children down in Badgery. His folks live in a magnificent castle, with two doors. (*She becomes a little bewildered.*) I'm all mixed up.

(*The children are soon asleep. She wanders aimlessly to the door. The wall closes on the little room, and we now see her standing in the street. Our* POLICEMAN *returns and flashes his lantern on her.*)

CINDERELLA. It's you!

POLICEMAN. It's me. But there's no Godmother. There's not a soul . . . No. . . . Good-night, Cinderella. Go inside.

CINDERELLA (*doggedly*). Not me! I don't feel the cold – not much. And one has to take risks to get a Prince. The only thing I'm feared about is my feet. If they was to swell I mightn't be able to get the slippers on, and he would have naught to do with me.

POLICEMAN. What slippers? If you won't go back, I'll stop here with you.

CINDERELLA. No, I think there's more chance of her coming if I'm alone.

POLICEMAN. I'm very troubled about you.

CINDERELLA (*wistfully*). Do you think I'm just a liar? Maybe I am. You see I'm all mixed up. I'm sore in need of somebody to help me out.

POLICEMAN. I would do it if I could.

CINDERELLA. I'm sure. (*Anxiously.*) Are you good at riddles?

(*He shakes his head.*)

There's always a riddle before you can marry into a royal family.

POLICEMAN (*with increased gloom*). The whole thing seems to be most terrible difficult.

CINDERELLA. Yes. . . . Good-night.

POLICEMAN. You won't let me stay with you?

CINDERELLA. No.

(*He puts his lantern on the ground beside her.*)

What's that for?

POLICEMAN (*humbly*). It's just a sort of guard for you. (*He takes off his muffler and puts it several times round her neck.*)

CINDERELLA. Nice!

POLICEMAN. Good luck.

(*She finds it easiest just to nod in reply.*)

I wish I was a Prince.

CINDERELLA (*suddenly struck by the idea*). You're kind of like him.

(*He goes away. She sits down on the step to wait. She shivers. She takes the muffler off her neck and winds it round her more valuable feet. She falls asleep.*

Darkness comes, and snow. From somewhere behind, the shadowy figure of CINDER-ELLA'S *Godmother, beautiful in a Red Cross Nurse's uniform, is seen looking benignantly on the waif.* CINDERELLA *is just a little vague, huddled form – there is no movement.*)

GODMOTHER. Cinderella, my little godchild!

CINDERELLA (*with eyes unopening*). Is that you, Godmother?

GODMOTHER. It is I; my poor god-daughter is all mixed up, and I have come to help her out.

CINDERELLA. You have been long in coming. I very near gave you up.

GODMOTHER. Sweetheart, I couldn't come sooner, because in these days, you know, even the fairy godmother is with the Red Cross.

CINDERELLA. Was that the reason? I see now; I thought perhaps you kept away because I wasn't a good girl.

GODMOTHER. You have been a good brave girl; I am well pleased with my darling godchild.

CINDERELLA. It is fine to be called darling; it heats me up. I've been wearying for it, Godmother. Life's a kind of hard.

GODMOTHER. It will always be hard to you, Cinderella. I can't promise you anything else.

CINDERELLA. I don't suppose I could have my three wishes, Godmother.

GODMOTHER. I am not very powerful in these days, Cinderella; but what are your wishes?

CINDERELLA. I would like fine to have my ball, Godmother.

GODMOTHER. You shall have your ball.

CINDERELLA. I would like to nurse the wounded.

GODMOTHER. You shall nurse the wounded.

CINDERELLA. I would like to be loved by the man of my choice, Godmother.

GODMOTHER. You shall be loved by the man of your choice.

CINDERELLA. Thank you kindly. The ball first, if you please, and could you squeeze in the children so that they may see me in my glory.

GODMOTHER. Now let this be my downtrodden godchild's ball, not as balls are, but as they are conceived to be in a little chamber in Cinderella's head.

103

(She fades from sight. In the awful stillness we can now hear the tiny clatter of horses infinitely small and infinitely far off. It is the equipage of CINDERELLA. *Then an unearthly trumpet sounds thrice, and the darkness is blown away.*

It is the night of the most celebrated ball in history, and we see it through our heroine's eyes. She has, as it were, made everything with her own hands, from the cloths of gold to the ices.

Nearly everything in the ball-room is of gold: it was only with an effort that she checked herself from dabbing gold on the regal countenances. You can see that she has not passed by gin-palaces without thinking about them. The walls and furniture are so golden that you have but to lean against them to acquire a competency. There is a golden throne with gold cloths on it, and the royal seats are three golden rocking chairs; there would be a fourth golden rocking chair if it were not that CINDERELLA *does not want you to guess where she is to sit. These chairs are stuffed to a golden corpulency. The panoply of the throne is about twenty feet high – each foot of pure gold; and nested on the top of it is a golden reproduction of the grandest thing* CINDERELLA *has ever seen – the private box of a theatre. In this box sit, wriggle, and sprawl the four children in their nightgowns, leaning over the golden parapet as if to the manner born and carelessly kicking nuggets out of it. They are shouting, pointing, and otherwise behaving badly, eating oranges out of paper bags, then blowing out the bags and bursting them. The superb scene is lit by four street lamps with red glass. Dancing is going on: the ladies all in white, the gentlemen in black with swords. If you were unused to royal balls you would think every one of these people was worth describing separately; but, compared to what is coming, it may be said that* CINDERELLA *has merely pushed them on with her lovely foot. They are her idea of courtiers, and have anxious expressions as if they knew she was watching them. They have character in the lump, if we may put it that way, but none individually. Thus one cannot smile or sigh, for instance, without all the others smiling or sighing. At night they probably sleep in two large beds, one for ladies and one for gentlemen, and if one of the ladies, say, wants to turn round, she gives the signal, and they all turn simultaneoulsy. As children they were not like this; they had genuine personal traits, but these have gradually been blotted out as they basked in royal favour; thus, if the* KING *wipes his glasses they all pretend that their glasses need wiping, and when the* QUEEN *lets her handkerchief fall they all stoop loyally to pick up their own.*

Down the golden steps at the back comes the LORD MAYOR, *easily recognisable by his enormous chain.)*

LORD MAYOR. O yes, O yes, make way every one for the Lord Mayor – namely myself.

(They all make way for him. Two black boys fling open lovely curtains.)

O yes, O yes, make way every one, and also myself, for Lord Times.

(This is a magnificent person created by CINDERELLA *on learning from* MR. BODIE *that the press is all powerful and that the 'Times' is the press. He carries one*

hand behind his back, as if it might be too risky to show the whole of himself at once, and it is noticeable that as he walks his feet do not quite touch the ground. He is the only person who is not a little staggered by the amount of gold: you almost feel that he thinks there is not quite enough of it. He very nearly sits down on one of the royal rocking chairs: and the LORD MAYOR, *looking red and unhappy, and as if he had now done for himself, has to whisper to him that the seats under the throne are reserved.*)

O yes, O yes, make way for the Censor.[9]

(CINDERELLA *has had a good deal of trouble over this person, of whom she has heard a great deal in war-time, without meeting any one who can tell her what he is like. She has done her best, and he is long and black and thin, dressed as tightly as a fish, and carries an executioner's axe. All fall back from him in fear, except* LORD TIMES, *who takes a step forward, and then the* CENSOR *falls back.*)

O yes, O yes, make way everybody for his Royal Highness the King, and his good lady the Queen.

(*The* KING *and* QUEEN *are attired like their portraits on playing cards, who are the only royalties* CINDERELLA *has seen, and they advance grandly to their rocking chairs, looking as if they thought the whole public was dirt, but not so much despised dirt as dirt with good points.* LORD TIMES *fixes them with his eye, and the* KING *hastily crosses and shakes hands with him.*)

O yes, O yes, Make way every one, except the King, and Queen, and Lord Times, for His Highness Prince Hard-to-Please.

(*The heir apparent comes, preceded by trumpeters. His dress may a little resemble that of the extraordinary youth seen by* CINDERELLA *in her only pantomime, but what quite takes our breath away is his likeness to our* POLICEMAN. *If the ball had taken place a night earlier it may be hazarded that the* PRINCE *would have presented quite a different face. It is as if* CINDERELLA'S *views of his personality had undergone some unaccountable change, confusing even to herself, and for a moment the whole scene rocks, the street lamps wink, and odd shadows stalk among the courtiers, shadows of* MR. BODIE, MARION, *and the party in an unfinished coat, who have surely no right to be here. This is only momentarily; then the palace steadies itself again.*

The KING *rises, and in stately manner addresses his guests in the words* CINDERELLA *conceives to be proper to his royal mouth. As he stands waiting superbly for the applause to cease, he holds on to a strap hanging conveniently above his head. To* CINDERELLA *strap-hanging on the Underground has been a rare and romantic privilege.*)

KING. My loyal subjects, all 'ail! I am as proud of you as you are of me. It gives me and my good lady much pleasure to see you 'ere by special invite, feasting at our expense. There is a paper bag for each, containing two sandwiches, buttered on both sides, a piece of cake, a hard-boiled egg, and an orange or a banana.

(*The cheers of the delighted courtiers gratify him, but the vulgar children over his head continue their rub-a-dub on the parapet until he glares up at them. Even then they continue.*)

Ladies and Gents all, pleasant though it is to fill up with good victuals, that is not the chief object of this royal invite. We are 'ere for a solemn purpose, namely, to find a mate for our noble son. All the Beauties are waiting in the lobby: no wonder he is excited.

(*All look at the* PRINCE, *who is rocking and yawning.*)

He will presently wake up; but first I want to say – (*here he becomes conscious of* LORD TIMES). What is it?

LORD TIMES. Less talk.

KING. Certainly. (*He sits down.*)

PRINCE (*encouraged to his feet by various royal nudges*). My liege King and Queen-Mother, you can have the competitors brought in, and I will take a look at them; but I have no hope. My curse is this, that I am a scoffer about females. I can play with them for an idle hour and then cast them from me even as I cast this banana skin. I can find none so lovely that I may love her for aye from the depths of my passionate heart. I am so blasted particular. O yes! O yes! (*He sits down and looks helpless.*)

KING (*undismayed*). All ready?

(*The* LORD MAYOR *bows.*)

All is ready, my son.

PRINCE (*bored*). Then let loose the Beauts.

(*To heavenly music from the royal hurdy-gurdies the Beauties descend the stairs, one at a time. There are a dozen of the fine creatures, in impudent confections such as* CINDERELLA *has seen in papers in* MR. BODIE'S *studio; some of them with ropes of hair hanging down their proud backs as she has seen them in a hair-dresser's window. As we know, she has once looked on at a horse show, and this has coloured her conception of a competition for a prince. The ladies prance round the ball-room like high-stepping steeds; it is evident that* CINDERELLA *has had them fed immediately before releasing them; her pride is to show them at their very best, and then to challenge them.*

They paw the floor wantonly until LORD TIMES *steps forward. Peace thus restored,* HIS MAJESTY *proceeds.*)

KING. The first duty of a royal consort being to be *good*, the test of goodness will now be applied by the Lord Mayor. Every competitor who does not pass in goodness will be made short work of.

(*Several ladies quake, and somewhere or other unseen* CINDERELLA *is chuckling.*)

ONE OF THE STEEDS. I wasn't told about this. It isn't fair.

LORD MAYOR (*darkly*). If your Grace wishes to withdraw –

(*She stamps.*)

KING. The Lord Mayor will now apply the test.

LORD MAYOR (*to a gold* PAGE). The therm-mo-ometers, boy.

(*A whole boxful of thermometers is presented to him by the* PAGE *on bended knee. The* LORD MAYOR *is now in his element. He has ridden in gold coaches and knows what hussies young women often are. To dainty music he trips up the line of Beauties and pops a tube into each pouting mouth. The competitors circle around, showing their paces while he stands, watch in hand, giving them two minutes. Then airily he withdraws the tubes; he is openly gleeful when he finds sinners. Twice he is in doubt, it is a very near thing, and he has to consult the* KING *in whispers: the* KING *takes the* QUEEN *aside, to whisper behind the door as it were; then they both look at* LORD TIMES, *who, without even stepping forward, says 'No' – and the doubtfuls are at once bundled out of the chamber with the certainties. Royalty sighs, and the courtiers sigh and the* LORD MAYOR *sighs in a perfunctory way, but there is a tossing of manes from the Beauties who have scraped through.*)

KING (*stirring up the* PRINCE, *who has fallen asleep*). Our Royal Bud will now graciously deign to pick out a few possibles.

(*His Royal Highness yawns.*)

LORD MAYOR (*obsequiously*). If your Highness would like a little assistance –

PRINCE (*you never know how they will take things*). We shall do this for ourselves, my good fellow.

(*He smacks the* LORD MAYOR'S *face with princely elegance. The* LORD MAYOR *takes this as a favour, and the courtiers gently smack each other's faces, and are very proud to be there. The* PRINCE *moves languidly down the line of Beauties considering their charms, occasionally nodding approval but more often screwing up his nose. The courtiers stand ready with nods or noses. Several ladies think they have been chosen, but he has only brought them into prominence to humiliate them; he suddenly says 'Good-bye,' and they have to go, while he is convulsed with merriment. He looks sharply at the courtiers to see if they are convulsed also, and most of them are. The others are flung out.*)

QUEEN (*hanging on to her strap*). Does our Royal one experience no palpitation at all?

PRINCE (*sleepily*). Ah me, ah me!

LORD TIMES (*irritated*). You are well called 'Ard-to-Please. You would turn up your nose at a lady though she were shaped like Apollo's bow.

(*The* PRINCE *shrugs his shoulder to indicate that love cannot be forced.*)

LORD MAYOR (*darkly*). And now we come to the severer test.

(*With a neat action, rather like taking a lid off a pot, the* LORD MAYOR *lets it be known to the ladies that they must now lift their skirts to show their feet. When this devastating test is concluded, there are only two competitors left in the room.*)

LORD TIMES (*almost as if he were thinking of himself*). Can't have Two.

(*Cards such as* CINDERELLA *saw at the horse show, with '1st,' '2nd,' and '3rd' on them, are handed to the* PRINCE. *Like one well used to such proceedings, he pins 2nd and 3rd into the ladies' bodices.*)

QUEEN (*gloomily*). But still no first.

(The children applaud; they have been interfering repeatedly.)

KING. Come, come, proud youth, you feel no palps at all?

PRINCE. Not a palp. Perhaps for a moment this one's nose – that one's cock of the head – But it has passed.

(He drearily resumes his rocking chair. No one seems to know what to do next.)

MARIE *(to the rescue)*. The two Ugly Sisters! Monsieur le Roi, the two Ugly Sisters! *(She points derisively at the winners.)*

KING *(badgered)*. How did these children get their invites?

(This is another thing that no one knows. Once more the room rocks, and MR. BODIE passes across it as if looking for some one. Then a growing clamour is heard outside. Bugles sound. The LORD MAYOR goes, and returns with strange news.)

LORD MAYOR. Another competitor, my King. Make way for the Lady Cinderella.

KING. Cinderella? I don't know her.

GLADYS *(nearly falling out of the box)*. You'll soon know her. Now you'll see! Somebody wake the Prince up!

(The portals are flung open, and CINDERELLA is seen alighting from her lovely equipage, which we will not describe because some one has described it before. But note the little waggle of her foot just before she favours the ground. We have thought a great deal about how our CINDERELLA should be dressed for this occasion: white of course, and she looked a darling in it, but we boggle at its really being of the grandest stuff and made in the shop where the Beauties got theirs. No, the material came from poorer warehouses in some shabby district not far from the street of the penny shop; her eyes had glistened as she gazed at it through the windows, and she paid for it with her life's blood, and made the frock herself. Very possibly it was bunchy here and there.

CINDERELLA *then comes sailing down into the ball-room, not a sound to be heard except the ecstatic shrieks of the four children. She is modest but calmly confident; she knows exactly what to do. She moves once round the room to show her gown, then curties to the Royal personages; then, turning to the LORD MAYOR, opens her mouth and signs to him to pop in the thermometer. He does it as in a dream. Presently he is excitedly showing the thermometer to the KING.)*

KING. Marvellous! 99!

(The cry is repeated from all sides. The QUEEN hands the KING a long pin from her coiffure, and the PRINCE is again wakened.)

PRINCE *(with his hand to his brow)*. What, another! Oh, all right; but you know this is a dog's life. *(He goes to CINDERELLA, takes one glance at her and resumes his chair.)*

LORD MAYOR *(while the children blub)*. That settles it, I think. *(He is a heartless fellow.)* That will do. Stand back, my girl.

CINDERELLA *(calmly)*. I don't think.

KING. It's no good, you know.

CINDERELLA (*curtsying*). Noble King, there is two bits of me thy son hath not yet seen. I crave my rights. (*She points to the two bits referred to, which are encased in the loveliest glass slippers.*)

KING. True. Boy, do your duty.

PRINCE. Oh, bother!

(*Those words are the last spoken by him in his present state. When we see him again, which is the moment afterwards, he is translated. He looks the same, but so does a clock into which new works have been put. The change is effected quite simply by* CINDERELLA *delicately raising her skirt and showing him her foot. As the exquisite nature of the sight thus vouchsafed to him penetrates his being a tremor passes through his frame; his vices take flight from him and the virtues enter. It is a heady wakening, and he falls at her feet. The courtiers are awkward, not knowing whether they should fall also.* CINDERELLA *beams to the children, who utter ribald cries of triumph.*)

KING (*rotating on his strap*). Give him air. Fill your lungs, my son.

QUEEN (*on hers*). My boy! My boy!

LORD MAYOR (*quickly taking the royal cue*). Oh, lady fair!

(*The* PRINCE'S *palpitations increase in violence.*)

QUEEN. Oh, happy sight!

KING. Oh, glorious hour!

LORD MAYOR (*not sure that he was heard the first time*). Oh, lady fair!

(*The* PRINCE *springs to his feet. He is looking very queer.*)

LORD TIMES (*probably remembering how he looked once*). The Prince is about to propose.

LORD MAYOR. O yes, O yes, O yes!

KING. Proceed, my son.

PRINCE (*with lover-like contortions and addressing himself largely to the feet*). Dew of the morning, garden of delight, sweet petals of enchanted nights, the heavens have opened and through the chink thou hast fallen at my feet, even as I fall at thine. Thou art not one but twain, and these the twain – Oh, pretty feet on which my lady walks, are they but feet? O no, O no, O no! They are so small I cannot see them. Hie! A candle that I may see my lady's feet!

(*He kisses one foot, and she holds up the other for similar treatment.*)

O Cinderella, if thou wilt deign to wife with me, I'll do my best to see that through the years you always walk on kisses.

(*The courtiers resolve to walk on kisses for evermore.*)

LORD MAYOR. The Prince has proposed. The Lady Cinderella will now reply.

KING. Lovely creature, take pity on my royal son.

QUEEN. Cinderella, be my daughter.

LORD TIMES (*succinctly*). Yes, or no?

CINDERELLA. There's just one thing. Before I answer, I would like that little glass thing to be put in his mouth.

LORD MAYOR (*staggered*). The Ther-mo-mo-meter?

KING. In our *Prince's* mouth!

LORD TIMES. Why not?

CINDERELLA. Just to make sure that he is good.

PRINCE (*with a sinking*). Oh, I say!

QUEEN. Of course he is good, Cinderella – he is our son.

CINDERELLA (*doggedly*). I would like it put in his mouth.

KING. But –

PRINCE (*alarmed*). Pater!

LORD TIMES. It must be done.

(*The test is therefore made. The royal mouth has to open to the thermometer, which is presently passed to the* KING *for examination. He looks very grave. The* PRINCE *seizes the tell-tale thing, and with a happy thought lets it fall.*)

PRINCE. 99!

(*The joyous cry is taken up by all, and* CINDERELLA *goes divinely on one knee to her lord and master.*)

CINDERELLA (*simply*). I accepts.

KING (*when the uproar has ceased*). All make merry. The fire is going low. (*Recklessly.*) In with another shilling!

(*A shilling is dumped into the shilling-in-the-slot stove, which blazes up. The* PRINCE *puts his arm round his love.*)

LORD TIMES (*again remembering his day of days*). My Prince, not so fast. There is still the riddle.

PRINCE. I had forgotten.

CINDERELLA (*quaking*). I was feared there would be a riddle.

KING (*prompted by* LORD TIMES). Know ye all, my subjects, that before blue blood can wed there is a riddle; and she who cannot guess it – (*darkly*) is taken away and censored.

(*The* CENSOR *with his axe comes into sudden prominence behind* CINDERELLA *and the two other competitors.*)

My Lord Times, the riddle.

LORD TIMES. I hold in my one hand the riddle, and in the other the answer in a sealed envelope, to prevent any suspicion of hanky-panky. Third prize, forward. Now, my child, this is the riddle. On the night of the Zeppelin raids,[10] what was it that every one rushed to save first?

3RD PRIZE. The children.

LORD TIMES. Children not included.

(*The lady is at a loss.*)

PRINCE. Time's up! Hoo-ray!

(*He signs callously to the* CENSOR, *who disappears with his victim through a side door, to reappear presently, alone, wiping his axe and skipping gaily.*)

LORD TIMES. Second prize, forward. Now, Duchess, answer.

2ND PRIZE. Her jewels.

(LORD TIMES *shakes his head.*)

PRINCE (*brightly*). Off with her head. Drown her in a bucket.

(*The* CENSOR *again removes the lady and does his fell work.*)

LORD TIMES. First prize, forward. Now, Cinderella, answer.

(*The* CENSOR, *a kindly man but used to his calling, puts his hand on her shoulder, to lead her away. She removes it without looking at him.*)

CINDERELLA. It's not a catch, is it?

LORD TIMES (*hotly*). No, indeed.

CINDERELLA. There's just one thing all true Britons would be anxious about.

KING (*who has been allowed to break the envelope and read the answer*). But what, Cinderella – what?

LORD MAYOR (*hedging again*). What, chit?

CINDERELLA. Their love-letters.

KING and LORD TIMES (*together, but* LORD TIMES *a little in front*). The fair Cinderella has solved the riddle!

LORD MAYOR (*promptly*). Oh, fair lady!

CINDERELLA (*remembering the Venus*). There's just one thing that makes it not quite a perfect ball. I wanted Mrs. Bodie to be one of the competitors – so as I could beat her.

KING. Send for her at once. Take a taxi.

(*A courtier rushes out whistling, and returns with* VENUS, *now imbued with life. Her arms go out wantonly to the* PRINCE. *He signs to the* CENSOR, *who takes her away and breaks her up.*)

PRINCE. I crave a boon. The wedding at once, my lord.

(LORD TIMES *signifies assent.*)

KING. The marriage ceremony will now take place.

CINDERELLA (*calling to the children*). Bridesmaids!

(*They rush down and become her bridesmaids. At the top of the stair appears a penguin – a penguin or a bishop, they melt into each other on great occasions. The regal couple kneel.*)

PENGUIN. Do you, O Prince, take this lady to be your delightful wife – and to adore her for ever?

PRINCE. I do, I do! Oh, I do, I do indeed! I do – I do – I do!

PENGUIN. Do you, Cinderella, loveliest of your sex, take this Prince for husband, and to love, honour, and obey him?

CINDERELLA (*primly*). If you please.

PENGUIN. The ring?

(*It is* MARIE-THERESE'S *great hour; she passes her ring to* CINDERELLA, *who is married in it. Triumphant music swells out as a crown is put upon our Princess's head, and an extraordinarily long train attached to her person. Her husband and she move dreamily round the ball-room, the children holding up the train.* LORD TIMES *with exquisite taste falls in behind them. Then follow the courtiers, all dreamily; and completing the noble procession is the* LORD MAYOR, *holding aloft on a pole an enormous penny. It has the face of* CINDERELLA *on one side of it – the penny which to those who know life is the most romantic of coins unless its little brother has done better.*)

The music, despite better intentions, begins to lose its head. It obviously wants to dance. Every one wants to dance. Even LORD TIMES *has trouble with his legs.*)

KING (*threatening, supplicating*). Don't dance yet. I've got a surprise for you. Don't dance. I haven't told you about it, so as to keep you on the wonder.

(*In vain do they try to control themselves.*)

It's ices!

(*All stop dancing.*)

(*Hoarsely*). There's an ice-cream for everybody.

(*Amid applause the royal ice-cream barrow is wheeled on by haughty menials who fill the paper sieves with dabs of the luscious condiment. The paper sieves are of gold, but there are no spoons. The children, drunk with expectation, forget their manners and sit on the throne. Somehow* CINDERELLA'S *penny clients drift in again, each carrying a sieve.*)

None touches till one royal lick has been taken by us four. . . . (*He gives them a toast.*) To the Bridal Pair!

(*At the royal word 'Go!' all attack the ices with their tongues, greedily but gracefully. They end in the approved manner by gobbling up the sieves. It is especially charming to see the last of* LORD TIMES'S *sieve. The music becomes irresistible. If you did not dance you would be abandoned by your legs. It is as if a golden coin had been dropped into a golden slot. Ranks are levelled. The* KING *asks* GLADYS *for this one; the* QUEEN *is whisked away by* MR. BODIE. *Perhaps they dance like costers: if you had time to reflect you might think it a scene in the streets. It becomes too merry to last; couples are whirled through the walls as if the floor itself were rotating: soon* CINDERELLA *and her* PRINCE *dance alone. It is then that the clock begins to strike twelve.* CINDERELLA *should fly now, or woe befall her. Alas, she hears nothing save the whispers of her lover. The hour has struck, and her glorious gown shrinks slowly into the tattered frock of a girl with a broom. Too late she huddles on the floor to conceal the change. In another moment the* PRINCE *must see. The children gather round her with little cries, and, spreading out their night-gowns to conceal her, rush her from the scene. It is then that the* PRINCE *discovers his loss. In a frenzy he calls her sweet name. The bewildered girl has even forgotten to drop the slipper, without which he shall never find her.* MARIE-THERESE, *the ever-vigilant, steals back with it, and leaves it on the floor.*

The ball-room is growing dark. The lamps have gone out. There is no light save the tiniest glow, which has been showing on the floor all the time, unregarded by us. It seems to come from a policeman's lantern. The gold is all washed out by the odd streaks of white that come down like rain. Soon the PRINCE'S *cry of 'Cinderella, Cinderella' dies away. It is no longer a ball-room on which the lantern sheds this feeble ray. is the street outside* CINDERELLA'S *door, a white street now, silent in snow. The child in her rags, the* POLICEMAN'S *scarf still round her precious feet, is asleep on the doorstep, very little life left in her, very little oil left in the lantern.*)

III

The retreat in which Cinderella is to be found two months later has been described to us by our policeman with becoming awe. It seems to be a very pleasant house near the sea, and possibly in pre-war days people were at ease in it. None of that, says the policeman emphatically, with Dr. Bodie in charge. He could wink discreetly at Dr. Bodie in absence, but was prepared to say on oath that no one ever winked at her when she was present. In the old days he had been more than a passive observer of the suffragette in action, had even been bitten by them in the way of business; had not then gone into the question of their suitability for the vote, but liked the pluck of them; had no objection to his feelings on the woman movement being summed up in this way, that he had vaguely disapproved of their object, but had admired their methods. After knowing Dr. Bodie he must admit that his views about their object had undergone a change; was now a whole-hearted supporter, felt in his bones that Dr. Bodie was born to command: astonishing thing about her that she did it so natural-like. She was not in the least mannish or bullying; she was a very ladylike sort of person, a bit careful about the doing of her hair, and the set of her hat, and she had a soft voice, though what you might call an arbitrary manner. Very noticeable the way she fixed you with her steely eye. In appearance she was very like her room at the retreat, or the room was very like her; everything in cruel good order, as you might say; an extraordinarily decorous writing-table near the centre, the sort of table against which you instinctively stood and waited to make your deposition; the friendliest thing in the room (to a policeman) was the book-cases with wire doors, because the books looked through the wires at you in a homely way like prisoners. It was a sunny room at times, but this did not take away from its likeness to the doctor, who could also smile on occasion.

Into this room Mr. Bodie is shown on a summer afternoon by a maid with no nonsense about her in working hours.

MAID (*who knows that male visitors should be impressed at once*). This way, sir; I
    shall see whether Dr. Bodie is disengaged.
BODIE (*doggedly*). *Miss* Bodie.
MAID (*with firm sweetness*). Dr. Bodie, sir. What name shall I say?
BODIE (*wincing*). Mr. Bodie; her brother.
MAID (*unmoved*). I shall tell Dr. Bodie, sir.
BODIE (*a fighter to the last*). Miss Bodie.
MAID. Dr. Bodie, sir.
(*He is surveying the room with manly disapproval when his sister appears and
    greets him. She is all that the* POLICEMAN *has said of her, and more; if we did
    not have a heroine already we would chose* DR. BODIE. *At the same time it
    cannot be denied that she is enough to make any brother wince. For instance,
    immediately she has passed him the time of day, she seems to be consider-
    ing his case. Perhaps this is because she has caught him frowning at her
    stethoscope. There is certainly a twinkle somewhere about her face. Before*

113

he can step back indignantly she raises one of his eyelids and comes to a conclusion.)

DR. BODIE. Oh dear! Well, Dick, it's entirely your own fault.

(MR. BODIE *has a curious trick of kicking backwards with one foot when people take liberties with him, and a liberty has been taken with him now.*)

Kick away, Dick, but you needn't pretend that you have no faith in me as a medical man; for when you are really ill you always take the first train down here. In your heart I am the only doctor you believe in.

BODIE. Stuff, Nellie.

DR. BODIE. Then why did you put Cinderella under my care?

BODIE. I didn't know where else to send her when she was discharged from the hospital. Had to give her a chance of picking up. (*Thawing.*) It was good of you to give her board and lodging.

DR. BODIE (*sitting down to her day-book*). Not at all. I'll send you in a whacking bill for her presently.

BODIE (*kicking*). Well, I've come all this way to see her. How is she getting on, Nellie?

DR. BODIE. She is in the garden. I dare say you can see her from the window.

BODIE. I see some men only; I believe they are wounded Tommies.

DR. BODIE. Yes. There is a Convalescent Home down here. That is part of my job. Do the men look as if they were gathering round anything?

BODIE. They do.

DR. BODIE. Ah! Then that is Cinderella. She is now bossing the British Army, Dick.

BODIE. I might have guessed it. (*Chuckling.*) Does she charge a penny?

DR. BODIE. Not to the military.

BODIE. Nellie, I have had some inquiries made lately about her parents.

DR. BODIE. She doesn't know much about them herself.

BODIE. No, and we needn't tell her this. Her mother – ah well, poor soul! – and the father was a very bad egg. And from that soil, Nellie, this flower has sprung. Nobody to tend it. Can't you see little Cinderella with her watering-can carefully bringing up herself. I wish I could paint that picture.

(*Perhaps* DR. BODIE *sees the picture even more clearly than he does.*)

I see her now. She is on a bed, Nellie.

DR. BODIE. Yes. That is for convenience, for wheeling her about.

BODIE (*waving*). She sees me. And how is she, Nell?

DR. BODIE. She is always bright; perhaps too bright.

BODIE. Can't be too bright.

DR. BODIE (*controlling her feelings*). A girl who is found frozen in the street by a policeman and taken to a London Hospital, where she has pneumonia – poor little waif! You know, she is very frail, Dick.

BODIE. I know; but she will get better, won't she?

(*He has said it confidently, but his sister looks at him and turns away. He is startled.*)

Come, Nellie, she is going to get better, isn't she?

114

DR. BODIE (*shaking her head*). There isn't much chance, Dick. Her body and soul have had to do too long without the little things they needed.

BODIE. She shall have them now, I promise. What are they?

DR. BODIE. First of all, just food. She has been half starved all her life. And then human affection. She has been starved of that also; she who has such a genius for it.

(*She goes to the window and calls.*)

No. 7, bring Cinderella in here.

(CINDERELLA *in her bed is wheeled in through the window by the soldier,* DANNY. *She is wearing a probationer's cap and dressing jacket. The bed is a simple iron one, small and low, of the kind that was so common in war hospitals; it is on tiny pneumatic wheels with ball bearings for easy propulsion. Though frail,* CINDERELLA *is full of glee.*)

BODIE. Hurray, Cinderella!

CINDERELLA. Hurray! Isn't it lovely. I'm glad you've seen me in my carriage. When I saw there was a visitor I thought at first it might be David.

BODIE. David? I didn't know you . . . Is he a relative?

(CINDERELLA *finds this extremely funny – so does* DANNY; *even the* DOCTOR *is discreetly amused.*)

CINDERELLA (*to* DANNY). Tell the men that! He's not exactly a relative. (*She pulls* MR. BODIE *down by the lapels of his coat.*) He's just that great big ridiculous policeman!

BODIE. Oho! Our policeman again. Does he come all this way to see you?

CINDERELLA (*her shoulders rising in pride*). Twice already; and he's coming again to-day. Mr. Bodie, get the Doctor to take you over the Convalescent Home. There's a field with cows in it, a whole litter of them! And the larder? There's barrel upon barrel full of eggs and sawdust, and Danny says – this is Danny –

(DANNY, *who is slightly lame and is in hospital blue, comes to attention*).

Danny says the hens lay in the barrels so as to save time in packing.

(DANNY *finds the severe eye of the Doctor upon him and is abashed.*)

Mr. Bodie, look! (*displaying her cap*). The Doctor lets me wear it; it makes me half a nurse, a kind of nurse's help. I make bandages, and they're took away in glass bottles and sterilized. Mr. Bodie, as sure as death I'm doing something for my country.

DR. BODIE. Cinderella, you're talking too much.

CINDERELLA (*subsiding meekly*). Yes, Doctor.

DR. BODIE. Dick, I am going over to the hospital presently. If you like to come with me – *really* want to see it – no affected interest –

BODIE. Thanks, I should like it – Dr. Bodie.

DR. BODIE (*to* DANNY). You are not required any more, No. 7.

(DANNY *is going thankfully, but she suddenly pulls him forward to examine his face*).

No. 7, you are wearing that brown eye again.

DANNY (*who has a glass eye*). Yes, Doctor; you see it's like this. First they sent me a brown eye. Then some meddlesome person finds out my natural eye is blue. So then they sends me a blue eye.

DOCTOR. Yes, where is it?

DANNY. It was a beautiful eye, Doctor; but I had taken a fancy to little browny. And I have a young lady; so I took the liberty of having the blue eye made up into a brooch and I sent it to her.

DR. BODIE (*without moving a muscle*). I shall report you.

BODIE (*when the martinet and* DANNY *have gone*). Are you afraid of her, Cinderella? I am.

CINDERELLA. No! She sometimes dashes me, but she is a fearful kind lady. (*She pulls him down again for further important revelations.*) She's very particular about her feet.

BODIE (*staggered*). Is she! In a feminine way?

CINDERELLA. Yes.

BODIE. Hurray! Then I have her. The Achilles Heel! (*He is once more jerked down.*)

CINDERELLA. I have a spring bed.

BODIE. Ah!

CINDERELLA (*in some awe*). The first time I woke in hospital, an angel with streamers was standing there holding a tray in her hand, and on the tray was a boiled egg. Then I thought it was the egg you get the day before you die.

BODIE. What egg is that?

CINDERELLA (*who in the course of a troubled life has acquired much miscellaneous information*). In the Workhouse you always get an egg to your tea the day before you die. (*She whispers.*) I know now I'm not the real Cinderella.

BODIE (*taking her hand*). How did you find out?

CINDERELLA (*gravely*). It's come to me. The more I eat the clearer I see things. I think it was just an idea of mine; being lonely-like I needed to have something to hang on to.

BODIE. That was it. Are you sorry you are not the other one?

CINDERELLA. I'm glad to be just myself. It's a pity though about the glass slippers. That's a lovely idea.

BODIE. Yes.

CINDERELLA. Tell me about *Them*.

BODIE. The children? They are still with me, of course. I am keeping my promise, and they will be with me till you are able to take care of them again. I have them a great deal in the studio in the day-time.

CINDERELLA (*cogitating*). I wonder if that's wise.

BODIE. Oh, they don't disturb me much.

CINDERELLA. I was meaning perhaps the smell of the paint would be bad for them.

BODIE. I see! Of course I could give up painting.

CINDERELLA (*innocently*). I think that would be safest.

(MR. BODIE *kicks*.)

Are you kind to Gretchen?

BODIE. I hope so. I feel it's my duty.

CINDERELLA (*with a sinking*). It'll not be no use for Gretchen if that's how you do it. I'm sure I should get up. (*She attempts to rise.*)

BODIE. Now, now!

CINDERELLA. Are you fond of her, especially when she's bad?

BODIE (*hurriedly*). Yes, I am, I am! But she is never bad! they are all good, they are like angels.

CINDERELLA (*despairing*). Then they're cheating you. Where's my boots?

BODIE. Quiet! That's all right.

(*A pretty and not very competent* PROBATIONER *comes in at the window, carrying fishing rods, followed by* DANNY *with croquet mallets and balls.*)

PROBATIONER (*laden*). I want to shake hands with you, Mr. Bodie, but you see how I am placed.

CINDERELLA. Do your pretty bow at any rate.

(*The attractive girl does her pretty bow to* MR. BODIE. *It is one of the few things she does well, and will probably by and by bring her into some safe matrimonial harbour; but in her country's great hour she is of less value to it than a ball of twine. She is of a nice nature and would like to be of use, but things slip through her hands as through her mind; she cannot even carry a few lengths of fishing rods without an appeal to heaven. She is counting the pieces now with puckered brow.*)

DANNY (*one of the few men in the world who can carry four croquet balls in two hands*). You see, sir, there is a pond in the garden, and we have a fishing competition; and as there are not enough rods the men hides them so as to be sure of having a rod next day.

PROBATIONER. It is very unfair to the others, Danny.

DANNY (*warmly*). That's what I say, Nurse.

CINDERELLA. The Matron found a rod the other morning hidden beneath one of the men's mattresses.

PROBATIONER. The odd thing is how he could have got it to the house without being seen. (*Her counting of the pieces ends in her discomfiture.*)

BODIE. Anything wrong?

PROBATIONER. There are only nine pieces. A whole rod is missing!

CINDERELLA (*trembling for her*). Nurse, I'm so sorry!

BODIE. After all, it's a trivial matter, isn't it?

PROBATIONER (*her beautiful empty eyes filling*). Trivial! I am responsible. Just think what Dr. Bodie will say to me!

BODIE. Are you afraid of her too?

PROBATIONER. Afraid! I should think I am.

DANNY. And so am I.

(*Before* MR. BODIE *has time to kick, the terrible one reappears.*)

DR. BODIE. I am going over to the Home now, Dick. You must come at once, if you are coming.

BODIE (*cowed and getting his coat*). Yes, all right.

DR. BODIE. A great coat on a day like this! Absurd!

BODIE (*remembering what* CINDERELLA *has told him, and pointing sternly*). French shoes on roads like these, ridiculous!

(DR. BODIE *kicks this time – it is evidently a family trait. Delight of* DANNY.)

DR. BODIE. No. 7, you needn't grin unless there is a reason. Is there a reason?

DANNY. No, no, Doctor.

DR. BODIE. Fishing rods all right this time, Nurse?

PROBATIONER (*faltering*). I am so ashamed, Dr. Bodie; there is one missing.

DR. BODIE. Again. I must ask you, Nurse, to report yourself to the Matron.

PROBATIONER (*crushed*). Yes, Dr. Bodie.

DR. BODIE (*observing that* DANNY *is stealing away unobtrusively*). No. 7.

DANNY (*still backing*). Yes, Doctor.

DR. BODIE. Come here. What is the matter with your right leg; it seems stiff.

DANNY (*with the noble resignation of Tommies, of which he has read in the papers*). It's a twinge of the old stiffness come back, Doctor. I think there's a touch of east in the wind. The least touch of east seems to find the hole that bullet made. But I'm not complaining.

DR. BODIE (*brutally*). No, it is I who am complaining.

(*She feels his leg professionally.*)

Give me that fishing rod.

(*The long-suffering man unbuttons, and to his evident astonishment produces the missing rod.*)

DANNY (*without hope but in character*). Well, I am surprised!

DR. BODIE. You will be more surprised presently. Come along, Dick.

(*She takes her brother away.*)

DANNY (*the magnanimous*). She's great! Words couldn't express my admiration for that woman – lady – man – doctor.

PROBATIONER. How mean of you, Danny, to get me into trouble.

DANNY (*in the public school manner*). Sorry. But I'll have to pay for this. (*Seeing visions.*) She has a way of locking one up in the bathroom.

PROBATIONER (*with spirit*). Let us three conspirators combine to defy her. Carried. Proposed, that No. 7, being a male, conveys our challenge to her. Carried.

CINDERELLA (*gleefully*). Go on, Danny.

DANNY (*of the bull-dog breed*). I never could refuse the ladies. (*He uses the stethoscope as a telephone.*) Give me the Convalescent Home, please. Is that you, Doctor. How are you? We've just rung up to defy you. Now, now, not another word, or I'll have you locked up in the bathroom. Wait a mo; there's a nurse here wants to give you a piece of her mind.

PROBATIONER (*with the stethoscope*). Is that you, Miss Bodie? What? No, I have decided not to call you Dr. Bodie any more.

(*Alas,* DR. BODIE *returns by the window unseen and hears her.*)

Please to report yourself as in disgrace at once to the Matron. That will do. Goodbye. Run along. Heavens, if she had caught us!

DANNY. It would have meant permanent residence in bathroom for me.

(*It is then that they see her.*)

DR. BODIE (*after an awful pause*). I have come back for my stethoscope, Nurse.

(*The* PROBATIONER *can think of no suitable reply.*)

DANNY (*searching his person*). I don't think I have it, Doctor.

DR. BODIE. Don't be a fool, No. 7.

PROBATIONER (*surrendering it*). Here it is, Dr. Bodie, I – I –

DR. BODIE (*charmingly*). Thank you. And, my dear, don't be always Doctor Bodie-ing me. That, of course, at the Home, and on duty, but here in my house you are my guest. I am Miss Bodie to you here. Don't let me forget that I am a woman. I assure you I value that privilege. (*She lingers over* CINDERELLA'S *pillow*). Dear, you must invite Nurse and Danny to tea with you, and all be happy together. Little Cinderella, if I will do as a substitute, you haven't altogether lost your Godmother.

(*She goes, shaking a reproving finger at* DANNY.)

DANNY. We're done again!

PROBATIONER (*reduced to tears*). Horrid little toad that I've been. Some one take me out and shoot me.

(*The* MAID *comes with tea things.*)

DANNY. Allow me, maiden.

ELLEN. Dr. Bodie says I am to bring two more cups.

DANNY (*whose manner is always that of one who, bathroom or no bathroom, feels he is a general favourite*). If you please, child.

PROBATIONER (*as soon as* ELLEN *has gone*). Dr. Bodie is an angel.

DANNY (*quite surprised that he has not thought of this before*). That's what she is!

CINDERELLA. Danny, can't you say something comforting to poor Nurse.

DANNY (*manfully*). I'm thankful to say I can. Nurse, I've often had fits of remorse; and I can assure you that they soon pass away, leaving not a mark behind.

PROBATIONER. Dear Dr. Bodie!

DANNY. Exactly. You've taken the words out of my mouth. The only thing for us to think of henceforth is what to do to please her. Her last words to us were to draw up to the tea-table. Are we to disregard the last words of that sublime female?

PROBATIONER (*recovering*). No!

(*The extra cups having been brought, the company of three settle down to their wartime tea-party, the tray being on* CINDERELLA'S *lap and a guest on each side of her.*)

DANNY. Our plain duty is now to attack the victuals so as to become strong in that Wonder's service. Here's to dear Dr. Bodie, and may she find plenty to do elsewhere till this party is over.

PROBATIONER (*able to toss her head again*). After all, she put us in a false position.

DANNY. That's true. Down with her!

PROBATIONER. I drink to you, Danny.

DANNY (*gallantly*). And I reply with mine.

CINDERELLA. It's queer to think I'm being – what's the word? – hostess.

DANNY. All things are queer ever since the dull old days before the war; and not the unqueerest is that Daniel Duggan, once a plumber, is now partaking of currant cake with the Lady Charlotte something!

CINDERELLA (*nearly letting her cup fall*). What?

PROBATIONER. You weren't supposed to know that.

CINDERELLA. Does he mean you? Are you – ?

PROBATIONER. It's nothing to make a fuss about, Cinderella. How did you find out, Danny?

DANNY. Excuse me, but your haughty manner of wringing out a dishcloth betrayed you? My war-worn eyes, of various hues, have had the honour of seeing the Lady Charlotte washing the ward floor. O memorable day! O glorified floor! O blushing dishcloth!

PROBATIONER. That was just a beginning. Some day I hope when I rise in the profession to be allowed to wash you, Danny.

DANNY (*bowing grandly*). The pleasure, my lady, will be mutual. (*He hums a tune of the moment.*)

'And when I tell them that some day washed by her I'll be – they'll never believe me' –

PROBATIONER (*with abandon*). 'But when I tell them 'twas a jolly good thing for me – they'll all believe me!'

DANNY. And when I tell them – and I certainly mean to tell them – that one day she'll walk out with me –

(*In a spirit of devilry he crooks his arm; she takes it – she walks out with him for a moment.*)

PROBATIONER (*coming to*). No. 7, what are we doing!

CINDERELLA. It's just the war has mixed things up till we forget how different we are.

PROBATIONER (*with a moment of intuition*). Or it has straightened things out so that we know how like we are.

(*From the garden comes the sound of a gramophone.*)

CINDERELLA. David's a long time in coming.

DANNY. The four-twenty's not in yet.

CINDERELLA. Yes, it is; I heard the whistle.

DANNY (*sarcastically*). Would you like me to see if he hasn't lost his way? Those policemen are stupid fellows.

CINDERELLA. None of that, Danny; but I would like fine if you take a look.

DANNY. Anything to oblige you, though it brings our social to a close. None of these little tea-parties after the war is over, fine lady.

PROBATIONER. Oh dear! I'll often enjoy myself less, Danny.

DANNY. Daniel Duggan will sometimes think of this day, when you are in your presentation gown and he is on your roof, looking for that there leakage.

PROBATIONER. Oh, Danny, don't tell me that when I meet you with your bag of tools I'll be a beast. Surely there will be at least a smile of friendship between us in memory of the old days.

DANNY. I wonder! That's up to you, my lady. (*But he will be wiser if he arranges that it is to be up to himself.*)

PROBATIONER (*calling attention to the music*). Listen! No. 7, to-day is ours.

(*She impulsively offers herself for the waltz; they dance together.*)

DANNY (*when all is over*). Thank you, my lady. (*She curtsies and he goes out rather finely. It is not likely that her next partner will be equal to her plumber. The two girls are left alone, both nice girls of about the same age; but the poor one has already lived so long that the other, though there may be decades before her, will never make up on* CINDERELLA. *It would be grand to see this waif, the moment after death, setting off stoutly on the next adventure.*)

CINDERELLA. He is a droll character, Danny. (*Examining herself in a hand-mirror.*) Nurse, would you say my hair is looking right? He likes the cap.

PROBATIONER (*who will soon forget her, but is under the spell at present*). Your David?

CINDERELLA (*on her dignity*). He's not mine, Nurse.

PROBATIONER. Isn't he?

CINDERELLA. Hey, hey, hey! Nurse, when he comes you don't need to stay very long.

PROBATIONER (*in the conspiracy*). I won't.

CINDERELLA (*casually*). He might have things to say to me, you see.

PROBATIONER. Yes, he might.

CINDERELLA (*solemnly*). You and me are both very young, but maybe you understand about men better than I do. You've seen him, and this is terrible important. Swear by Almighty God you're to tell me the truth. Would you say that man loves little children?

PROBATIONER (*touched*). Don't frighten me, Cinderella; I believe him to be that kind of man. Are you fond of your policeman, dear?

CINDERELLA (*winking*). That's telling! (*Importantly.*) Nurse, did you ever have a love-letter.

PROBATIONER (*gaily*). Not I! Don't want to; horrid little explosives! But have you – has he – ?

CINDERELLA (*becoming larger*). In my poor opinion, if it's not a love-letter, it's a very near thing.

PROBATIONER. If I could see the darling little detestable?

CINDERELLA. Oh no, oh no, no, no, no! But I'll tell you one thing as is in it. This – 'There are thirty-four policemen sitting in this room, but I would rather have you, my dear.' What do you think? That's a fine bit at the end.

PROBATIONER (*sparkling*). Lovely! Go on, Cinderella, fling reticence to the winds.

CINDERELLA (*doing so*). Unless I am – very far out – in my judgment of men – that man is infatuate about me!

PROBATIONER (*clapping her hands*). The delicious scoundrel! Cinderella, be merciless to him! Knife him, you dear! Give him beans!

CINDERELLA (*gurgling*). I ill-treats him most terrible.

PROBATIONER. That's the way! down with lovers! slit them to ribbons! stamp on them!

CINDERELLA. Sometimes I – (*She sits up.*) Listen!

PROBATIONER (*alarmed*). It isn't Dr. Bodie, is it?

CINDERELLA. No, it's *him*.

PROBATIONER. I don't hear a sound.

CINDERELLA. I can hear him fanning his face with his helmet. He has come in such a hurry. Nurse, you watch me being cruel to him.

PROBATIONER. At him, Cinderella, at him!

DANNY (*flinging open the door*). The Constabulary's carriage stops the way.

(*Our* POLICEMAN *stalks in, wetting his lips as he does so.*)

PROBATIONER (*giving him her hand*). How do you do? You forget, I dare say, that I met you when you were here last; but I remember 'our policeman.'

(*He is bashful.*)

There she is.

(*The wicked invalid is looking the other way.*)

POLICEMAN. A visitor to see you, Jane.

CINDERELLA (*without looking round*). I thought it had a visitor's sound. (*She peeps at the* PROBATIONER *gleefully.*)

POLICEMAN (*very wooden*). You don't ask who it is, Jane?

CINDERELLA. I thought it might be that great big ridiculous policeman.

(DANNY *laughs, and our* POLICEMAN *gives him a very stern look.*)

POLICEMAN (*after reflection*). I'm here again, Jane.

CINDERELLA (*admitting it with a glance*). Perhaps you didn't ought to come so often; it puts them about.

POLICEMAN (*cleverly*). But does it put you about, Jane?

CINDERELLA. Hey! Hey! (*With a cunning waggle of the hand she intimates to the* NURSE *that she may go.*)

DANNY (*who is not so easily got rid of*). You had best be going too, Robert. The lady has answered you in the negative.

POLICEMAN (*lowering*). You make a move there.

(DANNY, *affecting alarm, departs with the* PROBATIONER.)

CINDERELLA. I like fine to hear you ordering the public about, David.

POLICEMAN (*humbly*). I'm very pleased, Jane, if there's any little thing about me that gives you satisfaction.

(*He puts down a small parcel that he has brought in.*)

CINDERELLA (*curious*). What's in the parcel, David?

POLICEMAN. That remains to be seen. (*He stands staring at his divinity.*)

CINDERELLA (*sneering*). What are you looking at?

POLICEMAN. Just at you.

CINDERELLA (*in high delight*). Me? There's little to look at in me. You should see the larder at the Home. You'll have a cup of China tea and some of this cake?

POLICEMAN. No, Jane, no. (*In a somewhat melancholy voice.*) Things to eat have very little interest to me now.

CINDERELLA. Oh?

POLICEMAN. I've gone completely off my feed.

(CINDERELLA *would have liked the* PROBATIONER *to hear this.*)

CINDERELLA (*artfully*). I wonder how that can be!

POLICEMAN. Did you get my letter, Jane?

CINDERELLA (*calmly*). I got it –

POLICEMAN. Did you – did you think it was a peculiar sort of a letter?

CINDERELLA (*mercilessly*). I don't mind nothing peculiar in it.

POLICEMAN. There was no word in it that took you aback, was there?

CINDERELLA. Not that I mind of.

POLICEMAN (*worried*). Maybe you didn't read it very careful?

CINDERELLA. I may have missed something. What was the word, David?

POLICEMAN (*in gloom*). Oh, it was just a small affair. It was just a beginning. I thought, if she stands that she'll stand more. But if you never noticed it – (*He sighs profoundly.*)

CINDERELLA. I'll take another look –

POLICEMAN (*brightening*). You've kept it?

CINDERELLA. I have it here.

POLICEMAN. I could let you see the word if it's convenient to you to get the letter out of your pocket.

CINDERELLA. It's not in my pocket.

POLICEMAN. Is it under the pillow?

CINDERELLA. No.

POLICEMAN (*puzzled*). Where, then?

(CINDERELLA, *with charming modesty, takes the letter from her bodice. Her lover is thunderstruck.*)

What made you think of keeping it there?

CINDERELLA. I didn't think, David; it just came to me.

POLICEMAN (*elate*). It's infallayble! I'll let you see the word.

CINDERELLA (*smiling at the ridiculous man*). You don't need to bother, David. Fine I know what the word is.

POLICEMAN (*anxious*). And you like it?

CINDERELLA. If you like it.

POLICEMAN. That emboldens me tremendous.

CINDERELLA. I don't like that so much. If there's one thing I like more than any other thing in the world –

POLICEMAN (*eager*). Yes?

CINDERELLA. It's seeing you, David, tremendous bold before all other folk, and just in a quake before me.

POLICEMAN (*astounded*). It's what I am. And yet there's something bold I must say to you.

CINDERELLA (*faltering genteelly*). Is there?

POLICEMAN. It'll be a staggering surprise to you.

(CINDERELLA *giggles discreetly.*)

123

I promised the Doctor as I came in not to tire you. (*With some awe.*) She's a powerful woman that.

CINDERELLA. If you tire me I'll hold up my hand just like you do to stop the traffic. Go on, David. Just wait a moment. (*She takes off his helmet and holds it to her thin breast.*) Here's a friend of mine. Now?

POLICEMAN (*despairing of himself*). I wish I was a man in a book. It's pretty the way they say it; and if ever there was a woman that deserved to have it said pretty to her it's you. I've been reading the books. There was one chap that could speak six languages. Jane, I wish I could say it to you in six languages, one down and another come up, till you had to take me in the end.

CINDERELLA. To take you?

POLICEMAN (*in woe*). Now I've gone and said it in the poorest, silliest way. Did you hold up your hand to stop me, Jane?

CINDERELLA. No.

POLICEMAN (*encouraged*). But I've said it. Will you, Jane?

CINDERELLA (*doggedly*). Will I what?

POLICEMAN. Do you not see what I'm driving at?

CINDERELLA. Fine I see what you're driving at.

POLICEMAN. Then won't you help me out?

CINDERELLA. No.

POLICEMAN. If you could just give me a shove.

CINDERELLA (*sympathetically*). Try Badgery.

POLICEMAN (*brightening*). Have you forgotten that pool in Badgery Water where the half-pounder used – No, you never was there! Jane, the heart of me is crying out to walk with you by Badgery Water.

CINDERELLA. That's better!

POLICEMAN. I would never think of comparing Mrs. Bodie to you. For my part I think nothing of uppers. Feet for me.

(*She gives him her hand to hold.*) My dear.

CINDERELLA. You said *that* was only a beginning.

POLICEMAN. My dearest.

CINDERELLA (*glistening*). I'm not feeling none tired, David.

POLICEMAN. My pretty.

CINDERELLA. Hey! Hey! Hey! Hey!

POLICEMAN. I don't set up to be a prince, Jane; but I love you in a princely way, and if you would marry me, you wonder, I'll be a true man to you till death us do part. Come on, Cinders. (*Pause.*) It's the only chance that belt of mine has.

CINDERELLA. No, no, I haven't took you yet. There's a thing you could do for me, that would gratify me tremendous.

POLICEMAN. It's done.

CINDERELLA. I want you to let me have the satisfaction, David, of having refused you once.

POLICEMAN. Willingly; but what for?

CINDERELLA. I couldn't say. Just because I'm a woman. Mind you, I dare say I'll cast it up at you in the future.

POLICEMAN. I'll risk that. Will you be my princess, Jane?

CINDERELLA. You promise to ask again? At once?

POLICEMAN. Yes.

CINDERELLA. Say – I do.

POLICEMAN. I do.

CINDERELLA (*firmly*). It's a honour you do me, policeman, to which I am not distasteful. But I don't care for you in that way, so let there be no more on the subject. (*Anxiously.*) Quick, David!

POLICEMAN. For the second time, will you marry me, Jane?

CINDERELLA (*who has been thinking out the answer for several days*). David, I love thee, even as the stars shining on the parched earth, even as the flowers opening their petals to the sun; even as mighty ocean with its billows; even so do I love thee, David. (*She nestles her head on his shoulder.*)

POLICEMAN. If only I could have said it like that!

CINDERELLA (*happily*). That's just a bit I was keeping handy. (*Almost in a whisper.*) David, do you think I could have a engagement ring?

POLICEMAN (*squaring his shoulders*). As to that, Jane, first tell me frankly, do you think the Police Force is romantical?

CINDERELLA. They're brave and strong, but –

POLICEMAN. The general verdict is no. And yet a more romantical body of men do not exist. I have been brooding over this question of engagement rings, and I consider them unromantical affairs. (*He walks toward his parcel.*)

CINDERELLA. David, what's in that parcel?

POLICEMAN. Humbly hoping you would have me, Jane, I have had something special made for you –

CINDERELLA (*thrilling*). Oh, David, what is it?

POLICEMAN. It's a policeman's idea of an engagement ring –

CINDERELLA. Quick! Quick!

POLICEMAN. – for my amazing romantical mind said to me that, instead of popping a ring on the finger of his dear, a true lover should pop a pair of glass slippers upon her darling feet!

CINDERELLA. David, you're a poet!

POLICEMAN (*not denying it*). It's what you've made me – and proud I would be if, for the honour of the Force, I set this new fashion in engagement rings. (*He reveals the glass slippers.*)

(CINDERELLA *holds out her hands for the little doves.*)

They're not for hands. (*He uncovers her feet.*)

CINDERELLA. They're terrible small! Maybe they'll not go on!

(*They go on.*)

CINDERELLA. They're like two kisses.

POLICEMAN. More like two love-letters.

CINDERELLA. No, David, no, – kisses.

POLICEMAN. We won't quarrel about it, Cinders; but at the same time. . . . However!

(*He presses her face to him for a moment so that he may not see its transparency.* DR. BODIE *has told him something.*)

NOTES

1 Unclear is this is an error in the original text or part of the humor.
2 Slavey is: 'a female domestic servant, esp. one who is hard-worked; a maid of all work'. *OED Online*.
3 The phrase 'a swell' is slang for a wealthy upper-class person.
4 The phrase 'talked sixteen to the dozen' is a variation of the more well-known phrase 'talked nineteen to the dozen', which means to speak rapidly and without stopping. See *Merriam-Webster Dictionary*.
5 This is a popular idiom for a small space, first recorded in the *OED* in 1665. The phrase 'swing a cat' originally referred to a space small enough to swing a whip called a 'cat-o-nine-tales'.
6 The term 'flunkey' here denotes a liveried servant, usually a contemptuous or derogatory term. *OED Online*.
7 The term 'blue jacket' may refer to convalescent soldiers during the First World War who were issued blue jackets as part of their uniform, though it was also a term used to describe service men wearing the emergency uniforms issued at the beginning of the war.
8 The allies here refer to the UK's allies during the First World War, particularly the French and Belgians.
9 The 'Censor' is a reference to the censorship imposed by the Defense of the Realm Act (DORA) of Parliament, passed on 7 August 1914 for emergency wartime powers during the First World War.
10 The Zeppelin was a German airship developed by Ferdinand Graf von Zeppelin in 1900, during the First World War, Zeppelins were used to bomb the UK. Bombings began in the United Kingdom in 1915.

Editorial Headnote

Williams, E., *Cinderella*, typescript, Emlyn William Papers, National Library of Wales (NLW), 1924.

George Emlyn Williams (1905–1987) was a Welsh actor and playwright, known for his macabre plays which were adapted into films including: 'A Murder Has Been Arranged' (1930), 'Night Must Fall' (1935) and 'The Corn is Green' (1938). Williams's 'Cinderella' precedes his popular dramas about murder. Although lacking the violence and death of later plays, the happily-ever-after unravels completely in the final act.

Williams was born in Welsh-speaking community; he learned English later in life and eventually attended Christ Church College, Oxford, in 1923.[1] 'Cinderella' was written during his second year at Christ Church College, perhaps for an amateur performance at the College. Williams's 'Cinderella' touches on the pantomime's tropes and moves beyond them.

The dangerous lure of Faery and the price it exacts haunts this dramatized version of Cinderella. Tropes of the other-worldly changeling circulate around the character of Cinderella. Her ability to hear music that no one else can hear and see beings no one else can see is a hallmark of the changeling being recalled to Faery.[2] The capricious fairy godmother resembles the dangerous queens of Faery, who sacrifice lovers when they finish with them.[3]

NOTES

1 Locock 2003.
2 Similar fairy-lore tropes are featured in Manx playwright Cushag's play 'Eunyce' (1908).
3 In the traditional ballad of Tam Lin, the fairy queen's lover is about to be sacrificed to pay the Tithe to Hell.

4

CINDERELLA

E. Williams

Source: Typescript, Emlyn William Papers, National Library of Wales (NLW), 1924

THE PERSONS IN THE PLAY

Cinderella, christened Claribella.
Annabella, her elder sisters, ladies.
Florizella,
The Prince.
The Strange Courtier.
His Wife.
A Page.
The lords, ladies and attendants at the ball.
The Fairy Godmother.

Act One The house of the three sisters.
Act Two The royal terrace.
Act Three The house of the three sisters.

The play extends over the night of the ball, beginning at sunset and ending at sunrise.

ACT ONE

The house of the three sisters. Night is falling; the stage is in darkness except for the dying glow of the fire and the shafts of light that come in from the street through a large window at the back. FLORIZELLA enters and stumbles over a chair.

FLORIZELLA
Annabella!

ANNABELLA (above)
Is that you, Florizella?

DOI: 10.4324/9781003034643-6

FLORIZELLA

I can't see a thing in this room. Where's the light? Where are the candles? Where's the lamp?

ANNABELLA (above)

What do you say?

FLORIZELLA

Have you got the lamp? . . . What? . . . I don't hear a word . . . . . Have you got the lamp? Come down immediately. Good gracious!

She sits down. Enter ANNABELLA with the lamp. The sisters are revealed. They are both of uncertain age, and both not as pretty as they were. Annabella has an air of primness about her. Florizella is painted and powdered.

ANNABELLA

Were you calling?

FLORIZELLA

Was I calling, indeed! Of course I was calling, and as high as I could. One would think everybody was deaf in the house. Here I come down for my hairpins and no fire and no light. Goodness! Why isn't there a fire and a light, when everybody's in a bustle dressing for the ball?

ANNABELLA

I don't know, sister. Where's Cinderella?

FLORIZELLA

Where's Cinderella! Yes, where's Cinderella! Haven't you seen her? She's a wicked and neglectful good-for-nothing. I come down for my hairpins and instead I fall over a chair. I might have just as well torn my red velvet and been stopped from going to the ball.

She has found the hairpins and is busy doing up her hair. Annabella manipulates with the fire and coaxes it into a faint flame.

ANNABELLA

I suppose she's gone for firewood.

FLORIZELLA

Nonsense. She must come immediately to do up the back of my red velvet. Cinderella! Cinderella! one would think the house was dead. Cinderella!

ANNABELLA

If she's not there, she won't hear you, sister.

FLORIZELLA

You're very impudent. But since she's not there, you'll have to fasten up.
Annabella fastens up.
I can't make out how you contrive to be ready so soon. I think you neglect yourself a little, my dear.[1]

ANNABELLA
I'm sorry you think so, my dear. And in what way am I neglected?

FLORIZELLA
I don't think your hair's as carefully powdered as it was. Or is it grey?

ANNABELLA
Grey? I'm not as old as that, I'd have you know, sister. It can't be grey.

FLORIZELLA
Oh yes you are as old as that. And when one's got grey hair, I've heard, one can't stop it's showing, even if one plasters one's head with the best powder. Besides, there's your face. Why *will* you not powder your neck? You need not think, sister, that its natural beauty deserves the absence of powder, because it doesn't.

ANNABELLA
I'll thank you to mind your own business, Florizella.

FLORIZELLA
You're mighty haughty. But I mustn't forget you're my elder. Besides, it's no use in the least quarelling on the night of the ball and getting untidy.

ANNABELLA
I'm not so much your elder as all that, while we're on the subject. One year isn't much difference.

FLORIZELLA
One year's one year! I'm younger than you because I *look* younger, and I'm younger than you by a good ten years. That's proved. Cinderella! The girl *won't* hear!. . . . Well, I suppose I'm about ready now. *I*'m wearing my ruby tonight.

ANNABELLA
It was only the other day that you said it was too small. Didn't you declare it hurt your finger?

FLORIZELLA
Yes, but I heard yesterday that it matches my cheeks to perfection. And now that I *am* ready, it's no use asking you how I look because you'll only say something very jealous. Is my hair curled at the back?

ANNABELLA
I should think it will do.

FLORIZELLA
Of course it will do!. . . . Tra-la-aa!. . . . As if it wouldn't!. . . . I don't think my red velvet looks as well as it did. I shall see that Cinders improves it for me. Sit down, sister, and don't gape at me.

ANNABELLA
You are very excited tonight, Florizella.

FLORIZELLA
Hasn't every young body a right to be excited over the great ball of the year?

ANNABELLA
Yes, every young body is bound to be in a flutter. But it doesn't explain why you
should be.

FLORIZELLA
And why doesn't it?

ANNABELLA
Because you're not young. What's the use of pretending? Isn't it enough to make faces
when there are others there to benefit by it? If we were as young as Cinderella –

FLORIZELLA
Cinderella, indeed! What's the time?

ANNABELLA
I don't know; besides, we're early, the trumpet hasn't blown yet. But we're not
young, like Cinderella, and we'll never again be so well-featured.

FLORIZELLA
Simplicity to the point of idiocy I will grant her; but beauty I refuse her on every
condition. Cinderella beautiful! Whoever heard of such a thing? If she were
once seen in court half the men would burst their sides with laughter. Thank
goodness she doesn't take after me; if someone told me we looked like each
other, I shouldn't be pleased. That's all I can say.

ANNABELLA
I can't understand you. That you should tell lies to a man, or before a man, is comprehensible; but you must keep up appearances. But why lie to me, even to
me, who've known you ever since you were born? Is it that you've repeated
these things so often that you've come to believe them? Have you made faces
so often that it's actually become a part of you?

FLORIZELLA
I am always myself.

ANNABELLA
You are never yourself.[2] We are both playing a part when there are others there,
because we are both getting old and we don't want to. We are both trying to
get out of our existence what enjoyment we can –

FLORIZELLA
And I am getting out of it rather more than you are, my dear. That is the only difference, but a considerable one.

ANNABELLA

Because you are bolder, my dear. But how many times you have to start again
being bold, until you've made another little conquest, and have a little rest!
The stuff of your heart must be worn threadbare by now.

FLORIZELLA

The stuff of yours must be brand new, my dear. You mustn't think that because I
broke last month I can't keep a lover. I was tired of him. A silly fool, who'd
talk of nothing but love, love, love.

ANNABELLA

Was it you who broke with him? There was talk at court, I hear, but of course talk
at court, one can never be certain –

FLORIZELLA

If it weren't for fear of smearing my hand with powder and paint, I'd slap your
face, sister. Did he ever look at you?

ANNABELLA

I never asked him.

FLORIZELLA

Did I?

ANNABELLA

Almost.

FLORIZELLA

Oh, do be quiet! You talk of my little conquests: you may be interested, my dear,
to hear that someone is coming to see me, before the ball begins. I expect my
visitor any moment now.

ANNABELLA

Indeed.

FLORIZELLA

Yes.

ANNABELLA

I shall leave as soon as she calls.

FLORIZELLA

She? It's a gentleman.

ANNABELLA

A man? A man, alone, in this house? I have permitted you much, Florizella, but
that I cannot and will not support. A man! I have my reputation to think of,
you must consider that –

FLORIZELLA

You suppose because I have none to think of for myself, it leaves me plenty of
time to think of yours?

ANNABELLA

I refuse, sister. I repeat, I have my reputation to think of. Besides, what would
Cinderella say?

FLORIZELLA

Cinderella! What business have you to drag in Cinderella? This is my house and
I shall see my visitor, so there's an end to the question. I despise you. . . . . It
may interest you to know who my visitor is?

ANNABELLA

I don't wish to know.

FLORIZELLA

Yes you do. And even if you did not I'd tell you all the same. It's the Prince.[3]

ANNABELLA

The Prince!

FLORIZELLA

Yes. Now who is getting old and wrinkled and playing parts? I hope you realize it
isn't everybody he goes to see at night, and alone.

ANNABELLA

Is he your . . . lover?

FLORIZELLA

He has been my lover for a week, my dear, but in great secret. Why, sister, there's
no reason to despair of being the sister of a queen, some day! That may perhaps bring you into a safe port after many storms. The prince has given me an
assignation before the ball.

ANNABELLA

I don't believe you.

The sound of trumpets.

There. That's the first call already. He's not coming and I believe you're telling a
mass of lies.

FLORIZELLA

I'm not telling a mass of lies, you ugly creature. You're as spiteful as Satan, and I
hate you. Of course he'll come! You're only jealous, you know very well he'd
never be coming here to see *you*!

ANNABELLA

He's late. Do your lovers never fall to come at the hour?

FLORIZELLA
Hush!
She tiptoes to the window.

ANNABELLA
There's nobody there.
A low knock.

FLORIZELLA
I told you! He's at the door. Oh joy! Leave me alone, sister. What a flutter!

ANNABELLA
Sister, you ought to be ashamed of yourself.
Exit ANNABELLA. Florizella goes to the door and lets in the PRINCE, wrapped
    in a long cloak.

THE PRINCE
I have come just in time before going to dress. You want to see me?

FLORIZELLA
Perhaps it was very foolish of me, dear, and perhaps you will be very angry. You
    remember. . . .

THE PRINCE
Yes?

FLORIZELLA
The night you swore you would do all – all I wished?

THE PRINCE
Yes.

FLORIZELLA
I doubted you. I have no great knowledge of men, I fear, and I have no curiosity;
    but I knew enough to doubt. So I asked you. . . . to come and see me, even if
    it was very inconvenient.

THE PRINCE
Yes?

FLORIZELLA
And you came. Don't think it was suspicion, my dear, but. . . . perhaps it was a
    little jealousy. O faithful lover!

THE PRINCE
So you did not wish to speak to me?

FLORIZELLA
I wished to prove your constancy. And it is proved! Was I foolish? Was I im-
    petuous? Ah, my dear prince-whom I used to call 'Your Majesty' – you will

find in me a difficult mistress. The warmth of my passion aches for an equal warmth in yours. But I forget myself. You *are* glad to see me?

THE PRINCE
Yes, madam. But it seemed to me strange that you should call for me . . . so. But the emptiness of my errand is recompensed by the sight of you, madam.

FLORIZELLA
I do not believe a word, but. . . . I cannot say anything in answer. Does my dress please you?

THE PRINCE
It is a beautiful dress, yes.

FLORIZELLA
Does its wearer please you too?

THE PRINCE
Yes.

FLORIZELLA
Ungrateful and cold answer!

THE PRINCE
A short and cold answer conceals more than fulsome compliment.

FLORIZELLA
I wonder! Ah, I wonder! I wonder, though I do not seek to know. Does my hair please you?

THE PRINCE
It is beautiful in its curls and sits most graciously upon your shoulder.

FLORIZELLA
Ah, while I remember, do we go in arm in arm from the terrace, or do we wait till we get to the door? I had quite forgotten. I have *such* a memory. I always forget everything.

THE PRINCE
Arm in arm?

FLORIZELLA
Of course, you foolish forgetful lover! Do you mean to say you did not ask me humbly to enter the ballroom on your arm?

THE PRINCE
But – ye-es.

FLORIZELLA
I have thought over it a long time. I told you, in the thoughtlessness of the moment, that I should. But afterwards I was tempted by the thought that it would mean

needless ostentation and set against me various ladies of the court whom I have already innocently wounded, I know not how. But again I considered, and to please you, I shall take your arm. Besides, sooner or later our . . . partiality must be revealed, must it not?

THE PRINCE
We shall go in arm in arm from the terrace, if it pleases you.

FLORIZELLA
Or from the door of the ballroom? From the terrace is so conspicuous!

THE PRINCE
From the terrace.

FLORIZELLA
Well, I suppose you know best. I shall have to summon all my self-control to my aid. . . . But the trumpet has sounded, in an hour we are all at the palace! You *must* leave me, you cannot stay any longer.

THE PRINCE
You are alone?

FLORIZELLA
Yes.

THE PRINCE
You – you – your sister is not here?

FLORIZELLA
My sister's in her room, spreading and preening herself before her looking-glass. You must know how Annabella is: so secret and so jealous and so vain, and more and more secret and jealous and vain as she grows older.

THE PRINCE
But . . . you have another sister?
A pause.

FLORIZELLA
Yes, I should like to have another sister, or even a brother. Annabella really is graceless at times, she tries even my patience. You must know how very unconsequential I am, mother always used to say I should never really grow up. Well, she's continually scolding me in her capacity of elder sister, and it's occasionally intolerable. But I put up with it as best I can, one has to forgive so many things in this world –

THE PRINCE
I asked if you have another sister.

FLORIZELLA
Oh, whoever made you think of her? There's a little sister whom we call Cinderella, she has such domestic habits. Such a harmless dear child! and she's

137

much to be pitied, for she was born without either talent or good looks. Whoever told you of her? She's so timid that no-one's ever seen her. Was that the trumpet again? Oh no it wasn't. The trumpet frightens me, it brings war to my mind and chills my blood. I cannot bear it. All I love is violin music. Violin music! A gift from heaven, it seems to me.

THE PRINCE
But where is she now? Someone told me of her; I'd heard nothing of her and I was just curious because nobody else seemed to have heard of her either.

FLORIZELLA
She's sewing in her room, I expect. Such a dear harmless child! A little simple, but I hope devoutly it will pass away as she grows older. . . . . Do you know, I could almost be sure you came to see her and not me, if I did not know different.

THE PRINCE
Oh no. No no. How could you think that, I wonder? Ha ha!

FLORIZELLA
You know I'm as jealous as a child. Of course it isn't true. . . . But go, my Prince! And . . . I have something to say. I have reproached myself a thousand times for giving myself to you. . . . the other night: but it was not without a deep struggle with myself. What harm cannot Love do?

THE PRINCE
Oh, do stop; I'm completely out of patience. Why do you make me come here for nothing at all, and talk the utterest rubbish while I am here? Things have happened between us, and what's the use of making up all this rigmarolle? I'm sick to death. What's the use of pretending?

FLORIZELLA
I don't know. I suppose it's just habit.

THE PRINCE
Then I'd advice you to get rid of it at once.

FLORIZELLA
But you will go with me? You will take my arm?

THE PRINCE
Yes yes. But I must give you to understand that just because of what has happened, you may not think you can depend on me for anything.[4]

FLORIZELLA
But you will?

THE PRINCE
Yes yes.

FLORIZELLA
There's someone coming. Tonight!

THE PRINCE
Tonight, madam. I kiss your hand.

She lets him out. She listens a moment, then sits down a little heavily. There is a
pause of silence. A door opens softly, and CINDERELLA enters. The child
we all know. . . . She goes to the fire and rakes it together.

FLORIZELLA
You're there at last.

CINDERELLA
I've been for firewood, sister, and I got lost. I think it got dark sooner than I
expected. But I found my way back by the west wall –

FLORIZELLA
Don't talk so much. It's all nonsense about the dark, it's your wicked care-
lessness. Why weren't you there to do me up? Spite, that's what I call it.
Where's Annabella? It's time to start almost. Nobody' there when I want
them. You might at least say something about how I look, now that you
are here.

CINDERELLA
It's a very pretty dress, sister. It matches your eyes, and your hair is pretty too.
Waltz music far off.
Is that the ball, sister?

FLORIZELLA
The music is starting this very minute. Where's Annabella? She must hurry up. I
get so impatient waiting round for selfish people like this.

CINDERELLA
It sounds so beautiful. Do they play that when the people dance?

FLORIZELLA
Of course they do.

CINDERELLA
Sister dear, don't you think your blue from last year would fit me?

FLORIZELLA
No. It's too long.

CINDERELLA
I could shorten it in ten minutes.

FLORIZELLA
No you couldn't. What then?

CINDERELLA
Sister dear, can't I go with you to the ball?

FLORIZELLA
What did you say?

CINDERELLA
Can't – can't I go to the great ball tonight?
Enter ANNABELLA

FLORIZELLA
I never heard such impudence. Sister Annabella, here's Cinders wants to go to the
ball, if you please.

ANNABELLA
Why, no, our little Cinders must stay at home and keep the fire, and go to bed like
a good little girl. Are you back long, dear? Did you get lost in the woods? It's
very dangerous, you mustn't stay out so late any more.
A noise of bells.

CINDERELLA
They're all going to the ball. Everybody's going to the ball. . . . .

FLORIZELLA
If you want to put me in a fury and shake all the gold powder out of my hair you
are about to succeed. Put such ideas into the fire immediately. You'd cut a
pretty figure! What would the people say? Why, half of them –

CINDERELLA
I could hide my face behind my fan.

FLORIZELLA
And where do you get your fan?

CINDERELLA
There's Grandmother's –

FLORIZELLA
You can't dance a step –

CINDERELLA
I learnt from the girl next door last –

FLORIZELLA
Don't dare answer back. Don't let me hear another word? If I hear any more of
your foolish notions, as sure as your name's Cinderella –

CINDERELLA
I will answer back! And don't dare say my name's Cinderella again, or I'll
scratch you! It's you who gave me that ugly name, and I was christened

Claribella – Claribella, Claribella! Why don't you give me pretty dresses and take me to see the grand court? Why do you make me rake ashes till you come home, and do your work for you? I hate you, I hate you![5]

She bursts into tears. A petrified silence.

FLORIZELLA

Really – I – I can't make out. I'm totally overcome. What *has* come over the girl? Never, never have I heard such language in all my life. Sit down and control yourself. I'm intensely shocked.

ANNABELLA

Do be quiet, sister, you talk far too much. Stop crying, my love, and look at me. There, Now will you be good and not cry any more?

FLORIZELLA

It's no good coaxing her. She's totally incorrigible.

CINDERELLA

Why can't I se the lights and hear the music, and dance till I'm tired? The days and nights pass away, and I see everybody going to dance and play; and I work and go to bed like an old woman or a simple creature. Why can't I put flowers in my hair and perfumes in my sleeve and beautiful rings on my fingers? I ought to be going to the ball. The music's calling me. I must go to the ball!

FLORIZELLA

You shall *not* go to the ball, if I have to tie you up. Do you want to disgrace both of us?

CINDERELLA

Please go away.

ANNABELLA

Yes. You only make things worse, Florizella. I shall calm her far better when you're not there.

FLORIZELLA

Before I go, my dear, it may interest you to hear about my visit. I know you're dying to hear.

ANNABELLA

What visit?

FLORIZELLA

Don't pretend you've forgotten. You may be interested to know that I shall figure quite prominently in the ball with a certain high personage. Did you call the coach?

ANNABELLA

Go away. What do I care about your visit? Oh, go away!

FLORIZELLA

I wish you what you probably won't have, my dear. I wish you many many cavaliers at the ball.

She goes out, banging the door. The coach passes the window and the noise dies slowly away.

ANNABELLA

You won't cry any more, will you, Cinderella?

CINDERELLA

There's the music.

The music trails into silence.

ANNABELLA

It's stopped. My dear, stay at home by your little fire and don't cry for all that. They'll all be useless tears, every one. You love the music: it stops playing, and you feel lost in the silence.

CINDERELLA

It'll begin again directly, for the ball. And I have learnt to dance far better than Florizella! She's stiff on her feet, I know, I've watched her for hours trying to get into a pretty step, and she can't because she's too old. And I'm seventeen, and I've wasted years and years already knitting your stockings and making you delicate food. And soon I shan't be seventeen any more.

ANNABELLA

You're growing up, Cinderella. You don't talk as you did.

CINDERELLA

Do you expect me to live on always, without a single word? I've never said anything all this long long while because I've been half asleep.[6] But when I see all the beautiful dresses fluttering to the ball, and the music singing louder than all the birds, and sweeter, I feel words rising in my throat.

ANNABELLA

Hush, my dear. Do you feel a little better now?

CINDERELLA

Why don't you want me to go to the ball? Florizella, she's just spiteful, she's just treating me like everybody else only the young gentlemen. But you're not the same, Annabella, and I can't understand. . . . Is – is it true that I disgrace you both? Am I so ugly, and do I walk like a country girl? Is it true? If only you'd tell me – no! Don't tell me, for it would break my heart.

ANNABELLA

You're the most beautiful child in all the world, my little Cinderella.

CINDERELLA

Oh! Then why can't I go to the ball?

ANNABELLA

It – it isn't half as beautiful as you think. Most of the ladies are like Florizella, and the gentlemen are foolish and without education. You would not be happy in such society.

CINDERELLA

No. That's not the reason. There's something else.

ANNABELLA

What makes you think so?

CINDERELLA

Yes, there's something else. It's a reason I can't understand. But I know it's there, and it frightens you.

ANNABELLA

Don't be silly, child. I think you really are given to dreaming all sorts of foolish things, you must stop immediately. What are you waiting for, Cinderella?

CINDERELLA

I thought I heard something.

ANNABELLA

Where?

CINDERELLA

In the street.

ANNABELLA

I didn't hear it. Are you expecting the milk, so late, and on the night of the ball too? It's hardly likely.

CINDERELLA

No, I'm not expecting. . . . anything for sure.
A pause.

ANNABELLA

Are you feeling better now, my Cinderella?

CINDERELLA

Yes, much better. I'm sorry I was rough, Annabella, because I love you a great deal. . . . . Are you sure you can't hear anything?

ANNABELLA

No. Are you nervous?

CINDERELLA

No. I'm too often by myself at night for that. Are you sure?

ANNABELLA

I don't hear anything.

143

CINDERELLA
Not a sound?

ANNABELLA
No. I never remember the town so silent.

CINDERELLA
Not a sound?

ANNABELLA
No, The music stopped just now, you know, and it won't start again for a minute
or two. I must be setting out, the coach will be back for me directly.

CINDERELLA
I don't mean the music of the ball. I mean. . . . oh, I don't know what I mean.
Annabella looks suddenly frightened.

ANNABELLA
I think you're a little shaken, child.

CINDERELLA
No, I'm not shaken, Annabella. And I'm not angry any more.

ANNABELLA
Why?

CINDERELLA
Because I feel happy and contented.

ANNABELLA
Oh, Cinders, so you're going to wait for us to come home, like a sweet child?

CINDERELLA
I don't know. No, I wouldn't be content and happy if I were going to bed. But
I feel as if everything were going to be stopped, as if there is going to be a
great change –

ANNABELLA
Cinderella!

CINDERELLA
No, I'm not going to be Cinderella any more.

ANNABELLA
Somebody has been pushing wicked thoughts into your head. Whom have you
been meeting in the wood?

CINDERELLA
It's not what the witches have been telling me, because I've never seen them. I
don't know. It's a feeling that comes to me, like scents on the wind, when you
feel the flowers can't be far away.

ANNABELLA
Oh!

CINDERELLA
I feel happy now.

ANNABELLA
Oh, why isn't Florizella here, why isn't she here! My darling child!

CINDERELLA
I've never felt so happy, not since I first held a looking-glass in my hand and first knew that I was more beautiful than Florizella ever was.

ANNABELLA
My dear, you – you must put these ideas out of your head at once. It is very grave indeed to nurse such whimsicalities. Now take your sewing like a good girl and sit by the fire.

CINDERELLA
Yes, sister dear. Will there be moonlight tonight?

ANNABELLA
I don't know. Yes, there will.

CINDERELLA
I knew there would be.

ANNABELLA
Why?

CINDERELLA
I don't know, but I knew.

ANNABELLA
Cinderella, my love, have I ever been cruel to you?

CINDERELLA
No. You've been a dear sister to me, except when you wouldn't let me dress up and go into the world. But it doesn't matter now.

ANNABELLA
Oh, my darling! Listen to me, listen carefully –

CINDERELLA
What's the matter? You're all pale and worried. What's the matter?

ANNABELLA
Oh no, I'm not pale or worried. But you mustn't think of such ideas. Now promise me you won't. And – and if you hear of see – something when you're by yourself, you mustn't listen, even if it sounds – sounds very beautiful. Do you hear me, Cinders? Promise me, promise me! I've never done you

any harm, have I, but always been kind to you? So you'll promise, won't you, darling?

CINDERELLA
What sounds? What beautiful sounds?

ANNABELLA
Oh – nothing. Only there are often foolish drunken musicians on the night of a great ball, and they might do you harm. Promise me you won't listen.

CINDERELLA
I don't know.

ANNABELLA
Oh, promise, promise! See, tomorrow morning coming home from the ball, I'll bring you a beautiful gold chain which you can wear always. Will you promise?

CINDERELLA
I can't promise.

ANNABELLA
Oh, what shall I do, what shall I do! Why isn't Florizella here! Think of all my kindness to you, my dear, and all the sweet things I gave you, and all the smiles and tears, and promise. . . .

CINDERELLA
I can't promise. Something tells me I can't.
The trumpet sounds.

ANNABELLA
I must go. Oh, my darling, whatever happens, think of me, and. . . . kiss me, my dear.
They kiss each other. Annabella begins to cry.

CINDERELLA
You kissed me – I don't know – as if you never expected to see me any more. Why are you crying?

ANNABELLA
I don't know. And all my powder will be washed away. There's the coach. I must powder my face on the way. Goodnight, Cinderella.

CINDERELLA
Goodnight. A happy night to you, sister.

ANNABELLA
My darling – goodnight.[7]
She hurries out. The coach passes the window and rumbles away into the night. There is complete silence. The moon has risen and is beginning to creep into

the room. Cinderella stands still a moment, then puts out the lamp and sits by the ashes of the fire with her sewing. She begins to sew, very calm and deliberate. There are distant sounds of footsteps, snatches of song, a strain of music, and then silence again. A long time passes, Cinderella sewing as calmly and deliberately as ever. Then the silence is broken. Far away, on the other side of the world, the Song of the Fairy Godmother rises. Cinderella drops her sewing, slowly, as if she had been expecting to hear all the time. The song is made of beautiful dreams. Nearer and nearer. The Fairy Godmother is at the window. She is an old lady, like every old lady, but she too is made of beautiful dreams.

THE FAIRY GODMOTHER
Goodnight, Claribella.

CINDERELLA
Goodnight.

THE FAIRY GODMOTHER
Have you been waiting for me?

CINDERELLA
Yes.

THE FAIRY GODMOTHER
Have you been waiting for me a long time?

CINDERELLA
Yes.

THE FAIRY GODMOTHER
Who told you that I would come?

CINDERELLA
Nobody. I knew you would come tonight, because the moon is brighter.

THE FAIRY GODMOTHER
You've never seen me before. Aren't you afraid?

CINDERELLA
No, I'm not afraid. I've never seen you, but I know you.

THE FAIRY GODMOTHER
Who am I?

CINDERELLA
You are my Godmother.

THE FAIRY GODMOTHER
Ah! Who told you?

CINDERELLA
Nobody. I know you are.

THE FAIRY GODMOTHER
Where are your sisters?

CINDERELLA
They've gone to the ball. Annabella's just left. Didn't she see you?

THE FAIRY GODMOTHER
I saw her in the coach. She was crying and putting ugly powder on her tears. She
    seemed to be crying over someone who was dead, or over a great misfortune.
    Why was she sorrowful?

CINDERELLA
I don't know. Didn't she see you?

THE FAIRY GODMOTHER
She did not see me. Nobody can see me now.

CINDERELLA
But I can see you, standing in the moonlight. Won't you come in?

THE FAIRY GODMOTHER
You can see me, but the rest of the world cannot, Claribella. You are a beautiful
    child. Can you dance?

CINDERELLA
Yes.

THE FAIRY GODMOTHER
Then why are you not dressed for the ball?

CINDERELLA
I don't know. My sisters will not let me be dressed up in beautiful clothes and go
    into the world.

THE FAIRY GODMOTHER
Ah! I wonder why.

CINDERELLA
Why have you come to see me? I felt all day that something would happen when
    the moonlight came. Why did you come?

THE FAIRY GODMOTHER
I have come to send you to the ball.

CINDERELLA
Yes, Godmother.

THE FAIRY GODMOTHER
You are seventeen. What are your thoughts?

CINDERELLA
I am beautiful and I want to wear a beautiful dress and beautiful flowers in my
hair.

THE FAIRY GODMOTHER
Is thqt all? [*sic*]

CINDERELLA
In the shining of my needles I have seen the shining of jewels.

THE FAIRY GODMOTHER
Is that all?

CINDERELLA
In the click of the needles, too, as they worked in and out, I have heard the sound
of bells.

THE FAIRY GODMOTHER
Is that all?

CINDERELLA
I have often heard the singing of nightingales. Then I looked into my glass and
saw I was more beautiful than ever. That made me cry a little.

THE FAIRY GODMOTHER
Why?

CINDERELLA
Because I thought how sad it was that time should pass and I should mend my
sisters' torn stockings.

THE FAIRY GODMOTHER
Yes.?

CINDERELLA
But when the nightingales stopped singing in my heart, I stopped crying, and went
on with my work as if nothing had happened.

THE FAIRY GODMOTHER
And did the nightingales sing very often, and the shine of the jewels, did it come
often too?

CINDERELLA
Every day. Especially at the end, when the sun was tender and the moon was just
going to rise. Lately . . . oh, yes, very often.

THE FAIRY GODMOTHER
You have never asked the meaning of all that?

CINDERELLA
There were none to tell.

THE FAIRY GODMOTHER
Not even your own heart?

CINDERELLA
My heart has never told me its secrets.

THE FAIRY GODMOTHER
Do you think it will, soon?

CINDERELLA
I don't know. I am going to the ball! I am all changed. Am I Cinderella? Just
    because of a ball, and Florizella goes once a week!

THE FAIRY GODMOTHER
This ball is not like another, my dear.

CINDERELLA
Why?

THE FAIRY GODMOTHER
Does not a beating in your breast tell you that?

CINDERELLA
I am all trembling. I wonder why. I feel as if I was dreaming, and I know I am not
    dreaming.

THE FAIRY GODMOTHER
No. You are not dreaming. You are going to the ball, tonight, and you will be the
    most beautiful.

CINDERELLA
Where is my beautiful dress, dear Godmother?

THE FAIRY GODMOTHER
At the bottom of the garden, with a coach all in gold and footmen all in the best
    livery, in gold too, to take you to the ball. . . . . But before I leave you to go
    to the garden for your coach, there is one thing I must tell you. Listen, it will
    pay you well.

CINDERELLA
Yes, Godmother.

THE FAIRY GODMOTHER
You must not stay too long at the ball.

CINDERELLA
No, Godmother.

THE FAIRY GODMOTHER
When the clock strikes twelve, you must be outside the palace, and at the bottom of the garden.

CINDERELLA
And then?

THE FAIRY GODMOTHER
If you do not leave, if you linger wilfully, if you forget, then, when you leave the palace, there will be no coach, no footmen, and your dress will fall from you into the finest dust. You will be Cinderella again.

CINDERELLA
Cinderella again! And if I come away early?

THE FAIRY GODMOTHER
If you stay late, you will hear me sing, again. Then you will know that all will be over. You will hear me sing, again, very far away, very softly, and you will see me again, a little farewell look. . . . You will know it is the end.[8]

CINDERELLA
But if I come away early?

THE FAIRY GODMOTHER
Then, my dear, you would be the happiest on the face of the earth.

CINDERELLA
I shall be the happiest on the face of the earth! Then I shall be very happy. I am to go now?

THE FAIRY GODMOTHER
Wait a moment. Stand here, by the moonlight.
A sound of bells.

CINDERELLA
The ball. . . . At last, at last! Music, and the ringing of bells . . . Everything will be beautiful, tonight, and all the rest of my life. . . . . To think the old Cinderella will never come back! This hem will never be sewn together now. I'll never sit on my little stool and watch the fire, never any more. I am going to the ball! And yet to think I'll never sit on my little stool again. . . . It's like leaving a very old friend, to say goodbye to Cinderella. I am going to the ball! Goodbye, Cinderella, be good! Lady Claribella is on her way to the ball. Her coach is at the bottom of the garden. Goodnight, Cinderella, don't you hope I shall enjoy myself at the ball?
Bells and Music, A noise of wheels.

THE FAIRY GODMOTHER
Do you hear?

CINDERELLA

Yes. Wheels running over the cobblestones under the moon. It's going to pass the window. It's going to pass the window, and there's somebody in it, with footmen drawing it in front and footmen behind. I've seen it all before, of course I have! I remember now. Who is in the coach? It's somebody I know, it's somebody I know!

THE FAIRY GODMOTHER

The prince of all the land.

CINDERELLA

The prince of all the land!. . . . Of course I've seen it all before. It's coming nearer and nearer. Why do I feel all the old things slipping through my fingers? Cinderella, Cinderella, where are you? I've lost you for ever . . . Cinderella! Cinderella!

The Prince passes slowly in his coach, beneath the moonlight. The sound dies away.

THE FAIRY GODMOTHER

You saw him?

CINDERELLA

Yes. He passed in the moonlight, proudly, with the sound of running wheels under his feet. My heart is telling its secret at last. It has seen him a thousand times, in dreams, proud and brave, and he gave me a white flower that was his own soul. His calm beautiful face, it belongs to me, I have always owned it, though he never knew. And he too has always known me, in his dreams. I am going to him. I am going to him.[9]

Music.

THE FAIRY GODMOTHER

They're beginning to get ready for the dance, Claribella.

CINDERELLA

Yes. I'm not sad now. Cinderella, poor Cinderella by her fire, she can't know what I feel . . . Poor, poor empty life that she has! Oh, Godmother, am I really really beautiful? Sister Florizella said my hair was too yellow. It isn't true, is it? Is there red in my cheeks? Are there pretty slippers for my feet? They must be very light to dance, and I've got the smallest feet in the world, though Florizella gives me big boots to make people think I haven't. I shall dance in the moonlight, and it will be with him that I shall dance. My eyes must be more beautiful than ever they were to look into his. Florizella said they weren't very beautiful . . . Poor Florizella! If she could only feel what I feel!

Music.

The happiest on the face of the earth. . . . .

THE FAIRY GODMOTHER

Come after me.

The Fairy Godmother goes. Cinderella stands gazing into the room. Then, slowly, she follows. The curtain falls.

ACT TWO

The royal terrace, immediately afterwards. Through a door at the side the ballroom is to be seen, with gaily dressed people passing to and fro. The terrace is lit by festive candles. FLORIZELLA is standing at the balcony, as if looking out for someone. ANNABELLA enters.

ANNABELLA

Is that you, sister? I've been looking for you everywhere.

FLORIZELLA

You've arrived, have you? And why were you looking for me? It isn't long since you saw me, is it? Has the Prince arrived?

ANNABELLA

No, I don't think so. Were you waiting for him?

FLORIZELLA

Don't be absurd. I assure you however much he may be taken with me, I can never be so foolishly taken with him as to stand tiptoe by a wall like a stray creature. . . . Are you sure he hasn't arrived?

ANNABELLA

I don't think so. There's plenty of time. Why aren't you in the ballroom?

FLORIZELLA

I can't stand the heat, it ruins a delicate complexion. Besides, I never met such a vacant crowd of people; they buzz round one so it is enough to give headaches for a week.

ANNABELLA

Yet, if you become Queen, my dear, you will have to make your life with them. A queen, they say, passes her time in forgetting herself and being gracious to her subjects, however vacant they may be.

FLORIZELLA

Do you think so? And since you are so well disposed towards these dear people, why aren't you mingling your wit with theirs instead of pestering me?

ANNABELLA

Florizella, I have something to say.

FLORIZELLA
You usually have.

ANNABELLA
Something very serious.

FLORIZELLA
That is quite different.

ANNABELLA
Cinderella –

FLORIZELLA
Oh, if it's Cinderella, I won't hear a word. I protest, are my ears to be deafened
with talk of her even at the ball, when one wants to look and talk one's gay-
est? I ask you! Don't say a word.

ANNABELLA
Florizella, I'm sure Cinderella isn't – safe.

FLORIZELLA
Safe? What do you mean, safe? Safe from what?

ANNABELLA
Safe from what I've always tried to keep away from her ever since . . . You know
what I mean.

FLORIZELLA
Oh![10]

ANNABELLA
She talks wildly, and says something is going to happen, and she's not going to be
Cinderella any more.

FLORIZELLA
Stuff and nonsense! Just because she couldn't come to the ball! She wants to run
away, or something. Upon my word, it's time she was really and seriously put
down. I can't stand such frippery. Talking wildly, indeed!

ANNABELLA
No, it wasn't the ball, I could see that. There was something in her eyes, something I recognised, something I'd seen before.

FLORIZELLA
And where! In whose eyes?

ANNABELLA
Can you ask me in whose eyes, Florizella, and flutter your fan like a wild thing?
Is ten years such a very long time, that you can't remember when you looked
into my face, with such a far-away look, and said – Oh!

Florizella has struck her across the face with her fan and walked rapidly to the edge of the terrace.[11]
Have you gone mad?

FLORIZELLA (half crying)
If you dare speak to me of such things again, I'll do more than strike you. I won't hear, I won't hear!

ANNABELLA (powdering her cheek)
So I've shaken you: that's why I spoke. Do you realize Cinderella is just the same now, that something is going to happen? We *must* do something, we must take her away; perhaps then things will stop and she will be quiet.

FLORIZELLA
I shan't stir a finger. She shall go as I did. Why should I? Who was there to say to me, this is the way and not that, this is true and that is not true? The sooner she gets over it the better for everybody. How dare you come talking to me of these things? I've forgotten all about them. How dare you spoil my enjoyment?

ANNABELLA
Have you forgotten?

FLORIZELLA
Do you want me to strike you again?

ANNABELLA
I have tried to persuade her and warn her as much as ever I could, though I said nothing – nothing definite.

FLORIZELLA
I hope not, indeed. Such nonsense to stuff into a child's head, and especially such a child. *Hasn't* the Prince come? I think he might have enough respect for me not to be late; and yet it surprises me.
The STRANGE COURTIER has entered, walking about slowly, with an air of studied distraction.[12]
Who's that?

ANNABELLA
I don't know.

FLORIZELLA
Whoever it is, I must talk to him. That will pay the Prince back for his inconstancy, he wil be put out to see us together. And on the terrace, too! . . . Don't you know who it is?
And [*sic*]

ANNABELLA
I think – I think now he's a little familiar.

FLORIZELLA
Yes, I *do* know him. Look a little closer, my dear.

ANNABELLA
Oh!

FLORIZELLA
There's no need to say 'Oh' at all. You talk of your ten years, and you ask me if I have forgotten. And there he is. Can you look at him, and ask yourself if there is anything to remember.? I've always told you, my dear, they always come back, like the pigeons; however far you send them, you can remain quite quite calm: they will always come back. I'me sure Lady Doramon's new wig is beautiful to see, my dear.

ANNABELLA
Do you think so?

FLORIZELLA
Yes, my love, especially with the tapestry of the ballroom as a background.

ANNABELLA
Really?
Annabella walks with strained unconcern into the ballroom. With strained un-concern Florizella hums a tune. With strained unconcern also the Strange Courtier advances.

THE STRANGE COURTIER
I beg your pardon, Madam.
Florizella sighs thoughtfully, working her fingers through the interstices of her fan.
Madam?

FLORIZELLA
Oh! Sir! I am fainting . . .

THE STRANGE COURTIER
Oh, Madam!

FLORIZELLA
You have so frightened me. Please leave me at once.

THE STRANGE COURTIER
I must see your face first. Oh, whoever made fans, to hide faces, as parasols were made to hide the sun?

FLORIZELLA
That wasn't a very good one.

THE STRANGE COURTIER
Please show your face! One short look?

FLORIZELLA
There. Do you like my face?

THE STRANGE COURTIER
Florizella!. . . .

FLORIZELLA
Goodnight, my lord. I hope at least you are pleased to see me.

THE STRANGE COURTIER
I didn't see it was you, my dear.

FLORIZELLA
That was evident. I hope you're glad to see me, now that the parasol no longer
    hides the sun.

THE STRANGE COURTIER
I don't know if I *am* glad to see you, Florizella. Why do you make fun of every-
    thing I say?

FLORIZELLA
Because I think it is born in your mind, whether you know it or no, my dear, with
    the full intention of being laughed at, and laughed at most heartily. Have you
    come to the ball, my dear?

THE STRANGE COURTIER
Yes, my dear. Why are you laughing?

FLORIZELLA
Because we talk like cooing doves. And why have you come to the ball, my dear?

THE STRANGE COURTIER
I have been looking forward to coming, Florizella, for a long long time.

FLORIZELLA
Oh!

THE STRANGE COURTIER
Yes. It is over six months since I saw you.

FLORIZELLA
When did you come back? I never heard a word about you after you went.

THE STRANGE COURTIER
Did you think of me when I was away, my darling?

FLORIZELLA
No, I did not think of you when you were away, my darling.

THE STRANGE COURTIER
You are playing with me, Florizella.

FLORIZELLA
Oh! Don't you like it?

THE STRANGE COURTIER
No.

FLORIZELLA
I can't help that. (with temper) You *are* a fool, and I can't help treating you as such.

THE STRANGE COURTIER
You asked me why I came, Florizella.

FLORIZELLA
Did I? Yes, so I did?

THE STRANGE COURTIER
I thought I'd see you, I came to see you . . . After six months. . . .

FLORIZELLA
How time flies, doesn't it?

THE STRANGE COURTIER
Did you expect to see me?

FLORIZELLA
I wasn't thinking of you at all. Did you expect to see me?

THE STRANGE COURTIER
Oh no. . . . That is . . . Why do you laugh at me?

FLORIZELLA
You're as easy to trip up as a lame dog.

THE STRANGE COURTIER
I *am* a lame dog, at your feet, Florizella.

FLORIZELLA
By the way, who did you think I was, just now?

THE STRANGE COURTIER
Just now?

FLORIZELLA
When you said my face was the sun behind a parasol?

THE STRANGE COURTIER
Oh! I knew it was you all the time. Couldn't you guess that, Florizella?

FLORIZELLA
No I couldn't, unfortunately. I suppose I really look quite brand new and romantic in the shadow, and with my back to you . . . But up you come, and it's the

old Florizella you've kissed and fondled a thousand times, and got sick of a thousand times, and come back to every one of those thousand times, because there was nobody else. You thought you'd got somebody really new, just now? What a pity! You must always be content with Florizella.

THE STRANGE COURTIER
Content with Florizella! Ah, that would be enough –

FLORIZELLA
I was forgetting, my dear. I have expectations.

THE STRANGE COURTIER
Expectations?

FLORIZELLA
I am the mistress of the Prince, and I fully expect to be queen before long.

THE STRANGE COURTIER
Oh!

FLORIZELLA
What do you mean? You gaping fool! Why shouldn't the Prince want me, why shouldn't I give myself to him? You foolish creature, if you think because you've intrigued with me a little that the Prince is beyond my reach, you're mistaken. You idiot! The Prince wants me, do you hear? I can't come with you any more. You will have to try somebody else for tonight. There's the other terrace. You may find a beautiful lady hanging pensively over the balcony, and this time you may be sure it won't be Florizella. Florizella will be the queen, and you will come and kiss her hand. And if you dare breathe a word about what we've been together, or anything you know about me, I'll get you hanged and drawn ten times round the Palace wall.

THE STRANGE COURTIER
I congratulate you, my dear, on your good fortune.

FLORIZELLA
Fortune? What do you mean, fortune? Is there anything strange about my getting married?

THE STRANGE COURTIER
Oh no, my dear. But tonight. . . . tonight you will not forget me, Florizella? Just once?

FLORIZELLA
I shall do no such thing. Tonight I belong to the Prince: how can you think that I belong to you? So there's no need to call me 'my dear' any more. Besides, there are plenty of ladies in the court.

THE STRANGE COURTIER
Perhaps there are.

FLORIZELLA

If there were a hundred thousand you'd hardly rest until you'd had a good look at every one of them. Go away. You irritate me more every time I set eyes on you. You're the stupidest fool I ever saw. Go away.

THE STRANGE COURTIER

Do hush. I can see her coming across the ballroom. She's looking for me.

FLORIZELLA

She?

THE STRANGE COURTIER

My wife.

FLORIZELLA

You're – not – married?

THE STRANGE COURTIER

I thought you must have heard. Oh, do stop laughing, for Heaven's sake, you'll bring the whole crowd out on the terrace.

FLORIZELLA

That's the joke of the night. You married? And who is she? What is she?
Enter the WIFE OF THE STRANGE COURTIER.

THE WIFE OF THE STRANGE COURTIER

Is that you?

THE STRANGE COURTIER

Yes.

THE WIFE OF THE STRANGE COURTIER

Oh! You are with somebody.

THE STRANGE COURTIER

I am following immediately.

THE WIFE OF THE STRANGE COURTIER

Do hurry up. I have been accosted several times already.
Exit the WIFE OF THE STRANGE COURTIER.[13]

THE STRANGE COURTIER

Does she amuse you so much?

FLORIZELLA

Really, it's beginning most beautifully, the night of the ball. My sides are aching, positively paining me. So that's your wife. You're married. Married! Oh dear. . . . Oh dear. . . .

THE STRANGE COURTIER

She's a fool, but her father's got money.

FLORIZELLA

That her father's got money I knew before ever I set eyes on her, but that she's a fool is the precious crowning detail. 'Do hurry up!'. . . . Poor thing, she's *so* used to being jostled in crowds and left alone by her gallant husband, who is far too busy running about telling strange ladies that their face is like the sun behind a parasol.

THE STRANGE COURTIER

But sometimes the ladies are not as strange as they would seem.

FLORIZELLA

No.

THE STRANGE COURTIER

I must go.

FLORIZELLA

Is she virtuous, my lady? Is she hot, is she cold, my lady? Has she love of men of gold, my lady?

THE STRANGE COURTIER

She's a fool.

FLORIZELLA

Ah! That explains all. But you must hurry.

THE STRANGE COURTIER

Florizella!

FLORIZELLA

No.

THE STRANGE COURTIER

Florizella!

FLORIZELLA

Oh, go away!

THE STRANGE COURTIER

Florizella, you did not say 'go away' once upon a time.

FLORIZELLA

Ah?

THE STRANGE COURTIER

Ten years ago, Florizella –

FLORIZELLA

I'm afraid that you don't realize the lady is running every possible danger. How can you leave her alone, when the first wicked man may come creeping along and repeating in her ear the very ugliest things?

THE STRANGE COURTIER
Will you dance with me?

FLORIZELLA
Is there *nobody* tonight? But of course you're not as prepossessing as you were.

THE STRANGE COURTIER
Will you dance with me?

FLORIZELLA
No.

Exit the STRANGE COURTIER. Florizella stands motionless, then laughs to herself. A hubbub in the ballroom: the Prince has arrived. Florizella tiptoes hurriedly to the door of the ballroom and looks in. The crowd comes on to the terrace, and forms two ranks through which the PRINCE advances. He is gorgeously dressed, but looks annoyed. Florizella works her way through the crowd till she is almost at his side. There is quiet while the Prince makes his speech.

THE PRINCE
This is the great night of the year, my friends – such you are tonight, every one who graces my court, – every one with joy in his heart is my friend tonight, whoever he be. The ball will last till the first rays of the sun, till then we must all be at our best, for, my friends, it is carnival-time.[14] In one moment the music will begin. Every cavalier will offer his arm to his lady and we will enter the ballroom.

Loud applause, interrupted suddenly by bells ringing in the distance. Shouts of applause in the same direction.

What is that? Who is arriving? Why applause in the garden? Some foolish creatures have not seen me arrive and take the carriage of one of my subjects for my own. Idiots.

Everyone crosses to the balcony at the back except the Prince, and Florizella behind him.

What is it?

No answer.

This is intolerable. Why cannot people arrive by the entrance, instead of sneaking round through the garden? I will not hear of such conduct. Will no one answer me? Everyone turns his back to me! Such conduct, in my own subjects –

FLORIZELLA
I, my lord, I do not turn my back on you.

THE PRINCE
Oh! Goodnight, madam.

FLORIZELLA
Goodnight, madam? So cold?

THE PRINCE
We are not alone.

FLORIZELLA
We shall be alone. . . . It will not be the first time. . . . Do you remember?

THE PRINCE
I beg your pardon?

FLORIZELLA
Why will you mock me? Can it be that you are not true? Remember that I gave
myself to you, asking nothing in exchange. It is not an easy sacrifice.

THE PRINCE
Sometimes.

FLORIZELLA
Sometimes? Why do you turn away?

THE PRINCE
There is evidently something extraordinary going on in the garden. I must go to
see. Excuse me, madam.

FLORIZELLA
Stay a moment. Do you talk to me so often, when there are none to hear? What
if some visitor, to make himself known, is so foolish as to come to the ball
through the garden and ring a peal of bells to let everyone know he is on the
way? Stay with me. You will take me in on your arm, won't you? You haven't
forgotten? Or am I not beautiful enough to languish on the arm of a Prince?

THE PRINCE
Who will one day be King. . . . .

FLORIZELLA
Yes. . . . What do you mean? You will take me in, will you not?

THE PRINCE
Yes Yes. People will gossip if they see us talking like this.

FLORIZELLA
Oh, dear me, what if they do?

THE CROWD (at the balcony, in one cry of admiration)
Oh!

THE PRINCE
I must see.
He steps up to the crowd, which is slowly dividing into two ranks, leaving a
passage leading from the garden. Florizella, curious at last, steps aside. The
crowd is all in a murmur. Then, suddenly, there is dead silence. The music has

stopped. A rapid tap-tap of footsteps, and Cinderella is standing on the edge of the terrace, silhouetted against the night.

CINDERELLA
Goodnight, ladies and gentlemen.
Vague murmurs of 'Goodnight'.
I greet you with wishes for light hearts and light feet. I am a stranger here, and I am afraid I don't know my way about very well. Where shall I find the Prince?

THE PRINCE
Goodnight, madam.
They are separated from the rest. Cinderella looks into his eyes, very calm and assured; he looks into hers.

CINDERELLA
His Highness?

THE PRINCE
I am the Prince, my lady.

CINDERELLA
Goodnight, your Highness. I left my coach in the garden. Do you mind?

THE PRINCE
What a beautiful coach it must be, to have attracted such a crowd to the balcony!. . . . . Or was it the visitor in the coach?

CINDERELLA (laughing)
Oh! I could not tell, my lord.

THE PRINCE
I could, my lady.

CINDERELLA
I have come a very long way, in my coach, to dance with you tonight.
The music plays. The crowd is whispering in the background and staring at Cinderella. Florizella stands a little aside.

THE PRINCE
And your name, sweet lady?

CINDERELLA
My name? Ah, I've forgotten.

THE PRINCE
Have you?

CINDERELLA
Yes. Isn't it strange? You always always have the names of your visitors?

THE PRINCE
Yes. But yours I shall not ask.

CINDERELLA
But you have just asked me!

THE PRINCE
But I shall not ask a second time.

CINDERELLA
Why?

THE PRINCE
Because you are not an ordinary visitor.

CINDERELLA
No, I am not an ordinary visitor. It is very embarrassing. I can't tell you who I am because my chancellor –

THE PRINCE
Your chancellor?

CINDERELLA
Oh!

THE PRINCE
Your chancellor, my lady?

CINDERELLA
There now. It's no use hiding the fact that – hiding from you what I am. I am a Princess.

THE PRINCE
I knew it.

CINDERELLA
Oh! And how?

THE PRINCE
Who could see your step, your eye, and not know, my lady, that you are a Princess?

CINDERELLA
Oh! Do you really mean, seriously, that say for a moment I gave up all my beautiful clothes and went to clear the streets of leaves, or wash dishes, or knit stockings, that people would point and say – 'That is a Princess, she has the step and the –' The – ?

THE PRINCE
The eye.

CINDERELLA
'– the eye of a Princess'? Do you really believe it?

THE PRINCE
I do.

CINDERELLA
Ah! That's very comforting. I mean it would be very comforting if I lost my lands or if my chancellor died and I had to become a menial, wouldn't it? But are you sure you will permit me to come to your Ball?

THE PRINCE
Could I do otherwise? The Beautiful Unknown!

CINDERELLA
I can dance beautifully.

THE PRINCE
Ah!

CINDERELLA
Yes. Will you dance with me?

THE PRINCE
Will you have too many engagements to dance with me?

CINDERELLA
Oh no! – That is, yes, I generally have quite a number when I go to a dance.

THE PRINCE
Do you go to every dance in the character of the Beautiful Unknown?

CINDERELLA
My lord, there are secrets I cannot tell.

THE PRINCE
Would the chancellor –

CINDERELLA
Yes, you are quite right. My chancellor would be very put out.

THE PRINCE
Yes?

CINDERELLA
Yes. Don't you find your affairs of state very tiresome? I do.

THE PRINCE
Yes. So do I.

CINDERELLA
There are such a lot of papers to sign, aren't there?

THE PRINCE
Yes. Do you know what I often wish?

CINDERELLA
No?

THE PRINCE
I often wish I could be an ordinary man all day, say work in the fields or break
stones, and then all night, when there's a great ball with music, just become a
Prince quite automatically and go off to the ball. Don't you?

CINDERELLA (uneasy)
Yes. It would be rather an interesting experience, wouldn't it?

THE PRINCE
Yes, wouldn't it?

CINDERELLA
Why are they all looking at me?

THE PRINCE
Have you lived sixteen years and not found an answer to such an easy question?

CINDERELLA
Seventeen years, my lord.

THE PRINCE
I beg your pardon, Princess.

CINDERELLA
It must look so strange, arriving late and refusing to give one's name. But when
one has such a very uncompromising chancellor, I don't see how one could
do otherwise. Do you?

THE PRINCE
No. Will you lead the ball with me?

CINDERELLA
Lead the ball?

THE PRINCE
Go in first, arm in arm, in front of all the rest.

CINDERELLA
Oh, you are amusing! Whatever made you think I didn't know?

THE PRINCE
I don't know.

CINDERELLA
I'll go in on your arm if you like.

THE PRINCE
Thank you, Princess.

CINDERELLA
But perhaps one of the other ladies would like to?

THE PRINCE
Oh no!

CINDERELLA
Besides, what is a more fitting companion for a Prince than a Princess?

THE PRINCE
Unknown. . . .

CINDERELLA
Come from a far land. . . . Who is that pretty lady watching us, by herself?

THE PRINCE
What pretty lady? There's only the lady Florizella.

CINDERELLA
That's the one.

THE PRINCE
You know the lady Florizella?

CINDERELLA
Oh no! What made you think so?

THE PRINCE
What made you say 'That's the one'?

CINDERELLA
Did I? I'm sure I didn't.

THE PRINCE
Yes, you did. You said 'That's the one'.

CINDERELLA
I'm sure I must have meant 'Is that the one'.

THE PRINCE
I suppose you must. But she's not pretty.

CINDERELLA
I think she really is as pretty as a picture in her red velvet. I should love to speak
    to her.

THE PRINCE
Oh!

CINDERELLA
Why? Please call her.

THE PRINCE
Lady Florizella!

FLORIZELLA
My lord?

THE PRINCE
The Princess desires to speak with you.

CINDERELLA
Goodnight, my lady Florizella.

FLORIZELLA
Goodnight.

CINDERELLA
Do you mind my wishing to know you? I am a Princess come from a far land. I
    thought you were a very beautiful lady and wished to speak with you.

FLORIZELLA
Oh! I thank you, madam, but I wish you would keep your spite to yourself.

CINDERELLA
Spite? I speak the complete truth. Why should you think it spite?

FLORIZELLA
How old are you?

CINDERELLA
Seventeen.

FLORIZELLA
Then you'll learn when you're older why one woman says spite when another
    woman calls her beautiful.

THE PRINCE
My dear lady Florizella –

FLORIZELLA
I cannot support insult, my lord: even from a Princess come from a far land.

CINDERELLA
Oh! I'm so sorry.

FLORIZELLA
Is not the ball going to begin? The people are getting impatient. I am quite ready.

THE PRINCE
I shall be ready in a moment.

CINDERELLA
Won't you talk with us a little while?

THE PRINCE
I think I see your sister beckoning to you, lady Florizella.

FLORIZELLA
She can't be. Annabella's in the garden.

THE PRINCE
Then it must be someone else.
Florizella retires.

CINDERELLA
Poor lady! I wonder why she's so bitter, when there is music and joy all about her?

THE PRINCE
One becomes bitter with age, Princess.

CINDERELLA
I wonder if you and I shall be bitter when we're thirty? . . . Shall we say ugly
   things to each other and everybody around us?

THE PRINCE
You will never be thirty, Princess.

CINDERELLA
Why do you think so?

THE PRINCE
Who could think of you at thirty, when before their eyes you stand at sixteen?

CINDERELLA
Seventeen.

THE PRINCE
At seventeen.

CINDERELLA
It would be beautiful if we could stay young, if the night of the ball would
   never come to an end; if the moon would never get clouded or the stars
   dim; if the music would play the night away, spinning it out through all
   eternity. . . . .[15]

THE PRINCE
The ball is only just beginning.

CINDERELLA
Yes. Will it last long?

THE PRINCE
Till tomorrow morning. Is it not long enough for you?

CINDERELLA

No. It could never be long enough for me. But the moon always gets clouded, the sun always comes back, and the stars do go dim, till they are blown out altogether.

THE PRINCE

Why are you sad?

CINDERELLA

Am I sad? I don't mean to be, because I am very very happy.

THE PRINCE

Are you always happy?

CINDERELLA

Not always. . . . that is, always.

THE PRINCE

Why do you say 'not always'?

CINDERELLA

I was thinking of my chancellor. He's so disagreeable at times. He really makes my life a misery – just because I'm young.

THE PRINCE

He seems to play a large part in your existence?

CINDERELLA

Yes, he does, really. Yoy [*sic*] see, he's an old man, and he served my father the king, so naturally he's not a little obstinate. He's positively disrespectful to me at times.[16]

THE PRINCE

Really? To the ball! To the ball!

Everyone crowds around. Animation. Cinderella, Florizella and the Prince are in the middle of the stage. A march is played, within. Pages line up. Florizella comes up behind the Prince as if to take his arm. He pretends not to see her and offers his arm to Cinderella. She takes it. All enter the ballroom in procession, leaving Florizella alone with the Strange Courtier. He offers his arm to her; she accepts. They follow the rest.

The curtain falls to represent an elapse of two hours, and rises again immediately.

Enter the PRINCE, dragging CINDERELLA, who is laughing joyously. The music is still playing. The lamps have now gone, there is bright moonlight.

CINDERELLA

Why, whatever makes you think the dance is over? Listen, they're still playing! The people are still going round and round. Oh, what a pity, we've missed half a dance!

THE PRINCE
What is half a dance, Princess? Can you not dance a thousand times again?

CINDERELLA
I don't know. I feel – I feel as if it's not going to last. To miss half a dance seems
a tragedy.

THE PRINCE
You are sad again.

CINDERELLA
Oh no I'm not. I'm only philosophic. When one is philosophic does that mean that
one is sad? I don't think so. That's a beautiful tune, isn't it? It's like a brook
running through a cornfield as hard as ever it can. Don't you think so, Prince
of all the land? I'm not sad any more, I'm as gay as anything. I feel as if I'm
going to live for ever and ever, and I'll always wear this beautiful dress. No
I won't. I'll change it every night: every night it will be a do different colour.

THE PRINCE
Why?

CINDERELLA
To please you.

THE PRINCE
To please – ?

CINDERELLA
To please you. Every night it shall be a different colour, so that you may never
tire of it. Every night the music shall be different, so that you may never tire
of that either. And every night I shall be different too, so that you may never
tire of me.

THE PRINCE
Why do you speak so?

CINDERELLA
Can you not guess?

THE PRINCE
No.

CINDERELLA
You are as stupid as my chancellor.

THE PRINCE
O the Unknown Beautiful –

CINDERELLA
Don't call me the Unknown Beautiful. I am not unknown –

THE PRINCE
And you are a thousand times more beautiful than when I first saw you.

CINDERELLA
Two hours ago.

THE PRINCE
Is it two hours?

CINDERELLA
Hardly two hours. The coach drove up to the gate of the garden, and then the footman came, all in gold livery, and helped me to the ground. I came up the steps with the scent of the night flowers about me, and there were bells ringing all over the world. There were lights before me, and behind the lights, behind all the people, I saw you. To think it will never come back, never will it happen again! I can come up the steps again a thousand times, with bells and lights every time, but it can never be exactly the same again.

THE PRINCE
Why?

CINDERELLA
I don't know. Why don't those moments come back in a never-ending circle? They pass through my fingers and whirl away, never to come back.

THE PRINCE
But, Princess, why be sad?

CINDERELLA
Yes, why be sad? Why aren't we dancing like the others? I suppose I'm so happy that I'm sad. Oh! That music! Your face is in shadow . . . Move a little. Now I can see your eyes.

THE PRINCE
And I can look into yours.

CINDERELLA
Do you love me very much?

THE PRINCE
Very much indeed.

CINDERELLA
I have seen your face, many times, I am sure, when I was a tiny little girl, looking for pictures in the fire when the long winter nights came. You eyes have always followed me, and in them I read friendship and loyalty and the deepest love. Your voice, too, it was always in the voice of the wind, in the voice of the waterfalls. Then I did not know what it was, that strange sound that seemed to make me light of heart. But now I know. You were always there. Always. You will always be there.

THE PRINCE
Do you love me?

CINDERELLA
Can you ask that? I have always loved you. We shall always have each other, always. You will be the beautiful Prince, with the brave eyes of a man and the heart of a little boy, I shall be the beautiful Princess, with the kind eyes of a woman and the heart of a little girl. To think the world is so full of wickedness! Is it possible that men forget their father and betray the good name of a friend? Can it be that men forget their mother and buy for flesh the body of a woman? It's all hard to believe, when I hear the music, and there's the moonlight on the trees, and the wind rocking them to sleep. And you are there, sitting in front of me, your eyes shining. Can it last? Can it last?

THE PRINCE
Did you come to see me especially? Had you heard of me?

CINDERELLA
I came because I loved you and it was the moment to come. I, and I alone, was born to be your Princess, and your Princess I came to be this night. Speak to me, tell me I am beautiful, tell me you love me. . . .

THE PRINCE
I love you, and I shall love you always.

CINDERELLA
Do not say you will love me always. Does not love by itself mean 'for ever'?

THE PRINCE
Who taught you that?

CINDERELLA
No one. I know it.

THE PRINCE
Have you loved anyone before more than you love me now?

CINDERELLA
My mother I never knew.

THE PRINCE
Your mother? You loved no one – like me?

CINDERELLA
There was never anyone like you. How could there be? You were always at the door, with the key held jealously in your hand. We belong to each other, and that holds the past, the present and all that is to come.

THE PRINCE
Yes.

CINDERELLA
Tell me that you love me!

THE PRINCE
I love you. Can I tell you more than that? I love you, strange Princess come from
the night, I love you, I love you. Why are you crying?

CINDERELLA
To think, my love, that one day our voices will be silent, and we shall be rotting
under the ground. Your face will not be smiling in the ball any more, I shall
never dance any more, we shall both be very still and quiet, for we shall both
be dead, and the days of our love shall be past, past. . . .

THE PRINCE
Have we not each other now?

CINDERELLA
Do you hear that lilt in the music? It will never come back. Do you see the moonlight? It will never shine again like that.

THE PRINCE
But we have our own love.

CINDERELLA
Yes. But the first night will never come back, and though the rest will be more
beautiful, it makes my heart ache. . . . with regret.

THE PRINCE
Will not our love last for ever?

CINDERELLA
If you were to die, I could not live any more. But I would die now, by my own
hand, so that you could live. If only I could write that in a book, and give it
to heaven and earth to read!

THE PRINCE
But only we, only we are to know.

CINDERELLA
Yes . . . We belong the one to the other, and the rest of the world shall never know of it.

THE PRINCE
Lift your face to mine.

CINDERELLA
Yes, Will you kiss me? It is the kiss of all my dreams. . . .
They kiss. The clock begins to strike twelve. At the third or fourth stroke Cinderella turns in dismay. She starts up and is through into the garden in the
twinkling of an eye. The Prince sits where he is, bewildered, looking into the
darkness which has swallowed her. The last strokes die away. A page enters,

175

lights the candles, and goes in again without seeing the Prince. The music has stopped. Enter FLORIZELLA.

FLORIZELLA
You're by yourself? They'e [*sic*] going to lay supper here.

THE PRINCE
Yes. Who are you?

FLORIZELLA
Who am I? Don't you want to know me? I'm Florizella. Where's the beautiful lady?

THE PRINCE
She's gone.

FLORIZELLA
Gone, so soon? Where's she gone?

THE PRINCE
I don't know.

FLORIZELLA
You don't know? Then how are you going to follow her if she didn't tell you where to go?

THE PRINCE
I don't know.

FLORIZELLA
I think myself you've just gone stupid.

THE PRINCE
Perhaps I have.

FLORIZELLA
Much matter there is, too. I swear her complexion wasn't – what's that? She picks up Cinderella's Slipper.

THE PRINCE
What's that?

FLORIZELLA
She's left her slipper behind to let you know how small a foot she's got.

THE PRINCE
Is that her slipper?

FLORIZELLA
She must have terrible pains in her feet to wear a thing like that. Why, *my* foot wouldn't go into it. She must fill it to bursting. Why did she fly off in such a tearing hurry?

THE PRINCE

I don't know. She just went. An angel or a devil. No, it's a devil she is, and the prettiest and cleverest I ever saw. I can't find her tonight. I can't find her tonight!

FLORIZELLA

No. Why were you such a fool as to take her into the ball?

THE PRINCE

Because I wasn't such a fool as to take *you* into the ball.

FLORIZELLA

You'll never see her any more.

THE PRINCE

I must see her. She's from the town, I'm positive – some little adventuress with brains who's dying to come out.

FLORIZELLA

What do you say?

THE PRINCE

Nothing. I was talking to myself.

FLORIZELLA

Do you think she cares a rap for you? I don't like her eyes.

THE PRINCE

I do. And she told me she was in love with me, several times.

FLORIZELLA

I don't believe you.

THE PRINCE

Yes she did. Oh yes she did!

FLORIZELLA

I don't believe a word. And you won't find her again, so – so you may as well content yourself with me.

THE PRINCE

After her, do you think I could go along with you? And I will find her. Give me that slipper.

FLORIZELLA

You want a memento of the occasion when a woman slipped through your fingers? Oh strange catastrophe, unexplained event!

THE PRINCE

I will find her. Not one girl in a thousand could put her foot into that slipper. This very night I'll find her. She didn't leave it behind for nothing. Clever little kitten! Cleverer than you will ever be, my lady Florizella!

FLORIZELLA
I have no doubt.

THE PRINCE
I shall find her, and you shall see.

FLORIZELLA
I shan't be interested. Goodnight.
The Prince hurries into the palace without answering. Florizella sits down. Enter
the STRANGE COURTIER. The music has begun again.

THE STRANGE COURTIER
You're by yourself? They're going to lay supper here.

FLORIZELLA
Yes. Are you by yourself too?

THE STRANGE COURTIER
She's gone off with a lady friend of her mother's.

FLORIZELLA
Dear me!

THE STRANGE COURTIER
Where's the Prince?

FLORIZELLA
He's just gone in. I'm tired of him.

THE STRANGE COURTIER
So very soon?

FLORIZELLA
If I had that girl between my hands for two minutes I'd choke her to death. The
wicked deceiving little idiot! Come from a little hovel nobody's ever seen
by daylight, and comes to the ball, if you please, a Princess from a far land!
Where'd she got that dress? Where'd she earned the money? I daresay you,
for one, could say something on the point.

THE STRANGE COURTIER
I've never had the good fortune to set eyes on the girl. So you're tired of him?
Well, if you are, all I can say is you're uncommonly jealous of her.

FLORIZELLA
Don't be foolish. He drives me mad with his declarations of passion and such
lunacy. A silly fool who'd talk to me of nothing but love, love, love, and love
again. I've sent him packing.

THE STRANGE COURTIER
Oh?

FLORIZELLA

I'told him he'd looked too long at the creature, he told me he hadn't, so there we were. I refused to go into the ball on his arm. I'm glad she came, now I come to think of it; it was a good excuse to get rid of his foolishness. Men are so sickening when they get to that stage.

THE STRANGE COURTIER

Are you staying for supper?

FLORIZELLA

I'm not very hungry. Are you?

THE STRANGE COURTIER

Oh no. Are you going? Shall we go?

FLORIZELLA

I don't know if I'll go. I suppose I may as well. I can't go home now. I may as well go along with you as anyone else.

They go out slowly into the garden, arm in arm. The music ceases. The lords and ladies come out again on to the terrace. A hubbub as the curtain falls.

ACT THREE

The house of the three sisters, several hours later. It is still night, but the day is now not far off. CINDERELLA, dressed now in the costume of Cinderella and no longer in that of Claribella, is sitting on her stool at the window, looking into the night, very wide-awake and happy. She hears a sound. ANNABELLA passes the window in the coach and enters immediately, looking cross and tired, and also a little anxious.

ANNABELLA

Cinderella? Heaven, isn't she there? Cinderella!

CINDERELLA

Sister.

ANNABELLA

Oh, there you are! What a relief. . . .

CINDERELLA

Why? You're home early, aren't you, Annabella?

ANNABELLA

Why aren't you in bed?

CINDERELLA

I couldn't sleep, so I got up to wait for you. Did you enjoy the ball? Who danced with you? What were the dresses?

ANNABELLA

Oh, really I'm too tired to tell you. Have – have you had a quiet night?

CINDERELLA

Oh yes. It has been very pleasant. Sister, sister!

ANNABELLA

Why are you laughing?

CINDERELLA

I don't know. Was I laughing? I suppose it's because I'm happy, very happy indeed.

ANNABELLA

My dear, so you are quite content?

CINDERELLA

As content as I ever could be.

ANNABELLA

I'm very glad of that. And here, darling, is the pretty gold chain I promised you.

CINDERELLA

Thank you, dear Annabella. I don't understand why you wanted to keep me at home, but I know you love me very much.

ANNABELLA

But aren't you tired, waiting up for me? There's a kiss for being a dear child.

CINDERELLA

No, I'm not a bit tired. Are you going to bed straight away? Please stay here a minute and tell me everything that happened.

ANNABELLA

I'll stay a minute to please you. What shall I tell you about?

CINDERELLA

Whom did you dance with, to begin?

ANNABELLA

There was a very cold sedate gentleman to begin with, then a silly one who was very young and who couldn't find anyone else because he was so silly. I assure you, child, it was very dull.

CINDERELLA

Now tell me about the visitors, – the other visitors.

ANNABELLA

There was a gentleman who knew Florizella long ago, and his wife.

CINDERELLA

Oh! And who went in on the Prince's arm?

ANNABELLA

Oh yes. That was the great sensation of the night. A strange lady most beautifully dressed who came in through the garden. The Prince was very polite to her because she was very beautiful and very lady-like, so he took her in on his arm.

CINDERELLA

That's very interesting!

ANNABELLA

Why are you laughing again?

CINDERELLA

I was only thinking how jealous everybody else must have been.

ANNABELLA

Florizella was white with rage.

CINDERELLA

Oh! I didn't mean Florizella. Poor Florizella! Where is she now?

ANNABELLA

I don't know. Still dancing, I'll warrant me. She'll dance herself off her feet just now, for they're none too steady.

CINDERELLA

Tell me more about the Princess.

ANNABELLA

Who told you she was a Princess?

CINDERELLA

Didn't you? Well, I supposed she must be a Princess.

ANNABELLA

Well, she isn't. Everybody's positive, the Prince most of all.

CINDERELLA

Ah! Was he in love with her?

ANNABELLA

He seemed to be. Everybody said he was.

CINDERELLA

And yet he believed all the while she wasn't a Princess?

ANNABELLA

He said afterwards he didn't.

CINDERELLA

Then he must love her very much. But tell me more, Annabella.

ANNABELLA

He says she's a girl from the town who came to the ball, and he's made up his mind to find her again.

CINDERELLA

So if he's going to find her, what does it matter to her that the ball is over, and she's lost all her fine clothes and jewels for ever?. . . . And how do you think he's going to find her?

ANNABELLA

You'd never tell. She left her slipper behind and he's sending a page round to try the slipper on every girl's foot in the town.

CINDERELLA

Why?

ANNABELLA

Because the slipper's so small there's only one person it will fit, and that is the mysterious Princess.

CINDERELLA

That's very interesting. Will the page go everywhere?

ANNABELLA

Yes.

CINDERELLA

Will he come here?

ANNABELLA

Yes. It won't fit Florizella or me. As for you – let me see your foot.

CINDERELLA

My foot isn't really as big as that, – they're the kitchen-boots Florizella gave me.

ANNABELLA

In any case your foot can't be as small as that. So none of us have the chance of being taken for the Princess.

CINDERELLA

No. That's very sad, isn't it?

ANNABELLA

Why are you laughing this time?

CINDERELLA

I'm thinking of all the grand ladies who will be bursting the little slipper, with trying to push their feet into it, and what a heaving and a straining the poor page will be put to, trying to get their feet in.

ANNABELLA

I'm going to bed. But no, of course, everyone has to wait up till the page comes. It's really absurd.

CINDERELLA

He must be very deeply in love with this creature to run all over the town after her.

ANNABELLA

They say he's gone mad over her. Why am I stuffing your head up with such non-sense? Go to bed immediately.

CINDERELLA

But I should love to stay up and see the page going about with the slipper. Will he carry it on a little cushion? Tell me about the Prince. Was he confused, all dazed, when the lady flew away? Was he angry, or was he just sad? Did he wonder why she had gone? Did he tell everybody how beautiful she was? Did he tell everybody he loved her?

ANNABELLA

Cinderella, I shall scold you if you continue to gossip in such a manner. I don't approve of it in the least, it doesn't suit a good well-poised girl like you.

CINDERELLA

Then I suppose I'd better not talk like that any more. Isn't the moon lovely, Annabella? It's the same moon that was shining over the ball, isn't it?

ANNABELLA

Of course it is.

CINDERELLA

Is the page coming soon?

ANNABELLA

We were told he would start any minute.

CINDERELLA

He'll wake up all the town, and all the drowsyheads who'd been asleep – asleep! – when the whole mad train of the ball was galloping along. And the nightcaps will wonder what it's all about, and swear they've got no daughters, so as to get back into bed again. But they'll find her at last. And when he finds her, do you think he'll give her up, really, when he knows for sure she's not a grand lady? Suppose she'd gone into the ball in clothes that didn't belong to her, that she'd stolen, and she couldn't get the clothes back. Would it matter?

ANNABELLA

Oh no, it wouldn't matter a bit. But you're as silly as a moonstruck child, I never saw you so before. What does it have to do with us? Still I think really it is the height of absurdity to wake up the whole town at this unearthly hour. I think he's mad.

CINDERELLA

I think it's perfectly natural. And is he so much in love with her that that he cannot wait to see her till the sun comes and everybody is up?

ANNABELLA

I suppose he is.

CINDERELLA

I'm sure he is. The sun's going to rise soon, I seem to feel it coming up behind the hills. Everything will be rosy-red in the town. Will the page be long? I'm dying to see the little slipper. She must be a very dainty lady, to have such a very small foot, mustn't she? Even though she's not a real lady.

ANNABELLA

Do be quiet. Why isn't Florizella back? She lingers and loiters, I do believe she still thinks she's a young girl.

CINDERELLA

Poor Florizella! What a pity she isn't the missing Princess! It would make her so happy, wouldn't it?

ANNABELLA

Florizella's long past the age of ever being a missing princess, I assure you.

CINDERELLA

There are lights down the other street, can you see? There's a page, and several people behind him. That's the one, that's the one! How very exciting!? It won't be long before he comes here, will it? I've never been so excited and happy in all my life before . . . I've been up at this hour a thousand times, and yet I'd never noticed the smell of flowers – just the scent of the dawn that's on the way, cool and fresh. I've always been too busy cleaning the hearth or brushing shoes to notice. I wonder why I used to cry in the early mornings, as if each day wasn't bringing me nearer and nearer, nearer and nearer! But sometimes I used to feel that, and then I'd smile and say, 'I will wait and see'. I have waited, and I have seen too. What's the matter, Annabella?

ANNABELLA

What did you say?

CINDERELLA

You're nearly fast asleep, Annabella. Poor Annabella, why aren't you happy like me?

ANNABELLA

Do be quiet, once again. I'm tired to death.
Enter FLORIZELLA

FLORIZELLA
Is that child still up?

CINDERELLA
I got up to wait for you, sister. Was the ball very beautiful? Annabella said there
was a beautiful lady –

FLORIZELLA
There was a strange person who was neither beautiful nor a lady, if that's who
you mean. If you're in one of your talkative moods I'll go to bed without
a word. What has it got to do with you what the ball was, or who was in
the ball?

CINDERELLA
Poor, poor Florizella!

FLORIZELLA
What did you say?

CINDERELLA
Nothing, sister.

FLORIZELLA
Did I hear you say 'Poor Florizella'? For a girl of your age your impudence sur-
passes anything I ever knew. You should learn to posses yourself. I'm sick to
death. When is that fool of a page coming? Nobody dare stir a finger till he's
satisfied his precious master, who's worth about as much as the creature he's
running after, I'll be bound!

CINDERELLA
Oh, sister! How dare you say a word against him? How can you?

FLORIZELLA
He's a fool.

CINDERELLA
Poor Florizella!

FLORIZELLA
I think she's quite mad, if you ask me . . . Why must I sit up till that fool of a page
comes along with his slipper?

ANNABELLA
He said nobody was to go to bed till the girl was found.

FLORIZELLA
Such ideas! Enough to make one sick. That a ball should end in such fashion, I
can't understand it.

CINDERELLA

I can. It's only natural he should want to find her, don't you think? If he's in love with her, isn't it natural he should try to find her again?

FLORIZELLA

Is it you who've been putting such ideas into the child's head, Annabella?
A trumpet sounds. The Page passes the window.

ANNABELLA

There he is.

FLORIZELLA

Now at least we can go to bed. You may go upstairs, Cinderella.

CINDERELLA

Yes, sister.
Exit CINDERELLA.

ANNABELLA

I can't understand her. In such a state last night, and now as content and happy as ever she could be!

FLORIZELLA

A girl like that doesn't feel anything. She just lives as the wind blows. She gets on my nerves so.
Enter the PAGE, with the slipper on a cushion.

THE PAGE

Goodnight, ladies.

FLORIZELLA

Good morning, rather. You can tell your master from me that he's a complete fool. What does he mean sending people round to wake everybody when everybody's dropping to sleep? You may tell him from me –

ANNABELLA

Hush, sister. There is a limit to what one may say, after all.

THE PAGE

I am sorry, madam, but I am obeying orders, very strictly. I am not responsible for what my master wishes or does not wish. Your foot, madam.
He tries Florizella's foot.

FLORIZELLA

Do you expect to find the creature?

THE PAGE

We have no idea whatever, madam.

FLORIZELLA
Upsetting the whole town like this.

THE PAGE
Thank you, madam.

FLORIZELLA
It's only because my foot is slender, and therefore long. She has probably a short fat
foot which means vulgarity. And that's what the rest of her conduct means too.

THE PAGE
Your foot, if you please, madam.
He tries Annabella's foot.

FLORIZELLA
If mine wouldn't go, yours won't, my dear. Now I can go to bed.
Exit FLORIZELLA

THE PAGE
Thank you, ladies. Goodnight, ladies.
Cinderella is at the door, radiant with smiles.

ANNABELLA
What are you doing there? Didn't Florizella tell you to go to bed?

THE PAGE
I beg your pardon, madam. I have strict orders to try the slipper on the foot of
every lady in the town, and I must obey. Will you sit down, miss?

CINDERELLA
Yes, sir. Thank you. Shall I take my boot off?

THE PAGE
If you please.

CINDERELLA
Yes, sir. There.

THE PAGE
That's a very small foot! Why do you wear such big boots?

CINDERELLA
I don't know.

ANNABELLA
Cinderella, don't talk to the stranger. Please hurry up, boy.

THE PAGE
Yes, madam.
The shoe fits exactly.

CINDERELLA
Thank you, sir.

THE PAGE
Now I can go to bed.

ANNABELLA
What do you mean?

THE PAGE
Because I have found the lady.

ANNABELLA
You have found the lady?

THE PAGE
Cannot you see, madam? The shoe belongs to your waiting-maid.

ANNABELLA
Please leave the house immediately.

THE PAGE
But you can see for yourself, madam. I must go and tell my master.
Exit the PAGE, running.

CINDERELLA
Annabella, darling, *can't* you see for yourself?

ANNABELLA
What do you mean?

CINDERELLA
Can't you see? Can't you see it in my eyes, all brimming over? I thought you
would see that all that had happened, as soon as I came home from the ball.

ANNABELLA
The ball?

CINDERELLA
Yes. I am the missing Princess, and I am going to be the Queen. Annabella dear,
just think of it! You shall wear the most beautiful dresses and jewels, and
Florizella won't even be cross any more, because she'll be too busy being as
happy as the day is long. We'll all live together in the Palace. . . .

ANNABELLA
Did you hear the music? Far away?

CINDERELLA
Yes.

ANNABELLA
Did you see Her?

CINDERELLA
Yes. But what does it matter now, if I came away late? He is coming!

ANNABELLA
Poor, poor Cinderella!

CINDERELLA
Annabella, I kept it as a surprise, because I knew the page would come, that he
  would search for me . . .
Annabella, a little dazed, has slipped quietly out to fetch Florizella.
The sun! Look, Annabella, the sun. . . . It's coming up to shine on me and my happiness. My love, my love, soon I shall see your face again, soon your voice
  will speak. Like the wind and the stars we shall live for ever, and there will
  never be any pain between us. My love!
Enter FLORIZELLA, ANNABELLA behind.
I can see him coming. He is at the gate now, his hand on the latch. He is looking
  at me. He is going to come in. . . . .

FLORIZELLA
You poor little fool.

CINDERELLA
Oh, Florizella! How can you say such things to make me unhappy, when I'm hap-
  pier than all the world? Florizella, if only you'll be happy and kind to me,
  I'll give you the most beautiful clothes and you shall be the loveliest lady in
  the kingdom. Look! He's at the gate, with his bare head shining in the dawn.
  He's coming in for me.

FLORIZELLA
Poor little fool.

ANNABELLA
Florizella, Florizella. . . . .

CINDERELLA
How can you talk such untruths, to wound me? Are you very unhappy, dear Florizella? Don't you know I couldn't believe anything, if he told me himself just
  to tease me and see if I was true? Can't you see? He's coming up the path!
  He's at the door . . . He is there.
The Prince is standing on the threshold. Low, very far away, on the other side of
  the world, the Song of the Fairy Godmother rises.
. . . . Annabella, I wish you would see it stopped. It makes me feel – as if I was
  going to die.

ANNABELLA
My poor child! What's the matter?

CINDERELLA
Send her away.

ANNABELLA
Whom – whom must I send away?

CINDERELLA
There's an old woman at the street-corner, singing. Send her away. I feel as if I
    was going to die.

ANNABELLA
I can't hear anything.

CINDERELLA
Yes you can.

ANNABELLA
My poor love, I can't hear anything.

CINDERELLA
Then you must be deaf. Florizella, go and tell her to be quiet.

FLORIZELLA
I can't hear anything either.

CINDERELLA
Yes you can. Florizella, say you can? Don't you hear, it's coming nearer and
    nearer? Florizella darling, say you can?

FLORIZELLA
I don't hear. . . . a sound.

CINDERELLA
Then it is for me alone she is singing.
The Fairy Godmother passes the window in the cold dimness of the dawn. The
    Song dies away.

ANNABELLA
Cinderella?

CINDERELLA
Yes. What has happened?

THE PRINCE
Good morning, Princess.

CINDERELLA
Good morning, my lord.

THE PRINCE
You see I have found you, after all your little
intrigues! Are you glad to see me, Cinderella? So it was Cinderella, whom
nobody'd ever heard of! No wonder they wanted to stow you away! Such
beauty and brains I never did see, in the whole of my life.

CINDERELLA
Yes, my lord.

THE PRINCE
Why 'my lord'? Last night, my dear, it was something far better than 'my lord',
wasn't it?

CINDERELLA
Last night, my lord?

THE PRINCE
Yes, Perhaps you don't remember.

CINDERELLA
Yes. I remember.

THE PRINCE
Won't you kiss me good morning?

CINDERELLA
No.

THE PRINCE
And why the devil won't you, my little Princess?

CINDERELLA
I have never seen you before.

THE PRINCE
A joke's a joke, but I'll soon be out of patience, may you be a thousand times
prettier than you are.

CINDERELLA
Where is the boy who kissed me on the lips? His eyes were very deep and blue,
and he was smiling. Where is he? Why do you come with your swaggering
air and ugly lines under your eyes? He's dead and I shall never see him again.
Why do you ask me to kiss you? Why have you come to see me? Florizella
belongs to you; why don't you kiss her?

THE PRINCE
This is getting beyond my depth altogether. Here I hunt all night for a pretty girl
who's made me advances, and when I've paid her the compliment of finding her, and coming to her, she talks like a lunatic and adds insults into the
bargain.

CINDERELLA
Please, please go away.

THE PRINCE
Are you coming with me, or have you changed your mind? Must I take it for granted that I displease you?

CINDERELLA
You are a stranger. How can you understand? My love is dead and buried, before I could see his face to kiss him goodbye. I rushed away from his arms, but it was no use. It was too late.

FLORIZELLA
Too late. . . .

CINDERELLA
Oh, Florizella, how could you be so cruel, so cruel! I was waiting for him, I could see him coming up the path, he was smiling to me, and then a stranger came to the door. How could you, Florizella, how could you?

FLORIZELLA
Don't. . . . Don't. . . .

CINDERELLA
You cannot know what it is to have lost the one you loved, as I have lost him. I have no grave to weep over, no stone to deck with flowers, my love does not belong to me, he is alive though he is dead. I cannot shed tears over him, for he will never feel the tears dropping one by one on his poor dear bones. . . .

FLORIZELLA
Don't. . . . Don't. . . .

CINDERELLA
Oh, Florizella, you have never kissed, scenting in that kiss the smell of crushed violets. You have never felt what I have felt.

FLORIZELLA
Yes. . . .

CINDERELLA
What a cruel old woman! What a heartless trick to play! But you can never understand.

FLORIZELLA
I can understand. Once I, too, kissed as you have kissed. Once I, too, looked with my beautiful eyes into the eyes of a boy. He was young and strong and brave, for She had sung to me. And then I, too, stayed too long, and she sang, singing me back into life again. The boy is dead, I shall never see him again. In his place was a man with strange eyes and deep lines under them.

CINDERELLA
And you have never been happy again.

FLORIZELLA
He took my hands and he said he loved me. I gave him my life. And then the
song came back, cruel, and none could share my pain, for none could hear
it but I . . . I buried my happiness and gave my body to the stranger with the
strange eyes. We got tired. I was fretting after the boy who was dead, and I
gave my body to another. It was by a stream that I saw him, under a willow.
And now I am old and painted and alone, my hands are all wrinkled. . . .

CINDERELLA
So shall I be, some day. Because I came away too late!

FLORIZELLA
They all forget, they all come away too late. She sings them into forgetfulness.
And then they give up their dreams and live like the rest of mortals. They play
a game, from morning till night, from night till morning, till at last they are
taunted with a glimpse of the moonlight that was, of the things that belong
to death.

CINDERELLA
Yes.

FLORIZELLA
Last night I slept in the arms of the man who pretends he is the ghost of the boy
who died. And I slept without bad dreams. She called to me, and I answered,
because I did not know.

CINDERELLA
If you had known, would you have stopped on the way and turned back?

FLORIZELLA
I could never have turned back. . . . Perhaps, when I am dead, he will be waiting
for me, and I shall be young and beautiful again. All I can do now is wait. . . .
and forget.

CINDERELLA
Then I must go with the stranger and forget too.

ANNABELLA
No, you mustn't do that.

CINDERELLA
Why?

ANNABELLA
You have shattered dreams to piece together again. I have not even those. I have
been waiting for the voice to sing to me, and it has forgotten me. I have never

seen anything, I have never heard anything. I do not know why I am in the world, for I have never lived. I have always tried to keep it all away from you. Could I see you follow Florizella? But now that it is all over, Cinders darling, sit down and remember. . . .

CINDERELLA

Yes. I must piece my dreams together. I shall sit by the fire and try to remember them, as long ago I used to try and see them beforehand. I shall build them up, and this time they will not fall. Have I not the memory of the Night of the Ball? Shall I not have eternal music in my ears, eternal music in my heart?

FLORIZELLA

I have sold my memories. I have gone into the market and sold them.

CINDERELLA

The stranger came for my body, I know now. But my body he shall never have, he shall never soil it even with his eyes. I'll just sit by the fire and keep my love young for ever, even if my hair grows grey, and my eyes grow dim and ugly. I have my broken memories.

FLORIZELLA

I have nothing left. Nothing at all.

CINDERELLA

The night of the ball! I'll never be discontented any more. I'll just sit in the corner and do my work. The sun feels cold, but tonight – tonight I shall see the moon again.

FLORIZELLA

Don't you want to go to bed?

CINDERELLA

No. I'm not sleepy now. Oh; I wish – I wish he were there to speak to me! Just to say one word, to give me one smile! But I must have patience to wait, even if it's a long long time.

ANNABELLA

Farewell, my darling.

FLORIZELLA

Farewell. Will you kiss me?

CINDERELLA

Yes. Say 'Goodnight, Cinderella'.

FLORIZELLA

It's morning now, my dear.

CINDERELLA

Yes. The night is over.

FLORIZELLA
May I bless you, Cinderella?

CINDERELLA
Yes.

FLORIZELLA
Farewell, Cinderella.

CINDERELLA
Fare well, dear sister.

ANNABELLA and FLORIZELLA pass the Prince as if they did not see him. He goes out slowly. Cinderella sits on her stool, takes out her work, and begins to stich. Then she takes off the slipper, puts it on the ledge before her and looks at it a moment. She gives a little sigh and goes on with her sewing. The curtain falls.

NOTES

1 Cinderella's sisters, Florizella and Annabella, prepare themselves for the ball and take care of the house in Cinderella's absence.

2 The comic exchange between Florizella and Annabella is a winking allusion to the artifice of their Dame roles. This is a staple of the genre.

3 This is a distinctive addition to the Cinderella pantomime. The comment about Annabella's visitor being a woman may be tongue-in-cheek foreshadowing, since the Prince is traditionally a cross-dressing role.

4 This faithless Prince does not fit within the tradition of the cross-dressing principal boy in the Cinderella pantomime. Although kisses, embraces and flirtatious double entendres challenge chaste and 'asexual' (Holland, 'The Play of Eros', p. 199) readings of the romance between the principal boy and principal girl (Schacker, *Staging Fairy Land*, p. 193), the boyish lover is never a faithless rogue like the Prince in this pantomime.

5 This angry Cinderella who rejects her name also rejects the character that has been created for her in this scene, both the role created by her sisters' exploitation and the role created by the meek, patient role of the traditional Cinderella pantomime.

6 This seems to be a meta-commentary on the Cinderella pantomime genre and its longevity, perpetuating the youth and silence of the title character.

7 Annabella's fear and Cinderella's behaviour both resonate with changeling narratives and dramas. Fairy lore was frequently merged with mainstream Cinderella pantomimes. However, fairy activities were consistently positive in these dramas. By contrast, this more closely resembles changeling dramas like Cushag's 'Eunyce' (1908), where the magical music heard only by the changeling character calls her back to Faery after she is exposed to the cruelty of the world. Her loving parents try to protect her and keep her from leaving with the fairies, but the call of Faery is too strong.

8 The traditional Cinderella fairy-tale warning is replaced with a fairy-lore prohibition. Humans often lose their memories or their abilities to sense the world of fairy once they violate the fairy's rules.

9 Reminiscent of a scene from the story of Tamlane, in moonlight with the fey passing his human lover, usually called Burd Janet. Tamlane is the consort of the Fairy Queen and he needs Burd Janet to rescue him.

10 The parents of fey changelings and those touched by the fey are usually aware of the danger of the fey being recalled to Faery. This serious conversation is dramatically different than the comic exchanges of the two Dames in Cinderella pantomimes.

11 Although slapstick violence is a staple of the genre for the Dames in Cinderella, Florizella's slap is not comedic.

12 The introduction of the Strange Courtier upstages the lead boy, Prince Charming.

13 The Strange Courtier's fate seems to parallel that of the mortal lover of the queen of fairy, Tam Lin.

14 Carnival-time is the medieval season of misrule during the twelve days of Christmas.

15 Cinderella describes an enchanted ball in Faery.

16 This seems to be a winking reference to the traditional Dames of the pantomime.

Part 3

WONDER TALES
AND FAIRY LORE

Langston Hughes creates a new fairy-tale tradition entirely in his debut play, *A Gold Piece* (1921). There is no explicit magic in this drama, but the fairy-tale wonder that defines the genre is recreated with the actions of the children, who end the drama pondering the potential good of the future.

The first issue of *The Brownies' Book Magazine* opens with an African American child in a fairy costume (1920). The image resonates with a two-page photographic spread in the same issue featuring children in fairy costumes during Baby Week at Tuskegee (pp. 16–17). The sign in the photograph states: 'THE BABY: GIVE HIM A CHANCE' (p. 17). These images implicitly associate the fairy-play of the children with future hope. These fairy photographs are a sharp contrast with the absence of magical helpers in the fairy tales included in *The Brownies' Book Magazine*. Although children do not rely on outside help to rise, they are able to inhabit the power of the fairy within themselves.

Fairies were among the stock 'immortal characters' (Schacker, *Staging Fairy Land*, p. 11) in fairy-tale pantomimes. The two tragic fairy dramas here tap into distinctive Manx and Scottish fairy-lore traditions distinct from the fairies frequently incorporated into other pantomimes. The fairies from these regional traditions are at odds with the human societies surrounding them, enabling the playwrights to make social commentaries.

Neither drama seems to be written for the Christmas pantomime scene.

DOI: 10.4324/9781003034643-7

Editorial Headnote

Hughes, L., 'The Gold Piece: A Play That Might Be True', *The Brownies' Book Magazine*, 2:7 (1921), pp. 191–4.

See *Fairy-Tale Revivals in the Long Nineteenth Century* General Introduction for information about *The Brownies' Book Magazine*.

In *Children's Literature of the Harlem Renaissance*, Katharine Capshaw Smith identifies Langston Hughes's debut drama as a distinctly African American fairy tale:

> Not simply applying a black face to a white genre, fairy tales in *The Brownies' Book* offer children black values in fairy tale form. A most suggestive example is Langston Hughes's first published drama, 'The Gold Piece' (July 1921), which revisits the conventional wicked witch character and her relationship to trickster children.[1]

The realism, highlighted in the subtitle: 'A Play That Might Be True', does not change the sense of wonder that the drama creates. In the final scene, the children bask in the sense of hope that their gold piece will give another child a happy ending. The communal ethic here is especially important to Du Bois's emphasis on preparing children to become active citizens.[2]

As Capshaw Smith notes, this tale inverts the orphans' relationship with the conventional witch. Instead of tricking her for their own gain or survival, they secretly help her take care of a blind child who needs medical help.[3] This structure as well as the sense of wonder the tale creates are essential to its characterization as a distinctive fairy tale in *The Brownies' Book*.

NOTES

1 Smith, K. Capshaw, *Children's Literature of the Harlem Renaissance* (Bloomington: Indiana UP, 2004), pp. 30–1.
2 Smith, *Children's Literature of the Harlem Renaissance*, pp. 29–32.
3 Smith, *Children's Literature of the Harlem Renaissance*, p. 31.

5

'THE GOLD PIECE: A PLAY THAT MIGHT BE TRUE'

L. Hughes

Source: *The Brownies' Book Magazine*, 2:7 (1921), pp. 191–4

CHARACTERS

A Peasant Boy.
A Peasant Girl, his wife.
An Old Woman.

SCENE

THE interior of a hut by the roadside. It is twilight. A boy and a girl are lying before the fire-place, a gold piece on the floor between them. There is a door at the right of the fire-place and a window at the left. During the play the twilight deepens into darkness.

THE GIRL (*Looking at the coin*) – Just to think that this bright gold piece is ours! All ours! Fifty whole loren!

THE BOY (*Smiling happily*) – The ten old pigs were fat ones, Rosa, and brought us a fine price in the market.

THE GIRL – Now we can buy and buy and buy.

THE BOY – Sure we can. Now we can buy all the things we've wanted ever since we've been married but haven't had the money to get.

THE GIRL – Oh! How good, Pablo! It seems we've been waiting an awfully long time.

THE BOY – We have, but now we shan't wait any longer. Now we can get the wooden clock, Rosa. You know – the one that we've wanted since we first saw it in the old watch-maker's window. The one so nicely carved, that strikes the hours every day and runs for a whole week with a single winding. And I think there is a cuckoo in it, too. It will make our little house look quite elegant.

THE GIRL – And now you can buy the thick brown boots with hob nails in them to work in the fields.

THE BOY – And you may have the woolen shawl with red and purple flowers on it and the fringe about the edges.

THE GIRL – O-o-o! Can I really, Pablo? I've dreamed of it for months.

THE BOY – You surely can, Rosa. I've wanted to give it to you ever since I knew you. It will make you look so pretty. And we'll get two long white candles, too, to burn on Sundays and feast days.

THE GIRL – And we'll get a little granite kettle for stewing vegetables in.

THE BOY – And we'll get a big spoon to stir with.

THE GIRL – And two little blue plates to eat from.

THE BOY – And we'll have dried fish and a little cake for supper every night.

THE GIRL – And – but Oh! Pablo! It's wonderful!

THE BOY – Oh! Rosa! It's fine!

THE GIRL AND THE BOY (*Rising and dancing joyously around and around the little gold piece which glistens and glitters gaily on the floor before the open fire as if it knew it were the cause of their joy*) – Oh! How happy we are! Oh! How happy we are! Because we can buy! Because we can buy! Because we can buy and buy and buy!

    (*Just then an old woman's figure passes the window and there is a timid knock at the door. The dancing stops.* THE BOY *picks up his shining gold piece and clutches it tightly in his hand.*)

THE GIRL (*With a little frown of annoyance*) – Who's there?

(*The door opens slowly and a bent old woman leaning on a heavy stick enters.*)

THE BOY (*Rudely*) – Well, Grandmother, what do you want?

THE OLD WOMAN (*Panting and weak*) – I've come such a long way today and am very tired. I just wanted to rest a moment before going on.

(THE GIRL *brings her a stool and she sits down near the fire-place.*)

THE GIRL (*Sympathetically*) – But surely, Old Woman, you aren't going any further on foot tonight?

THE OLD WOMAN – Yes, I am, child, because I must.

THE GIRL – And why must you, Old Lady?

THE OLD WOMAN – Because my boy is in the house alone and he is blind.

THE GIRL – Your boy is blind?

THE OLD WOMAN – Yes, for eighteen years. He has not seen since he was a tiny baby.

THE BOY – And where have you been that you are so late upon the road?

THE OLD WOMAN – I've been into the city and from sunrise I have not rested. People told me famous doctors were there who could make my blind boy see again and so I went to find them.

THE GIRL – And did you find them?

THE OLD WOMAN – Yes, I found them, but (*her voice becomes sad*) they would not come with me.

THE GIRL – Why would they not come?

THE OLD WOMAN – Because they were great and proud. They said, "When you get fifty loren, send for us and then perhaps we'll come. Now we have no time." One who was kinder than the rest told me that a simple operation might bring my boy's sight back. But I am poor. I have no money and from where in all the world could a worn out old woman like me get fifty loren?

THE BOY AND THE GIRL (*Quickly*) – We don't know!

THE BOY (*Keeping his fist tightly closed over the gold piece*) – Why, we never even saw fifty loren!

THE GIRL – So much money we never will have.

THE BOY – No, we never will have.

THE OLD WOMAN – If I were young I would not say that, but I am old and I know I shall never see fifty loren. Ah! I would sell all that I have if my boy could only see again! I would sell my keepsakes, my silken dress that I've had for many years, my memories, anything to bring my boy's sight back to him!

THE GIRL – But, Old Lady, would you sell your dream of a wooden clock, a clock that strikes the hours every day and need not be wound for a whole week?

THE OLD WOMAN – Yes, child, I would.

THE BOY – And would you sell your wish for white candles to burn on feast days and Sundays?

THE OLD WOMAN – Oh! Boy, I would even sell my labor on feast days and Sundays were I not too weak to work.

THE GIRL – And would you give up your dream of a woolen shawl with red and purple flowers on it and fringe all around the four edges of it?

THE OLD WOMAN – I would give up all my dreams if my son were to see again.

(*There is a pause.* THE GIRL, *forgetting for a moment her own desires, begins to speak slowly as if to herself.*)

But, Old Lady, would you sell your dream of a wooden clock?[1]

203

THE GIRL – It must be awful not to know the sunshine and the flowers and the beauty of the hills in springtime.

THE BOY – It must be awful never to see the jolly crowds in the square on market days and never to play with the fellows at May games.

THE GIRL – And the doctor says that maybe this boy could be made well.

THE BOY – And the Old Woman says that it would cost but fifty loren.

THE GIRL (*Suddenly*) – I have no need of a gay shawl, Pablo.

THE BOY – We have no shelf for a wooden clock, Rosa.

THE GIRL – Nor vegetables to cook in a granite kettle.

THE BOY – And a big spoon would be such a useless thing.

THE OLD WOMAN (*Rising*) – Before the night becomes too dark I must go on. (*She moves toward the door.*)

THE BOY – Wait a moment, Mother. Let us slip something into your pouch.

THE GIRL – Something bright and golden, Mother.

THE BOY – Something that shines in the sunlight.

THE GIRL – Something from us to your boy.

(*They open* THE OLD WOMAN's *bag and* THE BOY *slips the gold piece into it.* THE OLD WOMAN *does not see what they have given her.*)

THE OLD WOMAN – Thank you, good children. I know my boy will be pleased with your toy. It will give him something to hold in his hands and make him forget his blindness for a moment. God bless you both for your gift and, – Good-Bye.

THE BOY AND THE GIRL – Good-Bye, Old Woman.

(*The door closes. It is dark and the room is lighted only by the fire in the grate.*)

THE GIRL – Are you happy, Pablo?

THE BOY – I'm very happy. And you, Rosa?

THE GIRL – I'm happy, too. I'm happier than any wooden clock could make me.

THE BOY – Or hob-nailed shoes, me.

The Girl – Or me, a flowered shawl with crimson fringe.

(*They sit down before the fire-place and watch the big logs glow. The wood crackles and flames and lights the whole room with its warm red light. Outside through the window a night star shines.* THE BOY AND THE GIRL *are quiet while The Curtain Falls.*)

NOTE

1 Hilda Rue Wilkinson Brown (1894–1981) was an innovated educator and artist who worked in Washington D.C. In these illustrations, the children are depicted as Caucasian. However, most of her illustrations for *The Brownies Book Magazine* feature African American children. She lived in LeDroit Park in the 1920s, and knew Langston Hughes's family, who also lived there.

Editorial Headnote

Battey, 'Cover Picture', photograph, *The Brownies' Book Magazine*, 1:1 (January 1920), cover.

This is the first cover picture for *The Brownies' Book Magazine*, published in January 1920.

See *Fairy-Tale Revivals in the Long Nineteenth Century* General Introduction for information about *The Brownies' Book Magazine*.

6

'COVER PICTURE'

Battey

Source: Photograph, *The Brownies' Book Magazine*, 1:1 (January 1920)

DOI: 10.4324/9781003034643-9

Editorial Headnote

'Celebrating Baby Week at Tuskegee', photograph, *The Brownies' Book Magazine*, 1:1 (January 1920), pp. 16–17.

Photograph of children dressed as fairies and fantastic creatures at Tuskegee, celebrating the new year.

7

'CELEBRATING BABY WEEK AT TUSKEGEE'

Source: Photograph, *The Brownies' Book Magazine*, 1:1 (January 1920), pp. 16–17

DOI: 10.4324/9781003034643-10

Editorial Headnote

Morrison, S. 'Cushag', *Eunys, or The Dalby Maid* (Prospect Hill, Douglas, Isle of Mann: G&L Johnson, 1908).

Cushag is the *nom de plume* of Sophia Morrison, the most prolific and famous Manx author of the nineteenth century. According to the *OED Online*, 'cushag' is chiefly Manx English:

> Common ragwort, Jacobaea vulgaris. Also: the flower of this plant. Frequently regarded as or said to be the (unofficial) national flower of the Isle of Man, sometimes in ironic allusion to supposedly poor or wasteful agricultural practices.

The *nom de plume* is usually used in quotes, suggesting an ironic pen name that celebrates Manx identity.

Manx English is integral to this drama and all of Cushag's work. The Manx language is a Celtic language closely related to Scottish and Irish Gaelic. It was spoken by the majority of people on the Isle of Mann until it was replaced by English in the nineteenth century. Sophia Morrison and her brother worked to keep Manx alive during the late nineteenth and early twentieth century, before it was revived in the later twentieth century.[1]

Dalby is a small sea-side hamlet on the Isle of Mann. It faces the Irish Sea on the west side of Dalby Mountain.

The scenic St. James Anglican Church in Dalby was commissioned in 1839 by the Bishop of Sodor and Man. Unlike all other Anglican bishops in Great Britain, who are elected from the canons of the cathedral, the Bishop of Sodor and Man is appointed directly by the monarch by letters of patent and plays a role in the Legislative Council of the Isle of Mann. This makes the Bishop at St. James an outsider in the Manx community. The St. James Church itself has remained the centre of the Dalby community, serving as the schoolhouse and site for any community events.

NOTE

1 Tikkanen, A., 'Manx Language', *Encyclopaedia Britannica*, 25 October 2013.

8

EUNYS, OR THE DALBY MAID

S. Morrison, 'Cushag'

Source: Prospect Hill, Douglas, Isle of Mann: G&L Johnson, 1908

EUNYS, OR THE DALBY MAID.

(*Fisherman's Cottage. Little deep window looking over the sea. Juan and Nora sitting on either side of the "chiollagh"[1] listening and looking anxiously at each other. Music of "Arrane Ghelbee"[2] heard, increasing in sound and stopping abruptly.*)

JUAN. Did thou hear that, woman?

NORA. I did so. Deed yes, Juan.

JUAN. Did thou notice the tune was going furder this time?

NORA. Aye, furder still – always a lil bit an' a lil bit on – whatever is it meanin' at all!

JUAN. Did thou notice it different this time?

NORA. Was it louder like – as if it was takin' anger at us?

JUAN. Like enough. Thinkin' of to-morrow.

NORA (*lifting her apron to her eyes and weeping.*) To-morrow, to-morrow! What will we do at all to-morrow; an' black shame comin' on us for all the people to see.

JUAN. An' black shame put on the chile that's been like our own an' not sense at her even to be knowin' it.

NORA. Chile veen![3] Chile veen! As innocent as the lil lambs in the fiel' for all she's lookin' so weiss. That's the way the lambs is, too, lookin' so weiss, an' only knowin' the sun is in for to warm them an' yarb in for them to eat, an' never takin' no heed of what to-morrow may bring. And that's our Eunys the same – knowin' nothin' but jus' to be happy an' to be doin' what we are tellin' her. An' the name of Eunys that was put on her at th'oul' Pazon[4] was good too, for joy an' comfort an' happiness she has brought to us all these years.

JUAN. An' never an ill word or a cross look at her, but doin' lil things for others an' as good to read her book as any.

NORA. Aye, an' betthar[5] too than some that's jealous of her.

JUAN. An' Pazon that should be leadin' a sthray lamb tendhar, to be like puttin' spite on her for all! "Example," he was sayin', an' "Presented at the Wardens for loose talkin' an' foolish laughter, an' puttin' flowers in her hair like a heathen."[6] An' the chile lookin' at him so serious like, wontherin'[7] at all the big words, an' then smilin' at him till you'd have thought he must have seen she wasn' like others.

NORA. An' I believe Pazon is sorry for all. But he's a sevare man, an' not likin' to go back on his word. An' he always was for givin' ear to them that's tellin' crimes on others. Look at the way he was with his own childher, till they took an' lef' him an' the hearts jus bruk[8] at them. There's neither mirth nor music comin' from yandhar house, an' I believe there isn't a more unhappier man in the Parish than Pazon. An' I'm blamin' some wans a deal more till him.[9]

JUAN. Some wans; aye indeed. Them wans that has childher of their own an' should be more tendherer than given' heed to all the talk that's goin'. But them Wardens is hardening their hearts that's hard enough already. It's pride that's doin' on them, for, to be sayin' that so many has been presented is showin' how keen they are to be mindin' the Parish.

NORA. Only this everin' itself I have been thinkin' of the time she come to us. Do you min' Juan how the sun was shining sthraight over the sea an' the lil tune of the waves on the shore?

JUAN. An' us two down at the edge of the tide talkin' of the lil wans that was took, an' us lef' hungerin' for the feel of a chile's arms roun' our neck.

NORA. An' the quare[10] oul' boat comin' in urrov the sunset an' row, row, rowin' nearer an' nearer, an' the music comin', an' us wontherin' who could it be at all, an' the tune jus' like the waves goin' up an' down an' never gettin' no furder –

JUAN. An' the sun blazin' sudden in our eyes an' jus' puzzled with the light –

NORA. An' there at our feet on the wet san' the chile lyin', an' lookin' to be took up at us. Aw well, I don't know how can I bear it. Her to be took an' put at the Church dhure the same as them that has desarved it!

JUAN. I tell you woman I can't bear it, an' I'm goin' up to put a sight on Pazon again an' see can I peacify him and make him more lenient, an' take this black shame off of us that has never gone against him.

NORA. Aw Juan, Juan, I'm fearin' thou'll do no good, man. For he's hard terrible, an' it's example he's wantin' to make, an' the Bishop talkin', he says, of the scandal, an' (*crying and rocking herself*) it's our poor innocent lamb that's took without mercy.

JUAN (*preparing to leave the house*). Were you askin' Mrs. Cushlahan for the sheet when you were in this morning?

NORA. Aye Juan, an' the bes' sheet in the chiss[11] she said would not be too good for our Lhiannoo. She is a kind woman is Mrs. Cushlahan, an' vext turble that them Wardens has put such a thing on us. The bes' sheet that she has got, fine linen they'd had there, these years, an' lace trimming on the hem fit for a queen.

216

JUAN (*Going*). An' what good will fine linen and lace be doin' at all? It's sackcloth an' ashes that should be in for them that's desarvin' such punishment, an' them that's innocent like our Eunys isn't needin' no lace to set them off. (*Exit*)

NORA (*sol.*) Aw well; it's pleasin' the chile for all. The sowl! When I would be thryin' me bes' for to explain what them wans was sayin', an' tellin' her for why she was to be wearin' the white sheet at the Church dhure, all she was sayin' was: – "See the pretty lace, Granny veen – is it me that's to be dhressed so fine, an' all the people comin' to see!" Aw dear, dear, but Juan mus' be mindin' that she'll not be hearin' any ill words from wans that'll be mockin'. But there's no fear for all, for she would only be smilin' at them, an' never take in the meaning anyway of what they would be thinkin'. It's time the chile was home too. (*Sitting down and folding her hands patiently.*). Aw well, she'll not be long now.

CURTAIN.

II

Parson's study. Parson writing. Enter Juan.

PARSON (*drily*). Well, Juan Sayle, what is it you want?

JUAN (*feebly*). Good everin', Sir, good everin'.

PARSON. Yes, Yes. Good evening. What is it you have come for? You know I am always busy on Saturday evening.

JUAN (*gazing round*). Aye, aye. An' all these fine books. There'll be a sight of readin' in them too. Is any of them tellin' of the ways of shepherds with sthray lambs?

PARSON (*frowning impatiently*). What do you mean, Juan Sayle? Have you been taking too much again? (*Looking closely and severely at the old man.*)

JUAN. God forgive your Reverence. Taking too much again! It's well known in Dalby there isn't a soberer man in than me, unless it's your Reverence, an' indeed if there's a dhrop between us it's not me that's had it anyhow.

PARSON. Come now, I think you had better go home, and let the solemn thought of the coming morrow sober you and teach you to take more heed to the ways of your household.

JUAN (*standing stubbornly leaning on stick & gazing on floor*). Pazon! Pazon! You have known me these years, an' you cannot be sayin' that I have ever been consarned in dhrink, or unruly, or that my house was not regulated; an' the lil wan that was sent to us in place of them that was took was never no trouble to you in the Parish, but rared at me an' the wife as studdy an' God-fearing as we could do it. An' wherever she come from (*looking through window with far-away dreamy air*) she has been a good chile to us, an' its like there's wans in that'll be takin' heed that the like of her is not to be treated bad – (*Music of Arrane Ghelbee heard; Juan starts, holding up hand and listening*). Did you hear that, Sir? (*music gradually dying away*).

PARSON. Hear what, Juan Sayle? And what are you looking at me like that for? Come now! I can make allowance for the real trouble this light-minded girl

217

has brought upon you, but do not you forget your obedience to the Church and to me as your Spiritual Guide and Superior.

JUAN (*aside dreamily*). An' the tune goin' still, an' likely him not hearin' it afther all. Well, well! (*To Parson*) Is it light-minded you are callin' her, Sir? Light indeed – but the light of an innocent heart that knows no guile, an' her min' as the min' of a chile for all her eighteen years.

PARSON. If Eunys is really eighteen years, she is quite old enough to know that she is bringing trouble on you and your wife; and considering the circumstances of her birth, it is doubly to be desired that she should learn to conduct herself with modesty and soberness.

JUAN. Did you ever rightly know them circumstances, Sir?

PARSON. I know enough of the world, Juan Sayle, to find it only too easy to account for such circumstances. I also know that you and your wife took her as a foundling, and deserve praise for –

JUAN. Praise! – Us that's lovin' her!

PARSON. – for your care of her all these years. I also know from what has been told me, that you and your wife invented some foolish stories about your finding her as a baby; and that you deliberately checked any rumours that might have led to the discovery of her parents, and did your best to hide all traces of them by pretended mysteries, with which you thought to delude your neighbours. You know probably who those parents were, and, (if they were relatives of your own, whose shame you wished to hide) you are none the less guilty of having connived at fraud and deceit all these years.

JUAN. Will your Reverence have patience an' let me tell the story now. I am an old man, Sir, and I have lived honourable all my life, an' it's hard talkin' of shame an' deceit to them that's not desarvin' it.

PARSON. Well, Sayle, in consideration of your age and the trouble you are in, I will listen to you. But I warn you that you will not impose upon me as you did upon your simpler neighbours and friends.

JUAN. It's thruth I'm tellin' you, Sir, an' no lie, an' this is the way the chile come to us –

(*Parson fetches note-book & inkstand, Juan watching and waiting quietly till he settles*).

JUAN. Well, your Reverence – herself an' me was down at the tide that everin', an' the wather low, an' the sun goin' down; an' there was no soun' heard but the lil tune of the waves. An' out of the brightness of the sky we saw a boat comin' from the Wes' an' wan rowin' towards us, an' music comin' over the wather to us. We were hearin' no words, but music it was, sweeter than any bird could sing. An' the wife went down on her knees on the wet san', an' "Juan, Juan," I was hearin' her say, "Juan, Juan, look what the say has brought us, Juan." But I was takin' no heed for I was watchin' an' lookin' with my han' over me eyes, an' then I saw him like as if he was goin' back again, an' he rew, an' he rew, an' he rew – a mis' come over me eyes that I could not see him. An' I looked down at my feet and there was herself on her knees with

218

a chile in her arms. "Juan, Juan," she says, "look what the say has brought us in place of them that's gone." An' the babe looked up an' smiled as if it was come home. Aye, aye, that's the way it was.

PARSON. (*After a pause.*) And what did you do then?

JUAN. An' we went up the shore with it, an' a passel of folk was on the sthreet. But when we were tellin' them. – "Aw purr it back! purr it back where it come from" they were sayin' – "You'll never get no good from the like of yandhar" they were sayin'! "Purr it back. There'll be wans in to look afther it an' take it back." That's the way they were talkin'. But the music was soundin' loud again like as if it was takin' anger at us. I don't know was them wans hearin' it or not, but the wife an' me, we was hearin' it. – An' we went in an' shut the dhure, an' aw the joy we took of the chile. An' me sent up on the laff for th' oul' cradle, an' herself raeching down in the chiss for the lil caps an' coats an' shoes our wans had wore! Aw well, well! An' to think what's comin' on the chile now!

PARSON. Now Sayle, I have listened patiently to you because I promised to hear your story, but you cannot expect me to believe such a tissue of falsehood. –

JUAN. (*Doggedly.*) It's thruth I'm tellin' ye an' no lie. An' the babe christened nex' day at th' oul' Parson, an' us mindin' keerful that it was not took back before –

PARSON. I am not saying that you mean to speak falsely and I wish to be charitable as far as I can. It is probable that you and Mrs. Sayle have told your story so often that you have almost come to believe in it yourself – but I must tell you that I am very much shocked to find how much hold superstition still has upon you.

JUAN (*Going on as if he had not heard.*) An' he was askin' herself what would she call the chile, an' she answered an' said, – "Call her Eunys, for the Lord hath comforted His people." An' he did so an' the babe was named "Eunys" – that's like you'd be callin' Joy, Comfort, Happiness to, Sir, – an' the Sign of the Cross put on her – though I'm thinkin' them wans out yandhar, (*pointing towards sea*) was not bes' pleased, for the storm that was in that night was cruel urrov massy.[12]

PARSON. (*Getting up angrily.*) There now, that will do, this is mere profanity. Worse than ignorance, and heart-breaking after all the years I have laboured among you. All you say only convinces me that the Church needs to take severe measures in dealing with you and I shall take occasion to-morrow to speak very seriously about the terrible and heathenish superstition which binds you still in chains of darkness.

JUAN. (*Interrupting.*) Is there no chance at all of the penance being took off of her?

PARSON. I cannot go back from my word Sayle, nor has anything you have said given me any reason for so doing. The girl has been presented by the Wardens, who I have no doubt have grave reasons for taking such a step, and she must go through what is ordained for her own good and for the sake of example to others.

JUAN. (*Half-incredulous.*) An' is she, that's not even knowin' the meanin' of such things – is she to stand at the Church dhure in the white sheet for all?

PARSON. She must stand at the Church door in the white sheet of penance –

JUAN. You are calling it the white sheet of penance but when our Eunys is wearin' it tomorrow it will be the white robe of Innocence, an' the cannle in her han' will shine no brighter than the pure soul of her before the Angels that are in Heaven.

CURTAIN.

III

(*Fisherman's Cottage. Nora sitting waiting. Soft strains of music dying away as door opens and Eunys enters slowly, looking back, and with hand waving and lips moving as if speaking.*)

NORA. (*Watching.*) Who's thy company, chree?[13]

(*Eunys takes no heed but coming forward slowly takes stool at Nora's feet and looks up, affectionately caressing the old woman's face.*)

NORA. What's doin' on thee, chree?

EUNYS. (*Holding up hand and listening.*) Arn't you hearing it Granny veen, an' arn't you hearing them calling me all the time?

NORA. Who is it that's callin' my lamb? Hush thee, hush thee, chile veen. It's fancies an' fayries thass in. Stay quite now an' let Grannie talk to thee.

EUNYS. (*With far-away look.*) Still they're calling me, Granny, first thing when the sun comes slanting in on the wall an' the birds are singing, an' the leaves of the trees are whisperin' in at the window, they are crying, "Lhiannoo come away." In the morning down at the tide an' up in the Glen they're calling, "Lhiannoo[14] come away;" coming along the lane in the little everin', an' the waves all dancin' in the sunset, still I'm hearin' them calling "Lhiannoo come away, Lhiannoo come away!"

NORA. There, there, chile veen. Thou's tired an' fanciful. It'll be fayries that's callin' an' you musn' be mindin' them, Graih-ma-chree.[15] You wouldn' be for leaving me an' Grandaa at all?

EUNYS. Not only Fayries, Granny. There's more till Fayries too. The Stars were calling me to-day, Granny.

NORA. Chut! Chut! It's fancies the chile has got. Lizzen now till I tell thee again what we mus' be doin' to-morrow. –

EUNYS. (*Unheeding.*) I was over on Dalby Mountain a while ago, Granny, an' I was lyin' on the turf an' puttin' my ear to the ground in the place Grandaa was telling of. Do you mind Granny veen?

NORA. Aye deed. Aye deed. They're sayin' if you listen still an' quite you'll be hearin' the Stars tellin' the Secrets of the Infinite! I've heard my own Mother sayin' it, an' I'm thinkin' its what's meanin' in the Book where its sayin': – The Morning Stars sang together – Yes, yes chree, I know the place well. An' were you so far as that chile veen?

EUNYS. I was listening Granny an' for a long time I was only hearing the bees in among the heather, an' a lark was singing up in the sky, an' the lil flies rustling in the stalks of the grass – an' then, Granny villish,[16] I heard the Stars too, what they were saying. An' all the Stars were crying (*clasping her hands with an upward look*) "Lhiannoo come away, Lhiannoo come away."

NORA. Well now, an' was that all they had to say. "Come away home" its like they were meanin'. Home to me an' thy Grandaa that's longin' if the chile veen is out of our sight for an' hour. That's what the stars would be tellin' thee chree. Any way it's bes' for lil gels to be stayin' at home in th' everin'. There's wans on the mountains that's bes' not spoke of, an' there's wans talkin' too. Aye deed, an' a power of spite at them too, an' deed, Eunys, it's not well for thee to be goin' alone in them places so often, (*tenderly stroking the girl's hair.*)

(*Door opens and Juan enters with blaze of sunshine.*)

EUNYS. See, Granny veen, how the sunset Fayries are coming slidin' down the sun beams. Did they come with you Grandaa all the way from the sunset?

JUAN. (*Closing door and standing looking gravely at her.*) Thou'd bes' be goin' to bed, Lhiannoo veen. Its like thou'll be tired enough to-morrow.

NORA. (*Looking anxiously at him.*) Was it no good, Juan, man,

JUAN. No good at all, for obstinate turble he was. (*Sitting down wearily.*) Well, well! that's the way it iss! She mus' stan' at the Church dhure for all to see in the white sheet an' all. (*Leaning his head on his hand.*)

EUNYS. (*Springing up eagerly.*) Is it me Grandaa an' the white sheet.? Don't take on Grandaa – I'm not minding now, for Granny has got a fine dress for me to-mor-row. You should see the lace that's on it – Fit for a Queen isn't it Granny veen?

NORA. Aye deed. It's like the Queen isn' usin' no better.

EUNYS. Where is it. Granny, that Grandaa can see me in it, an' then he'll not be takin' on any more.

NORA. In the parlour it is. Take the cannle chile veen an' go keerful now. It's mid-dlin' dark in theer.

(*Eunys goes out and presently returns, slowly entering, draped in sheet and with lighted candle in her hand. Stands listening wistfully.*)

(*Chorus from without, accompanied by the rhythmical sound of rowlocks.*) – (*Air "Arrane Ghelbee."*)

Rowing, rowing from the Sunset
Where the water-fairies play,
We are come to bear thee homeward
Lhiannoo, Lhiannoo, come away.

EUNYS. (*Answering in clear distinct tones, sings.*)

I am coming, I am coming,
Hark they call me from the foam;

(*Turning to old folk yearningly.*)

> Oh, Fare-you-well! I may not linger,
> Stars and Sunset call me home.

curtain.
(*Chorus from without.*)

> Lonely, lonely will they wander
> On the ever-dark'ning shore;
> Softly sing the waves together
> But the Lhiannoo comes no more.
> Only from the Land of Sunset
> Flowing, flowing evermore,
> Oh! Sadly sing the waves together
> On the lonely Dalby Shore.

FINIS.

NOTES

1 'Chiollagh' is a Manx term that means 'chimney'.
2 'Arrane Ghelbee' is a Dalby tune.
3 'Chile veen' is a phrase that means 'child darling'. Veen is used as an endearing term through the play. *A Vocabulary of the Anglo-Manx Dialect* (1924), Sophia Morrison ed.
4 Pazon is a Manx colloquial spelling of parson.
5 Manx dialectic spelling of the phrase: and better.
6 In 1908, Anglican churchwardens were lay guardians of the parish, responsible for a wide range of church business including finances, provisions for services and order in the church. The power of the Wardens and Parson in the play reflect the centrality of St. James Church to the community of Dalby, a role it continues to hold in many ways (see '*Eunys, or the Dalby Maid*' Headnote).
7 Dialectic spelling of 'wondering'.
8 Dialectic spelling of 'just broke'.
9 'Wans' is a dialectic spelling of 'ones'.
10 'Quare' is a Gaelic term that means 'very'.
11 'Urrov' is a Manx term for 'Church'.
12 'Urrov' means 'out of'. *A Vocabulary of the Anglo-Manx Dialect.*
13 'Chree' is an endearment meaning 'heart' or 'dear'. *A Vocabulary of the Anglo-Manx Dialect.*
14 'Lhiannoo' is an endearment meaning 'child'. *A Vocabulary of the Anglo-Manx Dialect.*
15 'Graih' is an endearment meaning 'love'. *A Vocabulary of the Anglo-Manx Dialect.*
16 'Villish' is an inflection of 'millish' meaning 'sweet'. *A Vocabulary of the Anglo-Manx Dialect.*

Editorial Headnote

Noël-Paton, M. H., *The Hidden People: A Play Based on the Ballads of Tam Lin and Thomas the Rhymer* (London: George Allen & Unwin Ltd, 1933).

Author M. H. Noël-Paton was the granddaughter of famous Scottish painter and sculptor Joseph Noël-Paton, whose most famous plays deal with fairies and fairy lore.[1] This play is based on medieval ballads about Thomas the Rhymer and his experiences in Faery. It undermines the romance of the traditional Celtic fairy tale 'Tam Lin and Burd Janet', exploring the unravelling of their romance after decades of marriage, ending with Tam Lin's ultimate demise. It makes parallels between the capricious and meaningless fairy court and the human courts in its final acts. It is a mild critique of the structure of the local government, embodied in the characters of the Lord Provost and his Councillors.

Content warning: This play includes comic domestic violence within its critique of fairy-tale romance.

NOTE

1 'Joseph Noël-Paton', National Galleries Scotland.

9

THE HIDDEN PEOPLE:
A PLAY BASED ON THE
BALLADS OF TAM LIN AND
THOMAS THE RHYMER

M. H. Noël-Paton

Source: London: George Allen & Unwin Ltd, 1933

DRAMATIS PERSONÆ

TAM LIN
THOMAS THE RHYMER
THE FAËRY QUEEN
FAIR JANET
WILLIE WAME

TAM LIN'S CHILDREN: JO-ANN, ELPIE, ROBIN AND PETERKIN
*FOUR CITY COUNCILLORS
TWO MEN-AT-ARMS
SWORD-BEARER
TOWNSFOLK
*ELFIN KNIGHTS
TWO CHANGELINGS
FAËRY FOLK
DANCERS

(* These parts can be doubled if necessary)

DOI: 10.4324/9781003034643-12

NOTES ON THE PLAY

Introductory

THOMAS OF ERCILDOUNE, better known as Thomas the Rhymer, was a Border poet of the thirteenth century. According to popular legend, he was lying one day beside a wooded stream when

> "A ladie that was brisk and bold
>   Came riding o'er the fernie brae.
> Her skirt was of the grass-green silk,
>   Her mantle of the velvet fine,
> At ilka tett of her horse's mane
>   Hung fifty silver bells and nine.
> True Thomas he took off his hat,
>   And bowed him low down till his knee:
> 'All hail, thou mighty Queen of Heaven,
>   For your peer on earth I ne'er did see!'
> 'O no, O no, True Thomas,' she says,
>   'That name does not belong to me;
> I am but the queen of fair Elfland,
>   And I'm come here for to visit thee.'"

Thomas fell instantly in love with this beautiful being, and mounting her horse behind her rode off with her to Elfland. After a time, thoughts of the "middle-eard" come back to him, and he asks permission to revisit the land of mortals. The Queen of Faëryland grants it on condition that whenever she sends for him he will return to her. The Rhymer promises, and at their parting she bestows on him the three gifts of poetry, prophecy, and the true tongue (hence his nickname "True Thomas." One of the rhyming prophecies attributed to him, and – oddly enough – recently fulfilled, is: –

> "Betide, betide, whate'er betide,
> There'll aye be Haigs o' Bemersyde!")

The *Ballad of Tamlane* (or Tam Lin) – which tells of another mortal who is carried off to Elfland, and of his endeavours to escape therefrom when he discovers there are certain perils attached to being too good-looking (even in Faëryland!) – gives the other side of the picture so vividly that the play grew out of the contrasting characters of the two Thomases.

Though the historic Thomas of Ercildoune flourished in the thirteenth century, the *Ballad of Tamlane* (parts of which are incorporated in the play) is fifteenth or sixteenth century; and as this is a more picturesque period (and one, moreover, usually well represented in school "wardrobes"), I claim Shakespearian precedent for dressing the characters in the period when the tale was told.

It should be remembered that the faëry folk of the Border Ballads are not the gossamer-and-moonshine elves of Shakespeare's fancy, but "lords and ladies gay" who go a-hawking, and a-hunting, and a-wooing like any human, except that – being gifted with eternal youth – they are far more fascinating, irrational, irresponsible, and enchanting than any mere mortal can ever hope (or fear) to be.

Suggestions for Production

This play can be done in a curtain set; in fact better so, for – with a double-curtain or apron stage – Scene III (the interior of TAM LIN's cottage) can be played in front of the draw curtain while the Council Chamber is being set behind. (Incidentally, strong, bold, heraldic colours should be used for the Council Chamber, to contrast with the drabness of the cottage and the enchantment of the Glen.)

The scenes being comparatively short, it is essential that as little time as possible be wasted changing them.

In Scene I (the entrance to the Faëry Glen) the light should be subdued to suggest thick woodland. If anything, it should be brighter and more mundane on the side from which the humans enter, becoming greener and more mysterious on the faëry side. The only essential properties are a tree stump L. and a bush R. (behind which TAM LIN can hide) covered with bright berries.

In Scene II, when the faëry host ride by and THE QUEEN tries to work her spells on TAM, the apparitions can be done most effectively by using a projection lantern focussed on the backcloth of the scene, which should be dark. Take three blank slides, mask these with black paper, first cutting out of one the shape of a snake, out of the other a stag. Leave the third completely black. Paste these masks on to the blank slides, and at the right moment (having carefully focussed the lantern beforehand) slip in the snake and the stag at their respective cues, so that the lit forms flash across the darkness. The completely black slide must follow each to shut off the light from the lantern. The third phenomenon is a sudden red glow behind the cross which is best done from the stage.

The passing of the faëry host can be conveyed by making the sound of horses' hoofs with two half coco-nut shells. With a little practice it is quite easy to suggest walking, trotting, and cantering.

THE FAËRY QUEEN is always heralded by the jingling of the "silver bells" on her horse's mane.

Scene V should be a blaze of light (which, nevertheless, may be effectively dimmed during the speaking of the curse), for the faëries hold high festival on Midsummer's Eve. THE QUEEN, seated on a low daïs (covered with green to suggest a bank), is raised a little above her court, and should be the centre of light. A dance (by the Eurythmic class) might start the revels. (Brahms' Waltzes Nos. 8 and 15 make excellent music for this.) When the FIRST MESSENGER bursts in with his news THE DANCERS break their circle and scatter, terrified. They can either run off, or remain crouching in frightened groups; but they must keep perfectly still during the prouncement of the curse.

A double-curtained stage greatly simplifies the end of the play, for at the sign from THE QUEEN to shut the gates of Faëryland against TAM LIN, THE MESSENGERS rush to the draw-curtains at each side, and run with them as they swing together towards the centre. This leaves TAM LIN outside upon the apron stage, fumbling wildly at the crack where the curtains closed, before he falls.

The whole play should take about one hour and a quarter.

Music

The use of two songs from Rutland Boughton's *The Immortal Hour* (published by Stainer and Bell, Ltd., words by Fiona Macleod) greatly heightens the super-natural effect.

Scene II. – When the curtain rises on the semi-darkness of Miles' Cross, two verses of Eochaidh's song ("Where the water whispers," etc., down to "in dread of mortal sight") may be sung "off," ending just as JANET enters with the holy water in her hand.

Scene V. – When TAM LIN falls dead outside the Faëry Hill, the Old Bard's song: "I have seen all things pass" makes a fitting finish. In the original production of the play a hooded figure passed slowly in front of the curtain chanting this song, letting dead leaves, hidden in the wide sleeves of its black, monkish garb, drift to the ground.

N.B. – If it is desired to use these songs for a public performance, application should be made to the Performing Rights Society, Chatham House, George Street, Hanover Square, London, W., *stating where the performance is to take place.*

Costumes

THOMAS THE RHYMER should wear black velvet with if possible, a heron's plume in his hat. He is dignified charming, and perfectly at ease. His hair must be powdered in Scene IV to mark the passage of time, but in Scene V he is a young man once more.

TAM LIN in the first scene should be a gay gallant in green, or green and bronze. A gold circlet with a peacock's feather stuck in it adds a touch of the fantastic such as befits the favourite of THE FAËRY QUEEN. In Scene III it is a very different story TAM is in the frayed and shabby clothes of a poor yeoman; his hair is greying, and he has a ragged fringe of beard.

JANET, daintily dressed in Scenes I and II, would probably wear a coloured petticoat, mutch and shawl in Scene III; though she puts on her "braws" (such as they are, after twenty years' struggle with the feckless TAM!) to go to the Council Chamber. She, like TAM LIN and THE RHYMER, must be made up to look older in the later scenes.

WILLIE WAME should be in every possible way a complete contrast to TAM LIN: dull and plebeian in the first scene, pompous and prosperous in the third and fourth.

COUNCILLORS: furred scarlet gowns, scant grizzled locks, and decrepit gait.

FAËRY KNIGHTS: dressed like courtiers. In the first scene they must appear blue-chinned and decidedly unkempt; in the last scene they have shaved, recovered their poise, and are resplendent.

FAËRY QUEEN: In the earlier scenes she should be dressed in green velvet or silk, with a tall conical hat and veil of silver gauze. In the last scene she should wear gold tissue and a jewelled coronet. She might have a garland or bracelet of flowers.

FAËRY DANCERS: These should have bare arms and legs, and be clad in short, green tunics; each should wear a wreath of wild flowers. They should be chosen for their grace of movement primarily, and the dance should be rehearsed along with the other players in the last scene, as it requires careful timing.

NOTE. – Though there are a certain number of Scotticisms scattered through the play to retain the character of the original ballads, the general sense should be quite intelligible to an average English audience.

N.B. – The "g" in "gin" (meaning "if") is hard; "lie" in "the tongue that canna lie" should be pronounced "lee," and "gie" (meaning "give") should rhyme with it.

THE HIDDEN PEOPLE

Scene I

IN THE FAËRY GLEN. *A group of* ELFIN KNIGHTS, *somewhat blue-chinned and unwontedly grave, are grouped about two of their number who are dicing.* TAM LIN, *quite unconcerned, is among the idle watchers of the game.*

TAM LIN[1]

Why is it, Sirs, ye look so wan
    And little have to say?
Does all the elf-land laughter die
    When Thomas goes away?
           (*Banteringly*)

Am I not left? As braw a knight
    To dance beneath the moon?
And though I may not sing as he,
    I skip wi' lighter shoon!

FIRST ELF-KNIGHT (*ignoring* TAM LIN)

My turn to throw . . . aha! I win!

SECOND ELF-KNIGHT

Come, throw with me again –
    (*Half to himself*)

I'd barter half my elfin-hood
  To be a man with men!

TAM LIN

I've been a man with men, fine Sir,
  An' I can tell ye this:
Most men would leave their kith and kin
  To win the Elf-Queen's kiss.
    (*No response; the dicing continues gloomily.*)
'Twas so wi' Thomas[2] in the glen,
  And – seven years ago –
She reft me into Faëryland
  To be her love. . . .

FIRST ELF-KNIGHT (*suddenly*)

  I throw!
(*They continue playing in grim silence, the onlookers calling
the numbers softly as they turn up.*)

TAM LIN (*mockingly*)

Why have ye ceased to shave your chins,
  And curl your elfin locks?

FIRST ELF-KNIGHT (*viciously, over his shoulder*)

Do pigeons preen for the peregrine,
  Or pheasants for the fox?
    (*They continue dicing intently.*)

TAM LIN

What mean you?

SECOND ELF-KNIGHT (*looking up*)

  Every seven years
  We pay a fearful fee;
And every knight in Elfland quails
  For fear it may be he.

TAM LIN

A fee? To whom?

THIRD ELF-KNIGHT

Our tithe to Hell!

TAM LIN (*suddenly uncomfortable*)
Who is it like to be?

FOURTH ELF-KNIGHT
The sturdiest and comeliest knight
  Of all our companie.[3]

TAM LIN (*hastily*)
True Thomas is the Queen's dear love –

FIRST ELF-KNIGHT (*grimly*)
  Yet now he leaves her side
To seek once more the haunts of men. . . .

SECOND ELF-KNIGHT (*shuddering*)
I fear what may betide!

CHORUS OF KNIGHTS
So we have ceased to shave our chins
  Or curl our elfin locks,
For the cushat[4] dreads the peregrine
  And the pheasant fears the fox!
    (*They rise and gather up their things.*)

TAM LIN (*shaken*)
The Queen has ta'en me by the hand
  And kissed me on the brow,
And vowed I was her comely knight –
  Will she forswear it now?
The Queen has sealed me wi' a kiss
  Her own true knight to be. . . .

FIRST ELF-KNIGHT (*significantly*)
'Tis safer if thou kiss the Queen
  Than if the Queen kiss thee!

THIRD ELF-KNIGHT
Thomas alone dared buss those lips –

FOURTH ELF-KNIGHT
The Queen loves none so well.

SECOND ELF-KNIGHT

She is not like to pay with him
   the tithe we owe to Hell!
     (*Tossing their cloaks over*
     their shoulders they go out
     together, leaving TAM LIN
     to his own thoughts.)

TAM LIN (*repeats dully*)

Only True Thomas kissed those lips –
   The Queen loves none so well.
She is most like to pay with me
   The tithe she owes to Hell!
          (*Broods; then:*)

I will find me a human mate
   Before the direful day,
And gin she love me well enough
   I yet may win away.
     (*Frowning, starts to go slowly out, then, hearing voices approaching,*
     he whips behind the berry bush and peers through the foliage.)
     (*Enter* FAIR JANET, *L., half running, half dancing, followed at a little*
     distance, and a more sober pace, by WILLIE.)

WILLIE (*breathlessly*)

O Janet, Janet, come you back!
   I daur[5] no further go,
For whoso walks in the Faëry Glen
   Will drink his fill o' woe.

JANET

O Willie, ye've the wilting heart,
   And that I ne'er could bide,
And if ye will na[6] come wi' me
   I'll never be your bride!

WILLIE

O Janet, Janet, turn ye back!
   I love you far too well
To let you walk in the Faëry Glen
   That is the brink of Hell.

JANET

Whether ye let me walk or no
　I'm goin' to the Glen,
For there the brightest berries grow
　Far frae the haunts o' men.
An' if ye will na come wi' me,
　Ye chicken-hearted loon,
Ye are as like to wed wi' me
　As cock'rel wi' the moon!

WILLIE (*doggedly, coming to a standstill*)
'Tis little you reck[7] of honest love
　And faith securely tried,
That scorns to sit wi' her ain guid[8] man
　And bairns[9] at the fireside!

JANET

Oh you can have your hum-drum love
　Gin[10] you can find a bride.
The bairns I breed will dance in the woods,
　Not sit at your fireside!

WILLIE

Fareweel, fareweel, fair Janet then,
　Wi' heavy heart I go –
God grant no evil you befall,
　Though I fear it will be so.
　　　　　　(*Goes out L.*)

JANET

Oh Willie is a weary wight,
Weel quit o' him am I.
　(*With a delicious sense of forbidden freedom:*)
I would my love were an elfin-knight
　That gallops down the sky!
I would the steed my true-love rides
　Were fleeter than the wind,
Wi' moon-white siller[11] shod before,
　Wi' burning gold behind.
　　　(*She reaches out to pick some of the berries.* TAM LIN *comes up
　　　stealthily behind her and flinging his right arm round her so that her
　　　arms are pinioned, he covers her eyes with his left hand. She is too
　　　startled to cry out.* TAM LIN *bends over her and whispers in her ear:*)

TAM LIN

And if your love were an elfin gay,
    Janet, what would ye do?
Daur ye defy the Faëry Queen
    And to your love be true?

JANET (*without stirring*)

I would defy the Faëry Queen
    For one that I loved well,
Were he a saint from realms of bliss
    Or a fiend from nether Hell.
But how can I love what I have na seen?
    Let go, that I may tell!

TAM LIN (*his grip tightens*)

Oh I will neither let you go
    Nor will I let you see,
Until you swear by the Holy Rood
    That you'll keep faith with me.

JANET (*trying to pull his hand from her eyes*)

What is your name, you ranting knight?
    And what if I like you ill?

TAM LIN

'Tis Tam Lin holds you in his arms
    And ye maun[12] do his will!

JANET

Have ye a steed wi' siller shod,
    And burning gold behind?

TAM LIN

I have a steed wi' siller shod
    Rides faster than the wind.

JANET

Then I will gang wi' you, Tam Lin,
    And swear to do your will.

TAM LIN

Fair Janet, ye maun come wi' me

* Silver.

Unto the Faëry Hill,
And we'll plight troth by Eildon tree[13]
That knows nor good nor ill.

> (*They go out together R.,* TAM LIN *still holding her firmly by the wrist.*
> JANET, *half fearful, half joyful, cannot take her eyes from the dark hand-*
> *some face which, after the prosaic* WILLIE, *dazzles her almost as much*
> *as the thought of the "siller-shod" steed. They disappear among the*
> *trees of the glen.*
>
> *Presently there is the sound of silver bells far off in the woods. Their*
> *jingling comes nearer then suddenly stops, and enter* THOMAS THE
> RHYMER *and* THE FAËRY QUEEN *hand in hand.*)

FAËRY QUEEN

I've brought ye to the brink o' the Glen
    True Thomas, here we part.
Speed you well in the world o' men,
    But keep a lonely heart.
For whom I honour with my love
    Must ever walk apart.

THOMAS THE RHYMER

Sweet wanton, give me your honied lips
    To drink before I go,
Then folk will think, as I pass them by,
    That apple blossoms blow;
The leaves will bud on ev'ry bough,
    The throstle on the spray –
Though white with rime,[14] and winter time –
    Will sing as though 'twere May.
                    (*They embrace tenderly*)
And when you weary for your Knight
    With almost mortal pain,

                (THE QUEEN *frowns at this.*)
Send me a sign that I shall know,
    And I will come again.

FAËRY QUEEN

I'll send for you a royal stag,
    A stag and a milk-white doe,
And they will bring you back to me . . .
    But now, True Thomas, go –

Go, lest I take my promise back
   And find I do repent
That ere I let you from my side;
   And when your brow is bent,
Grieve not that halting human joys
   And carking[15] human care
Have ta'en the sparkle from your eye,
   The lustre from your hair;
For every Hallowe'en we ride,
   And on Midsummer morns
You'll hear upon the mountain side
   Our faëry hunting horns,
And you have but to turn your steps
   To the gate o' the Faëry Glen,
To win a kiss from my honied lips
   Will make you young again.
                (They kiss again.)

THOMAS

Love, when the solemn church bells toll,
   And mortal music swells,
I will be listening for the chime
   O' your sweet silver bells!

FAËRY QUEEN

Now will I give you gifts most rare
   To take with you along:
What is to be ye shall foresee,
   And blazon it in song –
And, that there may be none like you,
   A third gift will I gie,
'Twill keep you from the taint o' men –
   The tongue that canna lie. . . .

THOMAS

And what like gift is that to give
   To any mortal man?
Wi' it I'll no can buy nor sell
   Nor end what I began!
I daur na speak to prince or peer
   Or leddy[16] on the earth,

Where faëry gold is valueless
   And truth of little worth. . . .

FAËRY QUEEN

Then haud[17] your peace! What I have given
   I dinna take again.
So fare ye weel, my handsome knight,
   Fareweel, my man o' men!
Come back to be the dear delight
   Of all the Faëry Glen.
     (*He kisses her again and goes out L.* QUEEN *exits R.*)
      (*Enter from R.* TAM LIN *and* FAIR JANET *arm in arm like lovers,
     gazing fondly at each other.* TAM *has been telling her about the faëry
     folk.*)

TAM LIN

And pleasant is the faëry land
   For those that in it dwell,
But aye at end o' seven years
   They pay a teind[18] to Hell;
I am sae fair and fu' o' flesh
   I'm feared 'twill be mysel'.

JANET (*dismayed*)

O Tam!

TAM LIN (*quickly*)

But the night is Hallowe'en, Janet,
   The morn is Hallowday;
   (*Takes her in his arms.*)
Then win me, win me, an ye will,
   For weel I wat[19] ye may!

JANET

Ye say this night is Hallowe'en,
   When faëry folk do ride,
Then how may I my true-love win
   To have him at my side?

TAM LIN (*delighted to find his plan working so well*)
To Miles' Cross, Janet, go you down,
   'Twixt mirk* midnight and one;
With holy water in your hands
   Cast you your compass round.
And when the faëry host ride by
   I charge ye, stand your ground!

JANET (*a little nervously*)
I'll stand my ground for you, Tam Lin,
   But how long must I so?

TAM LIN (*holding her close to reassure her*)
The first and second company
   Heed not, but let them go.
Then kilt your kirtle,[20] to the knee
   And quickly breathe a prayer,
For when the third one passes by
   I, Tam Lin, will be there.

JANET
How shall I know you, my Tam Lin,
   At mirk midnight an' a',
Among a rout of uncouth knights
   The like I never saw?

TAM LIN
O first let pass the black, ladye,
   And then let pass the brown;
But quickly run to the milk-white steed
   And pull his rider down.
For some ride on the black, ladye,
   And some ride on the brown;
But I ride on a milk-white steed,
   A gowd[21] star in my crown:
Because I was an earthly knight
   They gie me that renown.

My right hand will be gloved, ladye,
   My left hand will be bare,
And thae's[22] the tokens I gie ye
   Nae doubt I will be there.

JANET

And when I've stopped the milk-white steed,
    And let the bridle fa'?

TAM LIN

The Queen o' Elfin she'll cry out:
    "True Tam Lin he's awa'!"

JANET

What if I fear the Elfin Queen?

TAM LIN

Then are we both undone!
    But gin ye do as I bid you
I will be safely won.
    They'll turn me in your arms, ladye,
Into a writhing snake;
    But hold me fast nor let me go,
For your love Tam Lin's sake!

JANET (*a little breathlessly*)
And then, Tam Lin? – And then . . . ?

TAM LIN

They'll turn me in your arms, ladye,
    Into a fallow deer,
But hold me fast, nor let me go
    For pity nor for fear!

JANET

And then, Tam Lin . . . what then?

TAM LIN

They'll shape me in your arms, ladye,
    An iron hot as fire;
But hold me fast, nor let me go,
    To be your heart's desire.

JANET

I'll hold you though you burn me, Tam
    Unto the very bone,
But shall I have you at the last
    To be my very own?

TAM LIN

They'll shape me in your arm, ladye
   A mother-naked man;
Cast your green mantle over me
   And so shall I be won.

JANET

Gin I do this for you, Tam Lin,
   Will you then swear to me
Ye'll gang nae mair[23] to Faëryland
   But my true husband be?

TAM LIN

I swear by oak and ash and thorn
   And the dark Eildon tree –
Gin you win me from Faëryland
   I'll your true husband be!

CURTAIN

Scene II

MILES' CROSS. *Centre back, on a raised bank (or steps), stands an old stone cross, silhouetted against a moonlit glade. The front of the stage is in darkness. (Enter L.* FAIR JANET, *a ghostly cloaked figure, clutching a stoup of holy water. She tiptoes cautiously across the stage with frequent anxious pauses.)*

JANET
(speaking softly to herself to keep up her courage)

'Tis Hallowe'en, and I have come
   My Faëry groom to win,
So here at Miles' Cross I maun* bide
   Until I spy Tam Lin.
With holy water in my hand
   I cast my compass round,
But canna still my beating heart
   For this is haunted ground.
     (Advances a few steps.)
We plighted troth, my love and I,
   Deep in the Faëry Glen;

* Disgusted.

He swore beneath the Eildon tree
  He would return to men. . . .
    (*Starts and looks round at a rustle in the bushes.*)
And should the Elfin Queen arise
  From out yon bush o' broom,
'Tis I maun strive wi' her to win
  Mysel' a bonny groom.
        (*Shivers.*)
Now comes the dead hour o' the night
  When I must do this thing –
    (*Begins to creep up stage.*)
So I will bide the cross beside
  Until the bridles ring.

    (*She settles down on the steps of the cross, silhouetted, like it, against
    the moonlit valley. The sound of silver bells and horses' hoofs are
    heard approaching.* JANET *crouches forward, her back to the audi-
    ence, and peers down at the track below her. The first company
    goes by at the canter; the second at the trot, the bells of* THE FAËRY
    QUEEN *jingling; the third comes at the walk and* JANET *leaps down
    out of sight. At the same moment there is a piercing shriek, and the
    lights go out.*
    *A thread of light flickers across the darkness. A voice is heard beyond
    the cross crying:*)

JANET

I clasp the snake
  For Tam Lin's sake!
    (*Suddenly a bush is lit up and from it rises* THE FAËRY QUEEN:)

FAËRY QUEEN

Oh had I known yestreen,[24] Tam Lin,
  What I have heard but now,
I'd made your heart a block of wood,
  Set stone eyes in your brow!
    (*The light goes out, but the form of a stag gleams for a moment in the
    dark, then vanishes.*)

JANET'S VOICE

The deer I hold,
  As Tam Lin told.

(*Again the face of* THE FAËRY QUEEN *appears in a bush:*)

FAËRY QUEEN

Oh had you thought yestreen, Tam Lin,
　What you have done this night,
You'd not have sold your elfin-hood
　For any mortal wight!
　　(*The face vanishes, but suddenly there is a dull red glow behind the cross.*)

JANET'S VOICE (*triumphantly*)

The iron burns,
　But Tam returns!
　　(*The red glow dies out, and once more* THE FAËRY QUEEN *appears. Her voice trails away in the last line and her face fades out:*)

FAËRY QUEEN

Oh had you but proved true, Tam Lin,
　As ye've proved false to-day,
I'd paid the tithe seven times to Hell
　Ere you'd been won away!
　　(*When* THE ELF-QUEEN *has vanished, two figures –* JANET *and* TAM LIN, *the latter wrapped in* JANET'S *cloak, his legs and arms bare – are seen groping their way past the cross and down the steps, silhouetted once more against the moon-lit woods beyond.*)

CURTAIN

Scene III

TAM LIN'S COTTAGE *twenty-five years later. It is poorly furnished. There is a wood fire in the middle of the floor; some three-legged stools; a broom stands in one corner, a long-bow (and possibly a spinning-wheel) in another. The entrance is R. A window, through which the sun shines, L.* TAM LIN'S *hair is turning grey, and he has grown a beard. He is shabbily dressed, and when the curtain rises he is seated on a stool by the fire, a bunch of feathers in his belt, fitting fresh goose-quills to some old arrows in his quiver. He straightens his back with a sigh and frowns at his work.*

TAM LIN

(*who has developed a habit of talking to himself*)

Five-and-twenty years, come Hallowe'en –
It seems like fifty!

The first few years went pleasantly enough.
Janet and I – we often disagreed,
but we were young,
and youth forgets.

(*Broods.*)

Then children came . . . too many, and too fast.
(*Rises impatiently and starts pacing up and down.*)

They had shrill voices, and ugly human ways. . . .
(those they got from Janet,
though their worst faults she always blames on me!)
Heigho! How things do change.
There was a time I'd not have thought it true
that Janet would become a scolding shrew!
> (*His pacing has brought him to the window. He pushes it open and the sunlight pours in. Leaning on the sill and gazing at the distant woods, he listens intently for a moment, then speaks with a sudden intake of the breath:*)

Midsummer morn! If I could only hear
The far-off echo of an elfin-horn
I would have that to help me through the year. . . .
(*Listens again.*)

Now I have threads of grey in beard and hair,
And even Janet is no longer fair.
> (*Turns away from the window and resumes his restless pacing.*)

She says I'm always talking to myself. . . .
Who else to talk to? In this stupid town
They have no thoughts for anything but pelf.[25]
They do not know a dew-drop on a leaf
Outshines the princeliest diamond.
They fight for gold –
(*Here he comes back to the window*)
and yet they cannot see
The golden largesse that each Autumn tree
Scatters abroad is fairer far than theirs. . . .
St. Christopher! There's Janet. . . .
(*Peers out cautiously.*)
And with her Willie Wame – the fat old man!
he eats too much!
I must away,
then they can cackle to their hearts' content. . . .
> (*Snatches up his quiver and feathers and his hat from a stool, and goes out R. A minute later* JANET *enters, accompanied by* WILLIE WAME. *The latter has grown portly; he wears a rich furred robe and a gold chain round his*

neck. His goatee beard is white. JANET, *wearing a much patched petticoat, has not improved with age. Her grey hair is dishevelled; she has a sulky, discontented mouth. Her high spirits have degenerated into petulance. She is shrilly recounting her grievances to* WILLIE:)

JANET

And he'll stand there babbling to himself, until the neighbours think he's daft! (WILLIE *shakes a disapproving head.*) He's aye talking to the birds, too – it's fair ridiculous! Why only yesterday I found him having a conversation with a robin . . . and shouting with laughter, too! It's enough to try the patience of a saint. (*She seizes the broom and starts sweeping vigorously. . . . After a few seconds:*) As for THE flowers: it's "my lady JASAMINE, my lady ROSE" And "Mistress EGLATINE, good day to you!" and he doffs his cap to them – but never a civil tongue in his head for the neighbours. I'm fair scunnered[26] at him!

WILLIE

(*lowering himself cautiously on to a three-legged stool*)
What for you ever married him beats me, Janet. He never treated you with the consideration you deserve. . . .

JANET (*breaking out again*)
There's never any money in the house. If he can scrape together enough for the next meal, he's quite content.

WILLIE (*soothingly*)
Aye, ye've had a hard life, Janet.

JANET (*almost tearful*)
I was a fool! A handsome face, a pleasant voice, and the trouble starts. (*Seizes her broom again.*) I hope when Jo-ann's old enough to wed, I will have knocked some sense into her head!

(*The door bursts open and* JO-ANN, ELPIE, ROBIN *and* PETERKIN *dance in, yelling:*)

CHILDREN

Da! Da! Where are you, Da?

JANET (*raising her broom threateningly*)

Haud your wheesht[27] and get out o' here. (THE CHILDREN *fall over each other in their efforts to get out quickly.*) As ram-stam[28] as their father!

WILLIE (*heaving himself up off the stool*)
See here, Janet, I've been thinkin'. My wife is dead, my sons are men. . . . I never loved her, Janet, as I once loved you; but my pride was hurt that you should scorn me so.

JANET

I was a fool – I know it now!

WILLIE (*smugly*)

I knew it then; but ye were aye a headstrong lass – ye were neither to haud nor bind* when you had the fancy on you. . . .

JANET (*bitterly*)

I've been cured of fancies. When you've had seven bairns you learn that money's worth more than moonshine!

WILLIE

I wish I could help you, Janet. (*Comes closer to her.*) I'm a man of means now . . . at least I've no done so badly for myself. To be Lord Provost at fifty . . . (*He swells with self-satisfaction.*) It's no everyone can manage that!

JANET (*admiringly*)

It is not, Willie. I'd have done better for myself if I'd married you instead of that feckless moon-calf Tam. . . .

WILLIE (*cautiously putting an arm round her waist*) If you mean that, give me a kiss, Janet. I've waited a long time.

> (JANET *is about to comply when* TAM LIN *enters suddenly, and stands with his thumbs in his belt staring moodily at them.* WILLIE *takes his arm away quickly, and opens and shuts his mouth once or twice like a fish.*)

TAM LIN

What have you come for, Willie Wame? Something to eat?

WILLIE

> (*his complacency a little shaken by the indignity of the situation*)

Eh? What? Me? No! (*Drops his velvet cap and picks it up again.* JANET *nudges him.*) Um! yes, er . . . As I was about to say (*recovers himself and becomes pompous once more*), what I came for was to see whether I couldna persuade you to reform your ways, Tam Lin, which are a scandal to the neighbourhood. . . .

TAM LIN

What d'you mean? – a scandal!

JANET (*opening fire*)

You know fine what he means, Tam Lin. Just you come down off your high horse and hear the truth for once. . . .

---

* Not to be restrained.

TAM LIN (*turning on her angrily*)

I get enough of it from you, ye cross-grained old besom! Ye're aye dinning it into my ears!

JANET (*becoming shrill*)

So that's all the thanks I get for working myself to the bone for you and your bairns – you lazy, good-for-nothing gangrel! What would the children get to eat if it wasna for me, I'd like to know?

TAM LIN (*sulkily*)

I brought them in a young cock'rel yesterday.

WILLIE

And where did ye get it, may I ask?

TAM LIN

That's none of your business.

WILLIE (*in his best magisterial manner*)

Tam Lin, unless you learn to mend your ways, it's no just your scallywag of a son we'll be hailing before the Council – it'll be yoursel'. . . .

TAM LIN

And what for have ye hailed my eldest son before the Council? What faddy, fin-icky law has he broken?

WILLIE (*pursing up his lips*)

It's easy to see who fathered him! (*Before* TAM LIN *can interrupt*) He is sum-moned before the Council on several heads, namely (*ticks them off on his fin-gers*) theft, arson, and assault and battery. His thieving ways have long been known; he is suspected of setting fire to the Beadle's ricks; and now he is under arrest for beating one of the worshipful Bailies – a most violent and unpro-voked attack!

TAM LIN

He's the only man in the toon wi' ony spunk in him. The rest of you pompous, law-abiding citizens are afraid of him – that's all there is to it!

WILLIE

Who wouldna be afraid of a young de'il who can run like the wind, jump like a deer, and climb like a cat? It's my belief – and not mine only – that he's fey. . . .

(*At the word "fey" TAM LIN winces and cries out:*)

TAM LIN

Fey! fey! Would that I were fey again! . . . Hst! Did you hear?
> (*He cocks his head and listens intently, holding his breath in his endeavour to catch the sound once more.*)

WILLIE (*who has heard nothing*)

What?

JANET (*plucking him nervously by the sleeve*)

Sh! dinna ask him!

TAM LIN (*dreamily*)

I thought I heard them. . . .
> (*Listens as though his life depended on his hearing. At this moment the door bursts open again, and* THE FOUR CHIL-DREN *march in two by two, one playing on a comb, one tootling through a cow's horn, two beating on improvised drums made out of pewter mugs or saucepans, and shouting lustily:*)

CHILDREN

Thomas the Rhymer is coming to town,
> Coming to town, coming to town;

Thomas the Rhymer is coming to town –
> Hey tiddley-i-do!
>> (TAM LIN'S *expression becomes murderous. Picking up a stool he raises it above his head and turns on his children, who scream and take to their heels.*)

WILLIE

> (*who had ducked instinctively when* TAM LIN *raised the stool*)

Would you attack your own bairns?

TAM LIN

> (*his rage subsiding as quickly as it arose lowers the stool shamefacedly*)

I cannot abide their noise . . . (*glances despairingly towards the window:*) Aye, when I'm listening for something I would hear, folk come and make a din.

JANET (*severely*)

One o' these days you'll murder someone!

TAM LIN (*looking significantly at* WILLIE)

Aye, so I will.

WILLIE (*hastily*)

Weel, I must awa'. Janet, this afternoon the Council are to confer the freedom o' the Burgh on a grand poet. Shall I keep a seat for you?

JANET

Aye, Willie, do. (*Casually*) What's the grand poet's name?

WILLIE

Thomas the Rhymer – he has won much fame.

TAM LIN (*violently*)

True Thomas! Here?

WILLIE

Aye, that's the name.

(*Departs, leaving* TAM LIN *staring before him.* JANET *shuts the window.*)

CURTAIN

Scene IV

ANTE-ROOM OF THE COUNCIL CHAMBER IN TAM LIN'S TOWN. *A crowd of townsfolk have gathered to see* THE COUNCILLORS *and* THE LORD PROVOST *go by in state, with the famous* RHYMER, *whom they are to honour. The entrance door is R., the window L. Centre back two or three steps lead up to the great doors of the Council Chamber; these are guarded by* TWO HALBERDIERS, *one on either side. Some of the people try to pass through the big doors, but are stopped by* THE MEN-AT-ARMS.

(*This scene gives great opportunity for the players to use their imaginations. Each individual member of the crowd should make up her mind as to who and what she is, her age, her outstanding characteristics, her usual occupation, etc., and act accordingly.*)

TAM LIN *is seen pushing his way eagerly through* THE CROWD, *and approaches the steps C.* THE GUARDS *cross their halberds to keep him from entering.*

FIRST MAN-AT-ARMS

No more are allowed in till the Councillors take their seats.

TAM LIN

But surely . . . I'm a friend of the Lord Provost's –

SECOND MAN-AT-ARMS

Name, please?

TAM LIN

Tam Lin.

(THE MEN-AT-ARMS *consult a list with much scratching of the head.* TAM LIN *impatiently.*)

SECOND MAN-AT-ARMS

Here it is – look! (*points it out to his fellow*) Lin (*reads it laboriously*) Mis-stress . . . Lin. . . . (*Stares at* TAM *suspiciously over the top of the paper.*)

TAM LIN (*correcting him*)

Tam Lin.

SECOND MAN-AT-ARMS

No. It doesna say "Tam Lin." It says "Mistress Lin."

TAM LIN (*irritably*)

Well, I'm her husband – (*Makes as though to enter.*)

FIRST MAN-AT-ARMS (*pushing him back*)

No, no! None of that! There's only one seat, and it's in Mistress Lin's name, so you just stand back

(TAM LIN *starts to dispute angrily when there is a stir at the entrance door, and several people cry:*)

A MAN

They're coming!

A BOY

Oh see, yonder's the Rhymer!

FIRST WOMAN

Which?

SECOND WOMAN

. . . Where?

A BOY

Yonder, the man in black, wi' a heron's plume.

THIRD WOMAN

I've heard say he's a grand singer.

FIRST WOMAN
FIRST WOMAN

Will we hear him sing?

SECOND WOMAN

. . . No!

A MAN

Sh! Here they come.

> (*They jostle each other in their efforts to see* THE RHYMER.)
> (*The procession of* COUNCILLORS, *headed by* THE LORD PROVOST *with* THE RHYMER, *preceded by a* HERALD,* *enter R., and advance towards the door centre back.* THE CROWD *throw up their caps and cheer.* TAM LIN *turns from the steps and, faci the approaching procession, catches sigh of* THOMAS THE RHYMER. *He steps forward with a cry.* THE RHYMER, *older and graver stops and looks questioningly at him; the procession halts, too.*)

TAM LIN

Thomas! True Thomas! (*Takes a few steps nearer*) Don't you know me? (*Pause*) I'm TAM LIN.

THOMAS (*looking closer at him*)

You've changed, Tam Lin.

TAM LIN

Yes, I have changed. I know I've changed.

THOMAS

I confess I hardly knew you.

WILLIE (*surprised and a little annoyed*)

So you have met before?

THOMAS

Yes, we knew each other – long ago. (*Crossing to* TAM LIN) In another life. . . .

TAM LIN

You've changed, too, Thomas; you are older!

THOMAS (*caressing his beard, now grey*)

Aye, Tam Lin, we are both older, but I wouldna say – wiser.

TAM LIN (*coming closer to him*)

So you – haven't gone back?

* Or sword-bearer.

THOMAS

Not yet, Tam Lin, but I am going – when she sends for me.

TAM LIN (*hoarsely*)

What if she never sends for you?

THOMAS (*quietly*)

When I am tired of this . . . (*with a swift gesture indicates the pomp of the procession*) . . . and the rest of the world's tinsel, I shall go home.

TAM LIN

So, it is "home" for you?

THOMAS

Of course. I am her subject still and owe her fealty. I pledged my word that when she sent for me, whatever I was doing, I would get up and go.

> (THE PROCESSION *reassembles.* THE COUNCILLORS *close in round* THE RHYMER. TAM LIN *catches at his sleeve to detain him:*)

TAM LIN

Tell me, did you never fear her?

THOMAS (*pausing to answer*)

There were times I feared her, but love proved ever stronger than my fear. She sealed me hers, and hers I shall remain.

> (THE PROCESSION *begins to move forward again.*)

TAM LIN (*holding desperately to* THE RHYMER'S *sleeve*)

I have heard that it is dangerous . . . going back . . . ? (THE GUARDS *push him aside.*)

THOMAS (*turning at the top of the steps says gravely*)
He who seeketh safety first,
Liveth all his life accursed.
(*They pass out into the Council Chamber.*)

TAM LIN

You ne'er spoke truer word, True Thomas! (*Turns sadly away.*)

> (THE CROWD *swarm up the steps into the Council Chamber,* THE TWO GUARDS *falling in behind, and* TAM *is left alone in the middle of the room.* JANET *enters R., hurrying, as she is late for the ceremony. She stops, annoyed at finding* TAM LIN *there.*)

JANET

What! Idling still, Tam Lin?

TAM LIN (*bitterly*)

So it's Willie you'll make a fool of next?

JANET (*in injured tones*)

You never loved me true, Tam Lin,
  'Twas just to win away;
Had you not feared the Faëry Queen
  You'd be an elf to-day!

TAM LIN

It wasna me you loved, Janet,
  'Twas just ye had a mind
To something others couldna get,
  Ye thought to ride the wind
Upon a steed wi' siller shod
  And burning gold behind. . . .

JANET

    (*angry at this reminder, which she knows to be true*)
I'm weary of your feckless ways!
  It hadna been for you
I might be livin' soft and fine,
  As other leddies do.

TAM LIN

You never liked my elfin-hood,
  Forbye it sounded fine;
The bairns are *yours* when they've been good –
  When little fiends, they're *mine*!

JANET

    (*working herself up into a state of righteous indignation*)
Think shame to talk like that, Tam Lin,
  For shame! Ye know full well
You might, had it no been for me
  Be roasting now in Hell!

TAM LIN (*wearily*)

I am no longer feared of Hell
  I taste it every day –
I hear no more the elfin-horns,
  I've lost the Queen o' Fay. . . .

JANET (*furious*)

Then get ye back to yon false witch
  Beneath her Eildon tree!
Ye've made me poor that once was rich –
  Ye'll get no more o' me,
I'm off to one that loves me yet –
  An ill wind go wi' ye!

> (*She flounces up the steps and into the Council Chamber.*)

TAM LIN (*left alone, sighs deeply*)

In Faëryland, in Faëryland,
  There's neither rich nor poor;
A man may ride the bitter wind
  That blows across the moor!

> (*Suddenly* THE CHILDREN *burst in R., yelling excitedly:*)

PETERKIN

Da! Da! Where are you, Da?
The strangest thing that ever I saw!

ELPIE

A hind and a hart come up the street!

JO-ANN

At ev'ry step o' their prancin' feet
There is a peal of silver bells,
And all the air of hawthorn smells. . . .

> (*They dart to the window and jostle there to see out.*)

ROBIN

Look! Look! There they come –
Where has Peterkin put my drum?

TAM LIN

> (*who has followed them to the window and is looking out
> over their heads, speaks in an awed voice*)

Down in the street a milk-white doe
And a royal stag pace to and fro . . .

> (*He turns and rushes to the door of the Council Chamber,
> shouting:*)

Thomas the Rhymer, rise and go!

> (THE CHILDREN *dance out again, squealing with joy.*
> THOMAS THE RHYMER, *surrounded by protesting* COUN-
> CILLORS, *appears at the top of the steps leading from the*

Council Chamber. He exchanges one look with TAM LIN, *who stands facing him pale and agitated.*)

THOMAS (turning to THE CHORUS OF COUNCILLORS) I grieve to disappoint you gentlemen, hut my Queen has sent for me. . . .

CHORUS OF COUNCILLORS
The Queen? The Queen! The Queen's in France.

THOMAS (*with dignity but finality*)
My Queen has summon I me and so (*settling his hat on his head*) Good day! (*Walks down the up and out R.*)

COUNCILLORS (*recovering from their astonishment*) Has he gone fey?

TAM LIN (*stung to desperation by the fatal word*) Fey! Fey!
(*Snatches up his cloak and hat*) True Thomas, wait for me!
(*Rushes out R., calling as he goes.* THE TOWNSFOLK, *crowding behind* THE COUNCILLORS, *can restrain themselve no longer, and they rush down the steps, keeping* THE COUNCILLORS *with them. Some run to the door; some to the window, where the voice of the young* HERALD *is heard:*)

HERALD (*at the window*)
The hart and the hind and the Rhymer are gone,
But there goes Tam Lin, running alone!
(*The rest turn from the window and dash to the door, leaving* THE PROVOST *still standing on the top of the steps, and* JANET, *with her back to him, down L., facing the audience. Fear and relief are in her face.*)

JANET (*as though speaking her thoughts aloud*)
Oh Tam Lin's gone to the hollow hill
    His elf-hood to retrieve –
The Faëry folk will take it ill
    For 'tis Midsummer's Eve,
and who so spies their revels out
    on forest, field or glen,
If he misplease the Faëry rout
    I never seen again. . . .

WILLIE (*holding out his arms to her*)
Janet!

JANET

Then shall I wed wi' Willie Wame,
The couthiest o' men!

> (*Turns and goes to him. As he takes her in his arms, she fingers* THE PROVOST'S *gold chain round his neck and smiles contentedly.*)

CURTAIN

Scene V

MIDSUMMER EVE, INSIDE THE FAËRY RING. THE FAËRY QUEEN, *surrounded by her Court, is welcoming* THOMAS THE RHYMER *back to Faëryland. As the curtain rises,* THE QUEEN *has risen from her throne before which* THE RHYMER *kneels, bareheaded, and bending forward takes his face between her hands and kisses him.*

THOMAS THE RHYMER

Five-and-twenty years, ladye,
  Have laid their frosts on me;
But at your kiss my youth comes back
  As May comes to the tree:
As sap stirs in the root, ladye,
  At the sweet touch of Spring –

> (*Rises and takes her in his arms, holding her hands to his heart*)

Till what was hoar and dead before
  Is white with blossoming!

FAËRY QUEEN

Five-and-twenty years, dear love,
  Have passed with leaden feet,
And every day my longing eyes
  Have looked your face to greet.
So I have called you back, Thomas,
  To be my man o' men,
The fairest knight and dear delight
  Of all the Faëry Glen.

> (*She seats him beside her and beckons* TWO LITTLE CHANGE-LINGS *to her*)

Now from my pretty changeling boys
  Choose one to be your squire,
That he may stand at your right hand
  To do your heart's desire.

255

THOMAS (*drawing* THE CHILDREN *to him*)
Come here to me, my bonny boys,
  And stand beside my knee;
And which of you can tumble best
  Shall be a squire to me!

> (*Revel and riot begin:* FAËRIES *dancing,* BOYS *somersaulting, etc.* THOMAS *selects the best somersaulter to be his squire; the other brings in the Queen's loving-cup, and* THE QUEEN *and* THE RHYMER *pledge each other. Into the midst of the dancing and revelry bursts a breathless* MESSENGER, *who runs to the Queen's daïs and drops on one knee before her, crying:*)

FIRST MESSENGER
Madam! A man has broken through
  Our barricade of whin . . .

> (*A* SECOND MESSENGER *dashing in, also falls on his knee before* THE QUEEN, *who raises her hand for silence. The music and dancing stop abruptly.*)

SECOND MESSENGER
Madam! A human sets his foot
  Within the Faëry Ring!

> (*A* THIRD MESSENGER *darts in and joins the panting group:*)

THIRD MESSENGER
A human blunders up the Glen. . . .

FAËRY QUEEN (*harshly*)
His name?

> (*As they hesitate to reply and look nervously at each other, she repeats, with rising anger in her voice:*)

His name?

MESSENGERS (*together*)
> (*as they say the fatal name, each throws up his arm as though to ward off an expected blow:*)

Tam Lin!

FAËRY QUEEN
> (*in a cold, hard voice, rising slowly to her feet*)

Tam Lin! False-hearted, faithless friend!
  You run upon your fate.

Although I loved you greatly once,
    Now do I fiercely hate.
        (THE ELVES *tremble. Only* TRUE THOMAS *dares to speak:*)

THOMAS

Sweet Queen, though his offence is dire –
    As none knows more than I –
Yet Mercy is a royal grace,
    Becometh sov'reignty!

FAËRY QUEEN

O rashly, rashly, do you speak!
    Have you so soon forgot,
True Thomas, there be human things
    That Faëry folk have not?
Mercy – scorn – or bartered love
    Our elves can never know;
No creature born can earn our scorn:
    No mercy do we show.

We never love for power or wealth,
    Or aught that it may bring,
And so our love is swift as fire
    And fragrant as the Spring –
When Faëry folk shall love for hire
    My bells will cease to ring!

Our Justice is not merciful,
    For Mercy is not just:
The rain that makes the young corn grow
    Will stain the sword with rust.
One law for corn: and one for steel:
    Till all things come to dust.

Tam Lin, who bartered my true love
    To buy his peace with men,
I'll see no more – Shut to the door
    That guards the Faëry Glen!
        (*Her* GUARDS *leap to obey. Raising her hands in malediction, she pronounces the Faëry curse:*)

FAËRY QUEEN

He who forsakes the Faëry Hill
  Without the Queen's consent,
Shall never enter it again
  Howe'er so he repent.
Though he may steal the night-wind's cry
  And weep with the bitter rain –
A rickle[29] of bones among the stones
  Is all that shall remain!

> (THE ELVES *cower as she recites the curse* THE RHYMER *bows his head to what he see is inevitable, and covers his eyes a* TAM LIN *rushes wildly in and the gate swing to in his face. Left outside the Faëry Hill,* TAM LIN *gives a great cry and falls to the ground.*)

CURTAIN

NOTES

1 'Tam Lin' is a traditional Irish ballad.
2 Thomas Rhymer was a Welsh medieval storyteller.
3 Alternate spelling of company.
4 Cusht is a Scot term for 'wood-pigeon' according to Noël-Paton's notes.
5 Daur is a Scot word for: dare. See *OED Online* and *Collins Dictionary*.
6 Here, 'na' is a Scot word for: no. See *Dictionary of the Scots Language* entry for 'na': *adv.*[1]
7 Reck is a verb meaning: 'To reckon, consider'. *Dictionary of the Scots Language*.
8 'Ain guid' means 'own good' here. *Dictionary of the Scots Language*.
9 'Bairn' is a Scot word that means a child or an offspring of any age or gender. *Dictionary of the Scots Language*.
10 Here 'gin' is a preposition meaning: 'by, before, by the time that . . . comes'. *Dictionary of the Scots Language*.
11 'Siller' means silver according to Noël-Paton's notes.
12 Here, 'maun' is an auxiliary verb that means 'must'. *Dictionary of the Scots Language*.
13 Eildon is a Faery location referenced in the James Hogg's *Hunt of Eildon* (1874).
14 Rime is white frost on a cold object. *OED Online*.
15 Carking here is a verb that means 'to complain peevishly'. *Dictionary of the Scots Language*.
16 Variant of 'lady'. *Dictionary of the Scots Language*.
17 Haud means 'hold' according to Noël-Paton's notes.
18 Teind means 'tithe' according to Noël-Paton's notes.
19 Wat here means 'know' according to Noël-Paton's notes.
20 'Kilt your kirtle' is a phrase that means to tuck up your shirt to free your legs. *Dictionary of the Scots Language*.
21 Gowd means 'gold' according to Noël-Paton's notes.
22 Thae's means 'from'. *Dictionary of the Scots Language*.
23 'Ye'll gang nae mair' means 'you'll go no more'. *Dictionary of the Scots Language*.
24 Yestereen means 'last night' according to Noël-Paton's notes.
25 Pelf means either material possessions or stolen goods. *OED Online*.

26 Scunnered means to get a 'feeling of aversion, disgust or loathing, to feel surfeited or nauseated'. *Dictionary of the Scots Language*.
27 Wheesht is a call for silence. *Dictionary of the Scots Language*.
28 Ram-stam here means: rash, rudely or unrefined. *Dictionary of the Scots Language*.
29 Rickle means a stack or pile, such as a haystack or a pile of leaves.

APPENDICES

Editorial Headnote

E. C., 'Two Jamaicans Write and Produce a Pantomime',
***The West Indies Review*, December 1949, p. 12.**

This is a review of the 1949/1950 premier of Bennett-Coverley's pantomime 'Bluebeard and Brer Anancy'.

APPENDIX A

'Two Jamaicans Write and Produce a Pantomime'

E. C.

Source: *The West Indies Review*, December 1949, p. 12

THIS year's pantomime must be assessed entirely upon its merits as a local effort. The production has considerable merit, but it also has faults which could have been avoided.

The entire play (it is scarcely a pantomime) revolves round the figure of the heroine, played by Miss Shirley Wood. She is pretty, has quite a sweet voice, and gives promise of acting ability. But why the authors and producer hung the entire effort upon that pair of fragile and inexperienced shoulders is beyond understanding. The principal girl in a sophisticated pantomime has little to do beyond looking pretty and dancing and singing a little. Miss Wood was given all the responsibility of a prima donna. It is not her fault that she failed in the gruelling test. I can never understand why year after year inexperienced young girls are forced into leading parts; and then, as soon as they begin to learn something, are shunted in favour of a newcomer.

Miss Louise Bennett is one of the authors of the pantomime. She did herself little service, for her own appearances gave little opportunity for the display of her talents. And why did not the producer make use of the Jamaican pantomime talent available . . . Clinton Nunes, Doris Duperley, Florence Reid, whose excellent singing was heard in the show but too seldom and to insufficient advantage . . . and others?

The burden of the production was sustained by Ranny Williams, who gave an excellent professional performance. I have never liked him better, for instead of the familiar cross-talk which cannot be understood except by bred and born Jamaicans, he was permitted to utilise his gift of comedy. Bob Verity, as a newcomer, showed that he too has a genuine aptitude for comedy. Orford St. John's lyric, "Queen of the Coast", was one of the highlights of the production, and Bob Verity put it over well, and will do it better with more experience.

The dancing was exceptionally well handled, and became part of the show. Most of us are tired of the irrelevant interpolation of little children, giving their dancing class routines in ballet costume, to the delight no doubt of their parents if of no-one else. This year, the ballet is used with artistry. The big ballet scene, Garden of Weeds, is very well done, though reminiscent of **Caribbean Rhapsody**. The chorus is good and lively, and reflects credit upon the producer.

The lyrics are good, and those of Orford St. John are really first rate. But it is necessary to read them to appreciate them, for the cast completely failed to put them over, with the one exception of "Queenie", already mentioned. Miss Barbara Ferland wrote some charming numbers, and composed some attractive music; but the show as a whole lacks swing and rhythm.

The pantomime gave pleasure to the packed first-night audience, which cannot be expected to be critical of details. It would have been a great deal better if the authors had considered the talent available – the supreme advantage to local writers for a local cast – and used it to good effect. If this is a first effort, Louise Bennett and Noel Vaz are to be congratulated upon considerable skill in compilation. Every playwright needs to see his work upon the stage, and they will have gained enormously by this oportunity. They might use the Jamaican background to better effect, while modifying the use of Jamaican dialect, so that the play will have local atmosphere and yet be comprehensible to the entire audience. And they should write their next play from the other end . . . that is to say, they should assemble their potential cast first. Thus they will have a well-nourished body with which to fit the dress of their invention, instead of a skeleton inclined to stagger under too heavy a load of responsibility.

As for the scenery, the painted backcloth land flats, although somewhat macabre for pantomime, were most effective. The other sets, showing the courthouse and other architectural designs, were less successful. There was the usual failure to create a completely satisfying decor, with sets, costumes and lighting coalescing into a harmonious design, and the dresses of the little heroine were not always successful.

I have not attempted to give a detailed consideration of the merits of the cast for there were many newcomers without wide experience, and the production really depends upon its effect as a complete conception. On the whole, it may be acclaimed a success; and no doubt after the first night the cast will have settled down to a more finished performance, with the music and lyrics given the value they deserve.

The attempt at original work deserves every encouragement, and it is a pity that the authors handicapped themselves by creating unnecessary obstacles which the producer, with the material he chose or which he decided was available, was unable to overcome.

E. C.

Editorial Headnote

'A Kiss for Cinderella' *Evening Express*

This notice for 'A Kiss for Cinderella' is included at the front of the *Evening Express* in the midst of headlines about troops lost during the Great War. This page gives the immediate context for the audience of *A Kiss for Cinderella* (1916) when it premiered in Great Britain.

APPENDIX B

'A Kiss for Cinderella'

Source: *Evening Express*, 6 October 1916, p. 2

The attraction next week at His Majesty's Theatre will be Mr Perov Hutchison and Miss Hilds Trevelyan in her original part in Sir James M. Barrie's fantasy play, "A Kiss for Cinderella."

If anyone doubts whether the magic of Sir James Barrie is as potent to-day as it was, say, twenty years ago, the doubt can be resolved by a visit to this beautiful dream play which the magician has given us. "A Kiss for Cinderella" will prove as perennially popular as "Peter Pan." There is the same quaint whimsical humour in both plays, the same pointed irony, the same tenderness, the same wholly indescribable blending of comedy and pathos. To describe the play as a work of genius is merely to state an obvious fact. "A Kiss for Cinderella" is not easily to be forgotten. It is a play of beauty – beautiful voices, beautiful dresses, beautiful thoughts that linger in one's mind and refuse to be banished.

Mr Percy Hutchison, who, by the way, is a nephew of Sir Charles Wyndham, has acquired the original production from Wyndham's Theatre, and travels with a company 50 strong. A matinee will be given on Saturday.

Editorial Headnote

'A Kiss for Cinderella', *The Bournemouth Graphic*,
1 September 1916, p. 4.

This review summarizes the action in the pantomime, identifying the conclusion
as a happy love scene rather than a tragic one.

APPENDIX C

'A Kiss for Cinderella'

Source: *The Bournemouth Graphic*, 1 September 1916, p. 4

Miss Emma Hutchison and Mr. Percy Hutchison's company will pay a welcome visit to the Theatre Royal on Monday next, for six nights and two matinees (Wednesday and Saturday), with Sir James Barrie's new play, "A Kiss for Cinderella," direct from Wyndham's Theatre, London.

The play is described as a fancy in three acts. Sir James Barrie is in his happiest vein of whimsical imagination – humour and sentiment. A Barrie fantasy is above all things hard to analyse. The underlying is to tell the tale of Cinderella as it exists in the mind of a poor little London drudge in these days of war. Little Miss Thing, as the Barrie Cinderella is called, is employed as maid-of-all-work in the studio of Mr. Bodie, a sculptor, where her duties include the scrubbing of a large statue – replica of the Venus of Milo – whom she nicknames Mrs. Bodie. Thither one night comes a policeman requiring Mr. Bodie to obscure the illumination from his fanlight. Our policeman suspects Cinderella of being a German spy, and tracks her to her abode, where it appears she carries on business as "the penny friend," a minder of other people's children. Our policeman comes in disguised for a penny shave, is unmasked, and sups with Cinderella on milk and potatoes while her changes in boxes on the wall make faces at each other. Later on, Cinderella, who is always dreaming of a fairy godmother and a grand ball and a prince charming, goes out in quest of them into the cold night, ill fed and ill clad, and falls into a swoon. Then follows a scene in which her dream of the prince is represented. Meantime she is found in the street by the policeman and is sent to hospital suffering from pneumonia. There she recovers, and the play ends with a delightful love scene between her and the romantic policeman, who, instead of a ring, gives her a pair of dainty slippers.

MR. PERCY HUTCHISON, *Proprietor and Producer of "A Kiss for Cinderella," appearing at the Theatre Royal next week.*

The whole of the production is being transferred from Wyndham's Theatre, with augmented orchestra. The cast includes Miss Hilda Trevelyan as "Cinderella" (her original character), and Mr. Percy Hutchison as "Our Policeman."

"A Kiss for Cinderella" has been drawing crowded houses for many months in London. The play is produced by Mr. Percy Hutchison, a statement which ensures perfection of staging and clever acting. Early booking is advisable.

INDEX